VISUAL QUICKSTART GUIDE

C PROGRAMMING

Larry Ullman and Marc Liyanage

◎ Peachpit Press

C Programming: Visual QuickStart Guide

Larry Ullman and Marc Liyanage

Peachpit Press

1249 Eighth Street
Berkeley, CA 94710
510/524-2178
800/283-9444
510/524-2221 (fax)
Find us on the Web at www.peachpit.com.
To report errors, please send a note to errata@peachpit.com.

Peachpit Press is a division of Pearson Education.

Copyright © 2005 by Larry Ullman and Marc Liyanage
Editor: Rebecca Gulick
Production Editor: Connie Jeung-Mills
Copy Editor: Liz Welch
Technical Editor: Andreas Signer
Compositor: Kelli Kamel
Indexer: Karin Arrigoni
Cover design: The Visual Group
Cover production: George Mattingly / GMD

ISBN 0-321-28763-0

9 8 7 6 5 4 3 2 1

Printed and bound in the United States of America

Dedication

With thanks for their friendship and in celebration of a joyful year,
Larry dedicates this book to the extended Chilton family:
John, Lorraine, Brian (and Sommar, Peyton, and Aubrey), Eric,
Mark (and Shauna), and Ali (and Mike).

Marc dedicates this book to his family and friends: Andy and Melek,
Andrew, Martina and Peter, Lionel and Nalini.

Acknowledgements

Larry sends one hundred *huzzahs* each to:

Rebecca Gulick, editor extraordinaire. Thanks for thinking of me for this title and for being there to make sure it's done right. If it weren't for your excellent guidance over the years, I'd still be writing bad haikus in a Midwestern poetry sweatshop.

Liz Welch, for her attention to detail, her ability to impose consistency on an inconsistent writer, and for letting me use the word *nefarious*.

Connie Jeung-Mills and Kelli Kamel, who turn the assortment of digital flotsam I create into a readable book.

Rebecca Ross, for tidying up the contractual messes.

All of the other very good people at Peachpit Press—like Nancy Aldrich-Ruenzel, Nancy Davis, Marjorie Baer, Suzie Lowey, Kim Lombardi, Gary-Paul Prince, Lisi Baldwin, Jim Bruce, and many others—who help turn a bunch of words in my head into a book on a bookshelf.

Andreas Signer, for a most excellent and thorough job with the technical review.

Marc Liyanage, my co-author. My sincerest thanks for stepping in when the chips were down and for giving the material the boost it needed.

And last but not least, on a personal note, a lifetime of thanks and all of my love to Jessica.

Marc would like to thank:

Larry Ullman, for inviting me to join this book project. I had a lot of fun and learned a lot along the way.

Andreas Signer, for the professional and detailed technical review.

TABLE OF CONTENTS

TABLE OF CONTENTS

INTRODUCTION

The C programming language was first invented in the early 1970s by Dennis Ritchie, an employee at Bell Labs. He created C as an outgrowth of the existing B programming language (in case you were wondering where the weird name came from). Despite the fact that C has been around for over 30 years and that newer languages have come along to improve upon C's functionality, C is still commonly used by many types of programmers.

Although C was written as a language specifically for programmers (unlike Pascal, which was designed to teach programming), even those without formal training or only modest computer skills can pick up the subject. This book was written as the no-frills, here's-what-you-really-need-to-know beginner's guide to the C programming language. Absolutely no programming experience is expected of you, but by following the examples and explanations we present here, you'll have some real-world know-how in no time.

Why Use C?

Numerous programming languages are available today, including C#, C++, and Java. Every language has its strengths and weaknesses, so you might well wonder how C stacks up before investing your time in learning it.

The primary benefits of programming with C are

◆ You can create compact, powerful programs.

◆ C applications tend to be comparatively fast.

◆ You can fine-tune your applications for optimal performance and memory usage.

◆ The C code itself is highly portable from one computer to the next.

◆ Many popular applications as well as parts of some operating systems have been written in C.

◆ An understanding of C is an easy way to gain appreciation for true programming in general and a good first step toward learning C++ and C#, in particular.

On the other hand, three of the more common issues people have with C are

◆ C code can be difficult to debug.

◆ C does not protect the programmer from making mistakes, nor does C automatically perform maintenance routines.

◆ The language lacks more contemporary features such as object-oriented programming.

Regardless of these relatively minor deficiencies, C is a great language with which to familiarize yourself. And, with the right book—like the one you're reading now—you'll be programming with C before you know it.

```
1     /* hello.c - Script i.1 */
2     /* This is a sample code file. */
3
4     #include <stdio.h>
5
6     int main (void) {
7
8         /* Say hello. */
9         printf ("Hello, world!\n");
10
11        /* Pause for user input. */
12        getchar();
13
14        return 0;
15
16    }
```

Script i.1 The format of a most basic C source file.

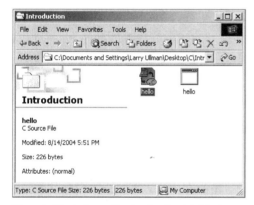

Figure i.1 The *hello* application (on the right) is the compiled result of the *hello.c* file (on the left).

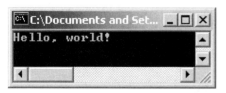

Figure i.2 Running the *hello* program on Windows.

How C Works

Creating applications in C is a multistep process. First you must understand what the end result is: what your application should do. By clearly stating your objectives, you can better determine your variable needs, what functionality must be present, and so forth. Every application in the book is accompanied by a brief description of its purpose.

The next step is to begin creating the C source code, a plain-text file that will look like **Script i.1**, for starters. Obviously the main focus of this book is to teach you what code you need to type to create the desired application.

Once you've created your source code, it needs to be *compiled*. Compilation is the process of turning a plain-text file of C code into a set of computer-readable instructions. The result of the compilation process—assuming it works—is an executable application, compiled specifically to work on that machine (**Figure i.1**).

If compilation did not work, you'll need to debug, debug, and debug. Errors can occur by inadvertently misspelling something, omitting a particular character, or out-and-out misusing a function. Rest assured that all of the code in this book has been debugged, meaning that if you follow the instructions exactly, your code will work too. But, the fact of the matter is that debugging is a good and necessary skill to have.

Once you have a compiled application, you can run it just as you would any other application: by double-clicking on its icon. All of the examples in this book will run in a console or terminal window (**Figure i.2**).

What You'll Need

The requirements for working with C are both free and minimal. For starters, you'll need a computer, but you probably already knew that. It doesn't matter what kind of computer you have, what operating system it's running, or really how much memory and hard disk space is available. If your computer can run, say, Microsoft Office, it has all the power you need for creating applications in C.

The most important—in fact, the only—requirement is that you have a qualified C compiler on your computer. This can be as simple as *gcc* (Gnu C Compiler), which is freely available, can run on most operating systems, and already comes on most Unix-derivative operating systems. Along with your compiler, you'll want a text editor and a command-line interface from which you'll run the compiler. Both of these tools are already present on every operating system.

Although you can use a text editor and a compiler to create your applications, a much easier option is to use an all-in-one integrated development environment (IDE) like Dev-C++ on Windows or Xcode on Mac OS X. Both of these tools are free and allow you to write, compile, debug, and execute your C code all within the one interface. Appendix A, "Installing and Using C Tools," covers the installation and basic usage of these tools, and we *highly* recommend you use either Dev-C++ or Xcode, depending on your operating system. Every one of the book's applications conforms to the C99 standard (see the sidebar) and has been tested using both IDEs. If you use either Dev-C++ or Xcode, following the examples will go more smoothly.

From you, the reader, nothing is expected except an interest and willingness to learn C.

Understanding the C Standards

The C language is a standardized technology, meaning that officially sanctioned versions are available. The first formal C standard was adopted by the American National Standards Institute (ANSI) in 1989. The International Organization for Standardization (ISO) approved a very similar version in 1990. Together, these are called C90.

Modifications to this standard eventually resulted in the C99 standard, which was adopted in 1999 (hence the name). The C99 standard supports a few new data types, works better with international languages, and covers up some gaps in C's functionality.

The standard you adhere to matters since different compilers and IDEs support different versions of C. The three primary applications used in this book—Dev-C++ on Windows, Xcode on Mac OS X, and gcc—all currently support the C99 standard. In other words, if you follow C99 rules, your applications should work.

For increased backwards compatibility, you can adhere to the stricter C90 standard. With this in mind, features that are new to the C99 standard will be described as such.

About This Book

This book attempts to convey the fundamentals of programming with C, without going into overwhelming details or bombarding you with irrelevant technicalities. It uses the following conventions to do.

The step-by-step instructions indicate what code you are to type or what other steps you are to take. The specific text you should type is printed in a unique type style to separate it from the main text. For example:

```
printf ("Hello, world!");
```

Because the column width in this book is narrower than the common text editor or IDE, some lines of code printed in the steps have to be broken where they would not otherwise break in an editor. A small gray arrow indicates when this kind of break occurs. For example:

```
printf ("Hello, world! How are you doing
→ on this rainy Saturday afternoon?");
```

With such code, you should continue to use one line in your scripts, or else you might encounter errors.

The complete C code is also written as its own separate script and is numbered by line for reference (see Script i.1). You shouldn't insert these numbers yourself, because doing so will render your code unusable. Most good text editors and IDEs will number lines for you. In these script blocks, we also highlight in bold the sections that demonstrate new or relevant concepts.

ABOUT THIS BOOK

You will also frequently see images showing the results of running an application (see Figure i.2), displaying a command you need to enter (**Figure i.3**), or demonstrating a particular subpart of an application (**Figure i.4**). All of the images were taken on either Windows or Mac OS X (the Mac OS X images and steps are similar to those for a Linux user). The exact appearance of an application will change from one computer to the next, but most of the content should be similar, as will all of the functionality.

Figure i.3 Invoking the gcc compiler in a Mac OS X Terminal window.

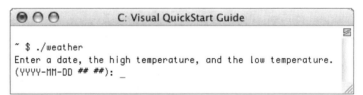

Figure i.4 Some images focus on the user interface.

Getting Help

Although this book was written with the intent of being the most down-to-earth, basic, get-going-now text around, you may run into problems and desire a little assistance on occasion. If you'd like some help regarding the content of this book, or C in general, you have options. Here are some choices, in order of likelihood for getting a fast response (fastest options are listed first):

◆ Search the Internet.

If you have questions about a particular function, header file, or concept, Google will often get you immediate answers.

◆ Use a C newsgroup or forum.

Appendix B, "Resources," lists a number of available outlets for when you have a specific question. If you ask a question wisely (see the sidebar), you should get the answer you need in a relatively short time.

◆ Check out the book's supporting Web site.

The book's official Web site can be found at www.DMCInsights.com/cvqs. There you'll find all the scripts from the book, links to other resources, and a list of any printing errors.

◆ Check out the book's support forum.

At www.DMCInsights.com/phorum/list.php?f=11, readers can post questions, get answers, see what others are doing, and so forth. We (the authors of this book) moderate this forum, which means we'll answer your question if someone doesn't beat us to the punch.

◆ Email the authors.

If all else fails, we gladly welcome your emails at cvqs@DMCInsights.com. A few words of caution, though: we can't do your job for you, we can't debug the 200 lines of code you wrote overnight, and it will take several days for us to get back to you. Still, if you do write, we will respond, and will try to assist as best as possible.

Asking Questions the Smart Way

Whether you're posting a message to the book's support forum, sending us an email, or asking a question in a newsgroup, knowing how to most effectively ask a question improves the quality of the response you'll receive as well as the speed with which you'll get your answer. To receive the best answer in the shortest amount of time, follow these steps:

1. Search the Internet, read the manuals, and browse any applicable documentation.

2. Ask your question in the most appropriate forum (newsgroup, mailing list, and so on).

3. Use a clear and concise subject.

4. Describe your problem in detail, show any relevant code, describe what went wrong, include what operating system you're running, and say what development environment (IDE, compiler, etc.) you're using.

For more tips and an enlightening read, see Eric Steven Raymond's "How to Ask Questions the Smart Way" at www.catb.org/~esr/faqs/smart-questions.html. The 10 minutes you spend on it will save you hours in the future!

GETTING
STARTED WITH C

When creating C applications, your first step is to decide what the application should do. Once you've done that, you write the C source code and compile it into an executable format. Finally, you can run the executable application.

But nothing is ever that easy—all too often you have additional steps to take: debugging and debugging, followed by more debugging. In this chapter, you'll learn how to follow these steps to create your first (very simple) C application. This information will be the basis of the book's remaining material—as well as the basis for your life as a C developer.

This chapter begins with the basic syntax and instructions for creating a quick C source file. Then you'll see how to compile and execute this application. Finally, you'll learn how to make the process easier—and make your work more professional—by mastering comments and judiciously spacing out your code.

Basic Syntax

Creating a C source file is simple, as long as you follow the standard syntax. A C document is just plain text—written in practically any text editor—with a *.c* file extension. The basic syntax of a minimal C file is

```
#include <stdio.h>
int main (void) {
    return 0;
}
```

The first line states that the *stdio.h* package should be included (this is a *preprocessor directive*, which you'll learn about in Chapter 8, "Using the C Preprocessor"). Including *stdio.h* has the same effect as making that file's contents part of this document (but without the extra typing or lines of code). The *stdio.h* file, which stands for *standard input/output*, brings fundamental functionality—such as the ability to take input from a keyboard and display output on the screen—to your C code.

The next three lines define a function called main(), which is always the first function *called* (or *run*, in layman's terms) by any C application. In this example, the function will return an integer value, as indicated by the preceding int. The function takes no *arguments*—values sent to a function for it to use—as indicated by the void. The contents of the function itself are placed between the opening and closing curly braces. For this minimal, downright pointless, example, all the function does is return the value *0*.

Because this is the standard template for the vast majority of the examples in this book, you should quickly write this up as your first C document.

```
1   #include <stdio.h>
2   int main (void) {
3   return 0;
4   }
```

Script 1.1 The basic structure of a minimal C source file.

To create a C source file:

1. Open your text editor or integrated development environment (IDE).

   C applications begin as plain-text source files. These can be written in any text editor that allows you to save files as plain text. Obviously some (like BBEdit for the Mac or Vi for Unix) are better than others. Some text editors, like TextEdit or WordPad, will always try to save files as Rich Text Format (*.rtf*) or with an extra extension. You should avoid using these editors for that very reason.

   There are some free IDEs you can use, like Eclipse (for Windows, Unix, and Mac) or Xcode (Mac OS X). Or, you can always invest in a commercial IDE like Visual Studio (Windows) or CodeWarrior (Windows, Unix, and Mac). Among the many benefits of a formal IDE over a text editor are built-in debugging, compiling, and execution. For more information on the available tools, see Appendix A, "Installing and Using C Tools."

   For the purposes of this book, we highly recommend—and all of the examples have been tested using—Dev-C++ on Windows and Xcode on Mac OS X, both of which are free and easy to use.

2. Create a new, blank text document.

3. Type the required `include` line (**Script 1.1**):

   `#include <stdio.h>`

   This line should be the first thing entered into your text file. Notice that there are no blank lines before it or even blank spaces between the number sign and the word *include*. Also—and you'll come to see why this is important in time—note that the line does not end with a semicolon.

   continues on next page

BASIC SYNTAX

4. Begin defining the `main()` function:

`int main (void) {`

Again, this line begins the definition of a user-defined function called `main()`. It takes no arguments (also called *parameters*) and will return an integer value. The opening curly brace marks the beginning of the function's contents.

5. Add the `return` line to the function:

`return 0;`

All functions in C should return a value, even if it's just the number *0*. This value is meant to reflect that no errors occurred. More complex functions might return a 1 to indicate that a problem occurred.

As you progress in your C learning, you'll have your functions do much, much more.

6. Close the `main()` function:

`}`

Don't forget the closing curly brace. This marks the end of the `main()` function definition.

7. Save the file as *template.c*.

Remember that C source files will always use the *.c* extension. This one will be called *template*, as it'll be the template for other examples.

✔ Tips

■ Some C source code files (although not those written in this book) will use the format

`main () {`

or

`void main () {`

to define the `main()` function. These variations are not C99 compliant and will work inconsistently across different compilers. For this reason this book uses the formal, standard

`int main (void) {`

■ Different operating systems have various restrictions as to how long a file's name can be. A basename (for example, *template* without the *.c* extension) is limited to 8 characters in MS-DOS and 14 on some versions of Unix, but Windows, Mac OS X, and most operating systems allow for a reasonably long name.

■ Although Windows and Mac OS X are not case-sensitive when it comes to filenames, Unix is. Treating your files as if case-sensitivity matters is a good programming habit and makes your code more portable. Hence, in this example, it's important that you use *template.c* as opposed to *template.C* or *Template.C*.

```
1    #include <stdio.h>
2    int main (void) {
3    printf("Hello, world!");
4    return 0;
5    }
```

Script 1.2 A simple *Hello, world!* example.

Printing Text

If you were to compile and run the *template.c* example (written in the previous section), it should work, but it won't do much. To take this up one notch, you'll have the application print a message when it's run. This example will teach you how to create a simple *Hello, world!* program, a staple of any programming text.

To print text in C, use the `printf()` function:

`printf("I could catch a monkey.");`

The `printf()` function is a printing function with formatting capability (hence, the *f*). Throughout the rest of the book, beginning with Chapter 3, "Working with Numbers," you'll see how to format text with `printf()`, but for the time being, it will be used in its most basic way.

Before getting into an example, you should revisit the exact syntax of `printf()`. The parentheses hold the arguments the function takes, the first (and in these early examples, only) argument being a string of text. This text is enclosed within straight double quotation marks. Finally, the line concludes with a semicolon, as every statement in C must.

To print text in C:

1. Open *template.c* (Script 1.1) in your text editor.

2. Within the `main()` function definition, before the `return` line, add the following (**Script 1.2**):

   `printf("Hello, world!");`

   Function names are case-sensitive in C, so be certain to type this exactly.

continues on next page

3. Create a new folder for your C files (**Figure 1.1**).

As you develop more complex applications, you'll want to get into the habit of keeping your files organized. As a suggestion, create a *C_code* folder for all of the code you'll be developing in this book. Then create a *Ch01* folder within *C_code* and a *hello* folder within *Ch01*. This will be the repository for all of the files in this example.

4. Save the file—within its proper folder—as *hello.c*.

So as not to overwrite the existing template, you should give this file a new name, one that is descriptive of what the file does.

✔ Tips

■ Another benefit of using an IDE is that it will normally organize your folders and all of your source files automatically for each project you do.

■ Statements in C, such as the use of the `printf()` function, can run over multiple lines. You can also put multiple statements on one line, as long as each is separated by a semicolon.

■ Make sure that your text editor does not use curly (also called *smart*) quotation marks—these can create problems for some compilers.

■ All of the examples in this book will print their messages to the command prompt window, where the application will be run. You can, using C, create conventional applications that print text within the context of a proper interface, but this is beyond the scope of the book as well as standard C, requiring a graphical user interface (GUI) builder, application programming interfaces (APIs), or other nefarious acronyms.

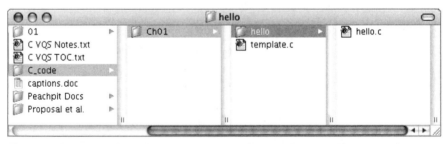

Figure 1.1 When you develop and program your own applications, keep your files organized in logical directories like these.

PRINTING TEXT

Compiling and Running C

Simply put, a compiler does the critical task of taking your C source code and turning it into an executable program (one that can be run). It takes high-level instructions and generates the proper low-level machine code that the computer can understand.

This process—also called *building*—involves linking together all relevant source files, reporting on errors, and much more. Most important, compilers take generic, possibly operating system–indifferent, C code and creates an executable file for that particular platform.

There are two ways you can compile and run your C:

◆ By using a command-line prompt with a stand-alone compiler

◆ By using the compiler and features built into an IDE

In the following steps, you will see how to use both methods. Obviously using an IDE is the easier method, but knowing how to use command-line tools is a worthy bit of info. Keep in mind that you can follow these steps only if you've installed a compiler or IDE on your system. For instructions (if you're not sure or have problems with these steps), see Appendix A.

Once you've successfully compiled an application (in other words, no errors were found), you are left with an executable file. Running this executable shows you the result of your C programming.

To compile and run C from the command line:

1. Open your command-line application.

   ▲ For Windows, you should click on the Start menu, select Run, type cmd in the Open text box (**Figure 1.2**), and press Enter. This will bring up the command-line console.

   ▲ For Mac OS X and Unix, use the Terminal application. Open it by double-clicking on its icon in the *Utilities* or *Applications* folder (depending on your OS).

2. Type cd /path/to/C_code/Ch01/hello and press Return (Mac) or Enter (PC).

   To begin compiling and running your work, you'll need to move yourself into the directory where the *hello.c* file resides. The proper syntax will have to change based on the location of the file and the operating system being used. You might end up using something like

   cd C:\Documents and Settings\Larry
   → Ullman\C_code\Ch01\hello (Windows)
   or
   cd /Users/*username*/Documents/
   → Programming/C_code/Ch01/hello (Mac OS X, where *username* is your username)

3. Type gcc -g -o hello hello.c and press Return or Enter (**Figure 1.3**).

   Assuming that gcc (*gcc* stands for GNU C Compiler) has been installed on your computer, this command will compile the *hello.c* file. See the sidebar "Command-Line Compilers" for more detailed information on the gcc syntax.

   If you do not have the gcc compiler on your machine (in which case, you'll see an error message saying as much), you'll need to use another compiler. See Appendix A for your options.

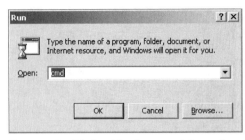

Figure 1.2 Use Windows' Run feature to bring up the command prompt.

Figure 1.3 Running the compiler in the Mac OS X Terminal application.

Figure 1.4 Checking that the new file (called *hello*) was created.

Alternatively, if the command indicated that the compiler could not be found, you may need to use an absolute path to the compiler in order to use it. For example:

```
/usr/bin/gcc -g -o hello hello.c
C:\Programs\gcc -g -o hello hello.c
```

4. Check the contents of the directory to make sure that the build worked.

   Step 3 will create a file called *hello.exe* or just plain *hello*, depending on your operating system and compiler. If no errors were reported, you should see this in the directory.

   You can either view the directory in the Explorer (Windows) or Finder (Mac OS X) or use the proper command-line prompt. This would be either

   ```
   dir (Windows)
   ```

   or

   `ls -a` (Mac OS X, as shown in **Figure 1.4**, and Unix)

5. Run the file.

   Once again, the syntax for running the file will depend on your operating system:

   `hello` (Windows; see **Figure 1.5**)

   or

   `./hello` (Mac OS X and Unix)

   continues on next page

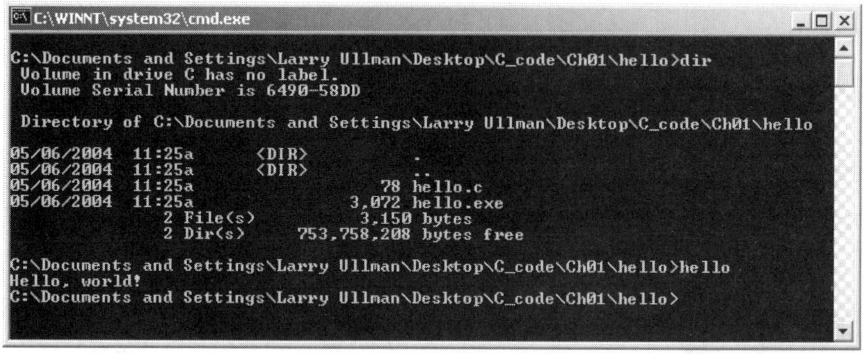

continues on next page

COMPILING AND RUNNING C

```
C:\WINNT\system32\cmd.exe                                        _ □ X

C:\Documents and Settings\Larry Ullman\Desktop\C_code\Ch01\hello>dir
 Volume in drive C has no label.
 Volume Serial Number is 6490-58DD

 Directory of C:\Documents and Settings\Larry Ullman\Desktop\C_code\Ch01\hello

05/06/2004  11:25a    <DIR>          .
05/06/2004  11:25a    <DIR>          ..
05/06/2004  11:25a                78 hello.c
05/06/2004  11:25a             3,072 hello.exe
               2 File(s)         3,150 bytes
               2 Dir(s)   753,758,208 bytes free

C:\Documents and Settings\Larry Ullman\Desktop\C_code\Ch01\hello>hello
Hello, world!
C:\Documents and Settings\Larry Ullman\Desktop\C_code\Ch01\hello>
```

Figure 1.5 Finally running the file and seeing the result of your first C program.

✔ Tips

■ If your compiler coughs up an error on the void argument in the main() function definition, this means that the compiler is not ANSI C compliant, and you should switch to a different one.

■ On many operating systems, gcc and cc are aliases for the same compiler.

■ Compilers also create object files during the build process (called, for example, *hello.o*). Some compilers will automatically delete these (if the build worked) and some won't (for example, if you're compiling multiple files at once).

■ As a compiler merely turns your C code into an executable application, the better your C code is, the better—in terms of performance and size—the resulting application will be. The examples in this book are oriented towards writing the most stable and efficient applications possible.

Command-Line Compilers

There are many free, good command-line compilers available—gcc and cc (C compiler) are two of the most popular. While it's generally easier to work entirely within an IDE, if you habitually use a command-line tool, you'll benefit by learning its full features.

On Unix and Mac OS X, the easiest way to see all of your options is to type man gcc or gcc --help in the Terminal (or man cc or cc --help).

The critical syntax for each compiler is

```
gcc -g -o hello hello.c
```

The g flag states that debugging should be enabled. The o flag is immediately followed by the name the resulting executable should have. (If you don't use the o flag, you'll end up with something named *a.out*.) Adding -W turns on warnings, whereas -ansi checks that the code is ANSI C90 compliant.

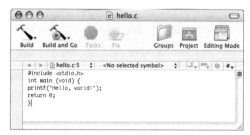

Figure 1.6 The *hello.c* file open in the Xcode IDE on Mac OS X.

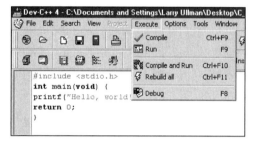

Figure 1.7 Use the Execute menu to compile and run a C program using Dev-C++ on Windows.

To compile and run C using an IDE:

1. Open *hello.c* in your IDE, if it's not already open (**Figure 1.6**).

2. Click the Build (or Compile) icon.

   Obviously the specifics will depend on the IDE being used, but most have a Build or Compile option (see Figure 1.6). Sometimes you'll find the command under an Execute or Build menu as well.

3. Click the Run icon.

   Again, the your IDE should have either a Run or an Execute option. This may be an icon or under a menu (**Figure 1.7**).

✔ Tips

- Most IDEs will include a tutorial on basic usage, which is well worth your time to go through. Also, there is ample documentation and examples online for using both Xcode and Dev-C++ in particular.

- As you might have already noticed, most IDEs have a Compile and Run (or Build and Go) option, which automatically runs the compiled application if it was built without error.

- For more advanced purposes, you can compile individual C modules and then link them all to create the final executable, but that notion is beyond the scope of this book.

- Technically, compilers both compile and link (tying all required code into one neat bundle). Although these used to be separate steps, most compilers now handle the whole shebang.

COMPILING AND RUNNING C

Keeping Your Application Open

If your application ran so quickly that you didn't even have time to see it, don't be surprised. The reason for this is that on some operating systems (think Windows here) the console application will open, the C executable will run, and the console will close again—that is, unless you do something to stop it.

So here's a little trick you can use if you are having this problem. Simply open your *hello.c* script and add the getchar() function to your main() function. This will make the application wait for the Enter or Return key to be pressed before continuing to execute.

To keep your application open using getchar():

1. Open *hello.c* (Script 1.2) in your text editor or IDE.

2. After the printf() line and before return, add the following line (**Script 1.3**):

   getchar();

   The getchar() function should be the penultimate line in the main() function, coming after the printf() but before the return. The end result of this is that the function will print the message, wait for a keystroke, and then return *0* and exit.

3. Save the file as *hello2.c*.

   Arguably you should create a new folder called *hello2* for this file to keep it separate from the other *hello* example, but how you organize things is up to you.

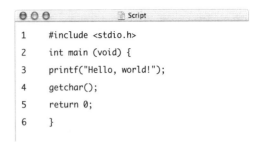

```
1    #include <stdio.h>
2    int main (void) {
3        printf("Hello, world!");
4        getchar();
5        return 0;
6    }
```

Script 1.3 The program now uses the getchar() function to pause its operation.

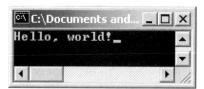

Figure 1.8 The application now pauses after saying "Hello, world!"

Figure 1.9 After pressing Return or Enter, the application will stop execution, either presenting the command line again or closing the console (or Terminal) window.

4. Compile and run *hello2.c* using the command-line or IDE method outlined earlier (**Figure 1.8**).

5. When you're done saying hello, press Return or Enter to finish running the application (**Figure 1.9**).

✔ Tips

- Once you've compiled an application, you can normally run it by just double-clicking on the new executable (within Windows Explorer or the Mac Finder).

- If you're keen on getchar(), you can add another one before printf(), so that the application will wait for your keystroke before doing anything at all.

- In Chapter 5, "Standard Input and Output," the getchar() function will actually be used to retrieve a typed character.

Adding Comments to Your Source Code

Although they do nothing for the functionality of an application, comments are still a critical part of any programming language. Comments are necessary to remind yourself—while you're initially developing an application or when you come back months later—why you did certain things. These are some of the most common uses for comments:

◆ Indicate the purpose of a file

◆ Document who created a file and when

◆ Note the thinking behind a function

◆ Clearly state the meaning of variables

◆ Explain why particular numbers are used

◆ Mark contingencies or assumptions being made

C supports two comment formats. The first allows you to write comments over multiple lines:

```
/* Multiline comments
have start and end delineators. */
```

Some programmers format these comments a little to make their commented nature clear:

```
/* Multiline comments
 * with spacing and
 * extra asterisks. */
```

The second comment type was added in the C99 standard. By using a double slash, you indicate that anything from that point until the end of the line is a comment:

```
// Single-line comment.
printf("Hello, world!"); // Comment.
```

With this in mind, let's rewrite *hello2.c* so that it's properly documented.

```
  ● ● ●              📄 Script
1     /* hello3.c - Script 1.4
2      * Created by Larry Ullman 5/6/2004
3      * This script says "Hello, world!"
4      */
5     #include <stdio.h>
6     int main (void) {
7     printf("Hello, world!");
8     getchar(); // Wait for the user
      ⇥ before continuing.
9     return 0;
10    }
```

Script 1.4 Judicious use of comments is critical to successful programming.

To add comments:

1. Open *hello2.c* (Script 1.3) in your text editor or IDE.

2. As the very first line, before the #include, start a new comment (**Script 1.4**):

   /*

   The combination of a slash and an asterisk indicates the beginning of a comment. Anything between this and the closing delineator (*/) will be a comment, and therefore not executed.

3. Add a description of the file and its purpose:

   * hello3.c - Script 1.4
   * Created by Larry Ullman 5/6/2004
   * This script says "Hello, world!"

   You can use comments for many things; this example is just a quick introduction to the possibilities. Your comments should clarify the code, making it easier to comprehend.

4. Type the ending delineator, completing the comment.

   */

   This closes out the comment so that any following code will be executed.

5. After the getchar() function, add a comment indicating its purpose:

   getchar(); // Wait for the user
   ⇥ before continuing.

   This simple comment states exactly why the function is being called. It's useful here, as nothing is ever done with the result of the function, which could be confusing when you revisit this code at a later date.

   continues on next page

ADDING COMMENTS TO YOUR SOURCE CODE

Not that, despite its appearance here and in Script 1.4, this comment is all on one line, with no Return or Enter being used within it.

6. Save the file as *hello3.c*.

7. Compile and run *hello3.c* using the command-line or IDE method (**Figure 1.10**).

✔ Tips

■ Despite the fact that we highly recommend adding oodles of comments to your scripts, the scripts in this book won't be as documented as we'd advise, in order to save valuable book space.

■ The multiline comment type can be a great debugging tool. You can use it to disengage sections of code while you're attempting to solve a problem.

■ While developing and inevitably altering your applications, always make sure that your comments continue to accurately reflect the code they comment on. If a comment indicates something different than what the code does, it'll only lead to confusion.

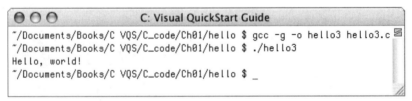

Figure 1.10 The addition of comments in no way affects the execution of a program, but it does make it easier to code and edit.

```
    ⊝ ○ ⊝              📄 Script
1       /* hello4.c - Script 1.5
2        * Created by Larry Ullman 5/6/2004
3        * This script says "Hello, world!"
4        */
5
6       #include <stdio.h>
7
8       int main (void) {
9
10          printf("Hello, world!\n");
11          getchar(); // Wait for the user
      → before continuing.
12          return 0;
13
14      }
```

Script 1.5 Add white space to make your code easier to read and comprehend.

Understanding White Space

The final concept covered in this chapter is that of white space. *White space* refers to blank lines, tabs, and spaces that add clarity to your coding, both during writing and running.

C, like many languages, is generally white space insensitive. This means that you can add blank lines to make your scripts easier to read. You can also add a little padding between a function call and its opening parentheses. Most important, you can use spaces to indent code, thereby indicating what code is a subset of what routines (for example, whether a line of code is part of a function or a conditional). This is a critical concept in making your code more approachable.

Finally, you'll learn how to add white space to the messages printed by an application. For example, to add a newline to the outputted message, print the newline character:

```
printf ("There will be a break here:\n");
```

To demonstrate this, you'll write the *Hello, world!* example one last time, as a proper source file should look.

To add white space to your file:

1. Open *hello3.c* (Script 1.4) in your text editor or IDE.

2. After the first comment, which ends on line 4, press Return or Enter once to add a blank line (**Script 1.5**).

    This blank line will help to separate out the initial comment from the meat of the code.

3. After the #include line, press Return or Enter again to add another blank line.

    This blank line differentiates the includes section from the functions.

continues on next page

4. After the initial function definition line, add another blank line.

5. Insert four spaces before each of the function's main lines: `printf()`, `getchar()`, and `return`.

   In order to mark that these lines are all part of the `main()` function, they'll be indented four spaces. This way, when glancing over the code, you can easily tell what sections belong with what functions. You'll see this method repeated frequently in this book.

6. Change the print line to read as follows:

   ```
   printf("Hello, world!\n");
   ```

   The addition of \n at the end of the print statement will create a break after that text, as if you pressed Return (or Enter). The end result will be a little bit clearer when the application is executed.

7. Add another blank line before the closing curly brace.

8. Save the file as *hello4.c*.

9. Compile and run *hello4.c* using the command-line or IDE method (**Figure 1.11**).

✔ Tips

■ Despite the fact that we highly recommend adding copious amounts of white space to your scripts, our scripts won't be as spaced out, again in an effort to save valuable book space.

■ Certain characters when escaped (preceded by a backslash) have special meanings (e.g., \n is newline). You'll learn about several others over the course of this book.

■ The reason four spaces are used for indentation instead of a single tab is for compliance across all text editors.

Figure 1.11 While the extra spacing didn't affect the executed result, the newline character made the cursor appear on the line after the *Hello, world!* message.

Introduction to Data Types

Before you can begin doing any serious C programming, you'll need a basic grasp of the available data types. The C language has several types—from numbers to characters and more advanced categories—each with its own specific purpose. What they all have in common is their ability to temporarily store information in memory, so that your applications can perform math, manipulate strings, take user input, and much, much more.

In this chapter you'll get a quick introduction to the most basic data types you'll be using throughout the rest of this book. In the process, you'll also learn about how to declare variables, assign values to them, and print their values.

Proper Variable Syntax

The overwhelming majority of data you'll work with will be in the form of variables (as opposed to constants, which you'll also learn about at the end of this chapter). To use a variable, you must first declare it—in other words, you state that a variable with a specific name will be of a certain type. The declaration statement looks like this:

datatype variablename;

For example:

```
int age;
float cost;
char answer;
```

The different types are listed in **Table 2.1**, along with what version of C they are allowed in.

The easiest to comprehend and use are the number types. For starters you have int, which is an integer. Then there are long and short ints, which increase and decrease the maximum size of their value (as well as how much memory each requires). Floats and doubles are two more types of numbers, each of which contains decimal points. Doubles are twice as precise as floats and therefore more reliable for many uses. Finally, all number types can be marked as signed or unsigned (those aren't actual types but rather modifiers for the different types). The former means that a number can be either positive or negative, whereas the latter asserts that the number is always non-negative (unsigned numbers can be 0 or greater in value).

Of the other types, char will be the only one demonstrated in this chapter. It lets you store other characters—like letters and punctuation—in variables.

Table 2.1 The basic variable types for use in the C language and what standard they fall under.

C Data Types	
TYPE	C STANDARD
int	All
long int	All
long long int	All
short int	All
unsigned	All
float	All
double	All
long double	All
char	All
signed	C90 and C99
void	C90 and C99
_Bool	C99
_Complex	C99 (optional support)
_Imaginary	C99 (optional support)

```
  ⊙ ○ ⊙              📄 Script
1      /* var1.c - Script 2.1 */
2
3      #include <stdio.h>
4
5      int main(void) {
6
7          int age; /* User's age in years. */
8          float hourly_wage; /* User's hourly
           ↪  wage in dollars. */
9
10         return 0;
11
12     }
```

Script 2.1 This minimal C file merely defines two different variables.

Besides deciding on a data type when declaring your variables, you also have to state their names, following specific rules. Variable names

◆ Can contain only letters, numbers, and the underscore

◆ Must begin with either a letter or an underscore

◆ Are case sensitive

◆ Can consist of up to 63 characters (as of the C99 standard)

◆ Cannot be the same as a reserved word (such as `int`, `return`, `main`, `printf`)

When you're trying to come up with variable name, there are many best practices to follow. For starters, variable names should be

◆ Descriptive of what information the variable represents

◆ Logically named, following consistent practices

◆ Documented by comments

To begin working with variables, let's create a simple application that declares a couple of them.

To declare variables:

1. Create a new, blank text document in your text editor or integrated development environment (IDE).

2. Begin by documenting the file (**Script 2.1**):

`/* var1.c - Script 2.1 */`

Remember that thorough and accurate comments are the key to professional, reliable programming. In this book you'll see more minimal notes like this one, but you should not hesitate to go overboard with your own documentation.

continues on next page

PROPER VARIABLE SYNTAX

3. Type the required `include` line:

```
#include <stdio.h>
```

This line should be part of practically all of your C programs; its purpose is to add standard functionality to your applications.

4. Begin defining the `main()` function:

```
int main (void) {
```

This line begins the definition of a user-defined function called `main()`, which will automatically be called first when the application is run. It takes no arguments and will return an integer value. The opening curly brace marks the beginning of the function's contents.

5. Define the variables to be used:

```
int age; /* User's age in years. */
float hourly_wage; /* User's hourly
→ wage in dollars. */
```

This function uses two of the number data types. Each is declared on its own line, terminated by a semicolon. Comments have also been added that detail the purpose of each, in case it's not otherwise clear.

6. Add the `return` line and close the `main()` function:

```
 return 0;
}
```

The function returns the value *0*, which indicates that the function ran successfully. Then, the curly brace marks the end of the `main()` function definition.

7. Save the file as *var1.c*.

If you want, you can create a new folder for this application, using whatever method you are using for maintaining your applications' source code.

length, but you'd probably only want to
make use of this if you really like typing.

8. Compile the application (**Figure 2.1**).
   Since this application doesn't actually do
   anything, it may not be worth your time
   to execute, but compiling will confirm
   that no errors occurred.

   Remember that how you compile a C
   application depends on what tools you
   are using to build them. See Chapter 1,
   "Getting Started with C," and Appendix A,
   "Installing and Using C Tools," for specific
   techniques.

✔ Tips

- Over the next few chapters you'll learn
  which data type to use when. Properly
  selecting a data type affects the memory
  requirements of your applications, how
  well they perform, and what they can do.

- There are two general naming conventions for creating compound variable
  names. One uses underscores to separate words; for example, `first_name` or
  `shipping_cost`. The second uses capitalization for this effect: `firstName` or
  `shippingCost` (or `FirstName` and
  `ShippingCost`). It doesn't matter which
  convention you follow as long as you
  remain consistent.

- The length of a variable's name should
  also be reflective of its importance.
  Temporary variables—like those used
  in loops—can have terse, almost random
  names like `i` or `num`. Important variables,
  however, should have full, descriptive
  names like `street_address` or `distance`.

- If you have multiple variables of the same
  type, you can quickly declare them all
  at once:

  ```
  double cost, budget, tax;
  ```

Assigning Values to Variables

Once you've declared a variable, you can *initialize* it, which means giving that variable a value. Assigning values to simple variables like numbers is very easy and requires only the assignment operator (=):

```
int model_year;
model_year = 2004;
float cost;
cost = 1.95;
```

Although you must declare a variable before assigning a value to it, C does allow you to perform both acts in one step:

```
int model_year = 2004;
float cost = 1.95
```

Let's build on the previous example by assigning values to the declared variables.

To assign values to variables:

1. Open *var1.c* (Script 2.1) in your text editor or IDE.

2. After declaring the variables but before the `return` statement, assign each variable a value (**Script 2.2**):

   ```
   age = 40;
   hourly_wage = 3.35;
   ```

   Obviously you can insert any value you want here, as long as it matches the variable's type. This means that integers don't have decimals or fractions and that floats must use a decimal point. As with all numbers, you must not use quotation marks when assigning these values.

3. Save the file as *var2.c*.

4. Compile the application (**Figure 2.2**).

```
1    /* var2.c - Script 2.2 */
2
3    #include <stdio.h>
4
5    int main(void) {
6
7        int age; /* User's age in years. */
8        float hourly_wage; /* User's hourly
      →  wage in dollars. */
9
10       /* Set the values. */
11       age = 40;
12       hourly_wage = 3.35;
13
14       return 0;
15
16   }
```

Script 2.2 Now each variable has been assigned a value, corresponding to its type.

Figure 2.2 Compiling *var2.c* using the command-line gcc tool.

✔ Tips

- One of the strengths of C is that you must declare every variable before you use it. Because of this, compilers will catch errors, such as referring to a variable by the wrong name.

- Some debuggers and IDEs have the capability to show you, on a line-by-line basis, the values of every variable in your file. You'll learn a little about debugging tools in Appendix A.

Table 2.2 These signifiers give the `printf()` function formatting cues for inserting values in their stead.

printf() **Signifiers**	
SIGNIFIER	MEANING
d	integer
f	floating point number
hd	short integer
ld	long integer
hu	unsigned short integer
u	unsigned integer
lu	unsigned long integer
lf	double
Lf	long double (not always available)
c	character
s	string

Printing Variables

Printing the values of variables will make use of the `printf()` function, which was used in Chapter 1 for creating a simple message. Sadly, you cannot simply place the variable names within the context of the message in order to print their values. Instead, you make use of different signifiers, which act as placeholders for the variables, and then follow the message itself with the list of variables to use. For example, the %d flag represents an integer:

```
int dob = 1947;
printf ("You were born in the year %d.",
→  dob);
```

When the application is run, the value of dob will be used in place of %d, resulting in the message *You were born in the year 1947.*

Table 2.2 lists the most important signifiers. As you'll discover, d, f, c, and s will suit most of your needs.

Since the `printf()` function is so critical, you should understand a few other things before using it. First, note that you can refer to multiple variables and types of variables in a single statement:

```
printf ("%s is %d years old.", name, age);
```

In that example, the value of name will be used in place of %s and the value of age will be filled in for %d.

You can also hardcode values, rather than use variables:

```
printf ("%s is %d years old.", name, 40);
```

Building on this, you can make calculations within the `printf()` function, rather than just printing variable values. For example:

```
printf ("The cost of %d widgets at $%f
→  price is $%f.\n", qty, cost, qty *
→  cost);
```

In that example, the value of qty is used in place of %d, the value of cost is used in place of the first %f (preceded by a dollar sign), and the result of the multiplication of these two variables is used in place of the final %f (again preceded by a dollar sign).

Finally, the printf() function can take formatting one step further. For example, using %0.2f formats a floating point number to two decimal places. This next example will demonstrate all of this information, and you'll learn more about printf() in Chapter 5, "Standard Input and Output."

To print variable values:

1. Open *var2.c* (Script 2.2) in your text editor or IDE.

2. After setting the variable values but before the return statement, print the value of the age variable (**Script 2.3**):

   ```
   printf ("You are %d years old.\n",
   → age);
   ```

   This statement will print out *You are 40 years old.*, replacing %d with the value of age (which was set at 40 earlier). Because age is an integer, %d is used as the signifier; see Table 2.2.

   The newline character is appended to the end of the statement so that the next statement will follow on the next line (see Chapter 1 for a refresher on white space in C).

3. Print out the hourly wage, along with an estimated yearly salary:

   ```
   printf ("Your hourly wage is $%0.2f.
   → This translates into approximately
   → $%0.2f per year.\n", hourly_wage,
   → hourly_wage * 40 * 52);
   ```

```
⊜ ⊜ ⊜                    📄 Script
1    /* var3.c - Script 2.3 */

2

3    #include <stdio.h>

4

5    int main(void) {

6

7        int age; /* User's age in years. */

8        float hourly_wage; /* User's hourly
         →  wage in dollars. */

9

10       /* Set the values. */

11       age = 40;

12       hourly_wage = 3.35;

13

14       /* Print the variable values. */

15       printf ("You are %d years old.\n",
         →  age);

16       printf ("Your hourly wage is
         →  $%0.2f. This translates into
         →  approximately $%0.2f per
         →  year.\n", hourly_wage,
         →  hourly_wage * 40 * 52);

17

18       getchar(); /* Pause for the user to
         →  press Return or Enter. */

19

20       return 0;

21

22   }
```

Script 2.3 Printing the value of a variable requires special syntax with the printf() function.

This print statement will make use of two inserted values. The first will be a float (a decimal), based on the value of `hourly_wage`. The second will also be a float but will be based on the result of multiplying the `hourly_wage` variable times 40 (hours per week) times 52 (weeks per year). In both cases the result is formatted to two decimal places and preceded by a dollar sign.

4. Add the `getchar()` function to make the application pause during runtime:

   `getchar();`

   This notion was also introduced in the previous chapter. It requires that the user press Return or Enter before the application stops running. This will ensure that the console or command-line window doesn't open and close before you have the chance to see the result.

5. Save the file as *var3.c*.

6. Compile and run the application (**Figure 2.3**).

✔ Tips

- If you use `%f` instead of `%0.2f` in this example, you'll see an odd result like that in **Figure 2.4**, as the entire float value is printed.

- Perhaps the best beginning debugging technique you can use as you program with C is to print out the values of variables as your applications execute. That will give you a peek into what's happening behind the scenes.

- C compilers will typically not generate an error if you have a mismatched number of formatting placeholders and variables in your `printf()` statements. Instead, you'll get odd results in the output such as pseudo-random numbers. You'll also see curious characters if you mismatch the type of placeholder and the associated value or variable.

- More `printf()` signifiers will be covered over the course of this book, and Appendix B, "Resources," contains the full list.

Figure 2.3 The result of the basic application, where each variable's value is printed.

```
C:\Documents and Settings\Larry Ullman\Desktop\C_code\Ch02\var3.exe
You are 40 years old.
Your hourly wage is $3.35. This translates into approximately $6968.00 per year.
```

```
C:\Documents and Settings\Larry Ullman\Desktop\C_code\Ch02\var3.exe
You are 40 years old.
Your hourly wage is $3.350000. This translates into approximately $6967.999802 per year.
```

Figure 2.4 Formatting variable values can be finely tuned using `printf()`. Compare the hourly wage and salary values here with those in Figure 2.3.

PRINTING VARIABLES

Introduction to Characters

The main data types used in C, including numbers, strings, and arrays, will each have its own chapter in this book, but a more basic type, the character, deserves a little discussion as well. Unlike the number types, character variables can be used for non-numeric characters such as letters and punctuation.

Creating a character variable is easy:

```
char initial;
```

Assigning values to character variables is only slightly more complicated, requiring the use of single (straight) quotation marks:

```
char right_answer;
right_answer = 'D';
```

Notice that a simple char variable contains only a single character. In the next section you'll learn how to make longer chars.

To print the value of a character using the printf() function, you'll need to use the %c marker.

To demonstrate this, you'll add a char variable to the existing C file.

To work with character variables:

1. Open *var3.c* (Script 2.3) in your text editor or IDE.

2. After declaring the other two variables, declare a char called gender (**Script 2.4**):

```
char gender; /* M or F */
```

This creates a single variable of type char. A comment is added indicating the values the variable is expected to take.

```
1    /* var4.c - Script 2.4 */
2
3    #include <stdio.h>
4
5    int main(void) {
6
7        int age; /* User's age in years. */
8        float hourly_wage; /* User's
     →  hourly wage in dollars. */
9        char gender; /* M or F */
10
11       /* Set the values. */
12       age = 40;
13       hourly_wage = 3.35;
14       gender = 'F';
15
16       /* Print the variable values. */
17       printf ("You are %d years old.\n",
     →  age);
18       printf ("Your hourly wage is
     →  $%0.2f. This translates into
     →  approximately $%0.2f per
     →  year.\n", hourly_wage,
     →  hourly_wage * 40 * 52);
19       printf ("Your gender was listed as
     →  %c.\n", gender);
20
21       getchar(); /* Pause for the user
     →  to press Return or Enter. */
22
23       return 0;
24
25   }
```

Script 2.4 This application now uses a third variable type for storing the user's gender as a single character.

3. After initializing the other two variables, assign a value to gender:

```
gender = 'F';
```

Remember that character variables can be assigned only a single character as a value and that this value is placed within single quotation marks.

4. Add a third print statement for this new variable:

```
printf ("Your gender was listed as
→ %c.\n", gender);
```

There's nothing terribly new here except for the fact that the %c formatting mark is used as a placeholder for the gender variable.

5. Save the file as *var4.c*.

6. Compile and run the application (**Figure 2.5**).

✔ Tips

■ Strings, a more complex data type, are assigned values using double quotation marks. You'll learn all about those in Chapter 11, "Working with Strings."

■ The char data type can also be used for small integers because, technically, it's an integer type, storing characters as their ASCII numeric equivalents. For example, the following lines are equivalent:

```
char initial = 'J';
char initial = 74;
```

Appendix B lists most of the ASCII characters along with their corresponding numeric values.

```
C:\Documents and Settings\Larry Ullman\Desktop\C_code\Ch02\var4.exe
You are 40 years old.
Your hourly wage is $3.35. This translates into approximately $6968.00 per year.

Your gender was listed as F.
```

Figure 2.5 Character variables—like gender here—can be printed just like numbers.

Using Character Strings

A more complex version of characters is the character string. Unlike strings you might have used in other programming languages, character strings are a sequence of individual characters.

The easiest way to create a character string is

```
char name[] = "David Brent";
```

This will create a variable called name, which contains the string David Brent. However, because character strings must end with the \0 character (which is the NULL character), name actually contains 12 characters.

Chapter 11 will discuss strings in all their glory. In the meantime, let's quickly add and print a character string in our working example.

To work with character strings:

1. Open *var4.c* (Script 2.4) in your text editor or IDE.

2. After declaring the other three variables, declare and initialize a character string called name (**Script 2.5**):

```
char name[] = "Franny Isabel";
```

```
1    /* var5.c - Script 2.5 */
2
3    #include <stdio.h>
4
5    int main(void) {
6
7        int age; /* User's age in years. */
8        float hourly_wage; /* User's
      →  hourly wage in dollars. */
9        char gender; /* M or F */
10
11       /* Create a character string and
      →  assign it a value. */
12       char name[] = "Franny Isabel";
13
14       /* Set the values. */
15       age = 40;
16       hourly_wage = 3.35;
17       gender = 'F';
18
19       /* Print the variable values. */
20       printf ("You are %d years old.\n",
      →  age);
21       printf ("Your hourly wage is
      →  $%0.2f. This translates into
      →  approximately $%0.2f per
      →  year.\n", hourly_wage,
      →  hourly_wage * 40 * 52);
22       printf ("Your gender was listed as
      →  %c.\n", gender);
23       printf ("Your name is %s.\n", name);
24
25       getchar(); /* Pause for the user
      →  to press Return or Enter. */
26
27       return 0;
28
29   }
```

Script 2.5 Characters variables can be used to create longer strings, like name here.

3. Add a fourth print statement for this new variable:

`printf ("Your name is %s.\n", name);`

Since the name variable is a character string, you'll need to use the %s signifier within the `printf()` function.

4. Save the file as *var5.c*.

5. Compile and run the application (**Figure 2.6**).

✔ Tip

■ The character string is actually an array of characters. You'll learn more about arrays in general (and use many more character arrays) in Chapter 6, "Working with Arrays."

Figure 2.6 Here a character string representing a person's name is printed out along with the other variables.

Introduction to Constants

The final data type introduced in this chapter is the constant. Unlike a variable, whose value can change over the course of an application, a constant's value never changes once it's been set. Still, you work with a constant much as you would a variable.

Constants, like variables, are of a certain type, like int or char. To declare a constant, start with the keyword const, followed by the type and name:

```
const type NAME;
const float TAXRATE;
const char RIGHT_ANSWER;
```

Although it's not required, it's commonplace to name constants using all uppercase letters as you see in these examples. Otherwise, the naming rules for constants are the same as those for variables.

After declaring a constant, assign a value as you would a variable:

```
MULTIPLIER = 4;
TAXRATE = 0.05;
RIGHT_ANSWER = 'B';
```

To demonstrate this, let's use a constant to convert degrees Fahrenheit to degrees Celsius. Although we haven't formally covered arithmetic yet, you should still be able to follow this example.

To use constants:

1. Create a new C file in your text editor or IDE.

2. Begin with the standard initial lines of code (**Script 2.6**):

   ```
   /* temperature.c - Script 2.6 */
   #include <stdio.h>
   int main(void) {
   ```

```
1    /* temperature.c - Script 2.6 */
2
3    #include <stdio.h>
4
5    int main(void) {
6
7        int fahrenheit = 212; /*
         →  Temperature to be converted. */
8        const int SUBTRACT_NUM = 32; /*
         →  Amount to subtract. */
9        const float RATIO = 5.0/9.0; /*
         →  5/9 converted to float. */
10
11       /* Calculate and print the
         →  conversion. */
12       printf ("%d degrees Fahrenheit is
         →  %0.1f degrees Celsius.\n",
         →  fahrenheit, (fahrenheit -
         →  SUBTRACT_NUM) * RATIO);
13
14       getchar(); /* Pause for the user
         →  to press Return or Enter. */
15
16       return 0;
17
18   }
```

Script 2.6 This application uses constants and number variables to convert temperatures.

3. Declare and initialize all variables and constants:

```
int fahrenheit = 212;
const int SUBTRACT_NUM = 32;
const float RATIO = 5.0/9.0;
```

This example makes use of one variable (an integer) and two constants (one an integer and the other a float). Each is assigned a value at the same time it's declared.

4. Make the conversion and print the results:

```
printf ("%d degrees Fahrenheit is
→ %0.1f degrees Celsius.\n",
→ fahrenheit, (fahrenheit -
→ SUBTRACT_NUM) * RATIO);
```

The print statement will indicate the initial degrees in Fahrenheit (which will be an integer, marked by %d) and the resulting degrees in Celsius (a float, formatted to one decimal place by %0.1f). This second value is calculated by subtracting 32—stored in the SUBTRACT_NUM constant—from the Fahrenheit number and then multiplying this by 5/9ths (stored in RATIO).

5. Complete the function:

```
getchar();
return 0;
}
```

continues on next page

6. Save the file as *temperature.c*.

7. Compile and run the application (**Figure 2.7**).

✔ Tips

- Doing mathematical calculations between integers and floats is surprisingly sensitive in C. This will be explained in more detail in the next chapter, but in the meantime, be sure to precisely follow the syntax used here.

- Admittedly, the previous example isn't the greatest use of constants, but it adequately demonstrates the basic concept.

- Another—in fact, an older—way to create constants is to use the #define syntax outside your function definitions. For example:

```
#include <stdio.h>
#define AREA_CODE 800
int main (void) {
```

The thinking behind this as well as many examples of this usage will be discussed in Chapter 8, "Using the C Preprocessor."

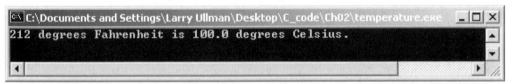

Figure 2.7 This application uses constants, which are printed like other variables: using a printf() signifier matched to the constants data type.

WORKING
WITH NUMBERS

3

One of the C programming language's strengths lies in working with numbers. For this reason, it's a very important data type to master. Although the fundamentals of doing arithmetic and such are simple, the nuances of selecting and working with the different number types can often bewilder the beginning C programmer.

In this chapter you'll learn all about the main number types and how to determine which type to use—and when. Then you'll go through quick examples demonstrating the principles of arithmetic and operator precedence. Finally, you'll learn more of the bugaboos of using the various types and how you can—inadvertently or not—switch among them.

Selecting a Number Type

Choosing the right type of number to use in a C application is critical, as it affects both the range of computational possibilities and the overall performance. Each of the available number types has its own strengths and weaknesses. More important, each has its own dangers, which can trip up even a thoughtful programmer.

C supports two broad types of numbers: *integers* (1, 2345, -8) and *floating points* (3.14, -0.8, 23.2). The latter always contain decimal points, whereas the former never do. Each of these is then further broken down into subtypes based on their size. Floats can also be represented as *doubles*, which are twice as accurate (more on this later). Also, integers (but not floats and doubles) can be defined as *signed*—meaning they can be positive or negative—or *unsigned* (in which case they cannot be negative).

The possible range of values for a specific number type depends on the operating system of the computer and how much memory is assigned to that type (**Table 3.1**). As a rule, int (the standard integer type) will always be the most efficient size (in terms of memory usage) for the computer on which the application is compiled.

Conversely, short ints tend to be only 2 bytes and long ints are 4. The actual memory usage will differ depending on the computer; the only thing you can assume is that a short int is smaller than or equal to an int and that an int is smaller than or equal to a long int. This also means that if a compiler gives the same amount of memory to a short int and an int, they'll both require 2 bytes of memory and have a range of -32,768 to 32,767. If the compiler gives the same amount of memory to both int and long int, they'll both require 4 bytes of memory and have a range of -2,147,483,648 to 2,147,483,647.

Table 3.1 This table represents the general range of values and memory requirements of the different number types for the average computer.

Number Types and Approximate Sizes		
TYPE	MEMORY USAGE	RANGE OF VALUES
short int	2 bytes	-32,768 to 32,767
unsigned short int	2 bytes	0 to 65,535
int	4 bytes	-2,147,483,648 to 2,147,483,647
unsigned int	4 bytes	0 to 4,294,967,295
long int	4 bytes	-2,147,483,648 to 2,147,483,647
unsigned long int	4 bytes	0 to 4,294,967,295
long long int	8 bytes	-9,223,372,036,854,775,808 to 9,223,372,036,854,775,807
unsigned long long int	8 bytes	0 to 18,446,744,073,709,551,615
float	4 bytes	-1e38 to +1e38
double	8 bytes	-1e308 to +1e308
long double	8 bytes	-1e308 to +1e308

C and Memory

One of the most complex aspects of programming in C is that you must judiciously manage memory usage (conversely, higher-level and scripting languages perform memory management for you). We deal with more complex memory management later in the book, but you should know now that selecting the right variable type will affect the amount of memory required by your applications.

Table 3.1 indicates the memory requirements of the different number types. For your reference, a *bit* is the smallest unit of memory, holding a single 0 or 1. A *byte* is equal to 8 bits. Therefore, a single byte can store up to 256 different combinations of zeroes and ones (either 0 or 1 in each of the eight slots). Your computer's memory is listed in *megabytes*, each of which is 1,024 kilobytes, where a kilobyte is 1,024 bytes. This may infer your C applications can go hog wild in memory usage, but a lot of memory is used by the operating system, so you shouldn't be writing applications that require 256 MB of RAM.

Finally, a *word* is the basic unit of memory for a particular computer. Hence, an old PC running MS-DOS has a word of 16 bits, or 2 bytes; most modern computers have a word of 32 bits, or 4 bytes; and something like Apple's new G5—which has a 64-bit processor—has a word of 64 bits, or 8 bytes.

All of this information is relevant because how much memory a type takes up—and therefore that type's possible range of values—depends on the computer's word. For starters, an `int` will normally require one word of memory. Most of today's computers, using 32-bit and x86 processors, have words of 4 bytes.

Floats normally require 4 bytes of memory and doubles 8. Computers are theoretically slower in dealing with floats (and more so for doubles), although most modern computers use a floating-point processor, which greatly minimizes the performance difference.

To select a number type:

1. Decide whether you will be working with a fraction.

   If you know that the number being manipulated will have a decimal, it must be a floating point type (`float`, `double`, `long double`). If it won't require a decimal, then you're working within the integer group.

2. If you will be using fractions, determine how important accuracy is.

   As stated before, doubles are twice as accurate as floats. If you'll be working with numbers whose accuracy is paramount, go with a double. If fair approximations are acceptable, stick to the smaller float. In the next few examples you'll get a better sense of each type's level of accuracy.

3. Consider what the maximum possible value for a number will be.

   For example, if you wanted to store a U.S. zip code as an integer, you couldn't use a `short int`, as the maximum zip code value (somewhere in the 90000 realm) would be larger than the maximum `short int` size (32,767). When making this decision, err on the side of selecting a type too large over one that might be too small, particularly as you are just learning C.

continues on next page

SELECTING A NUMBER TYPE

4. Finally, determine if the number can ever be negative, assuming it's an integer type. If the value will never be negative (like a zip code, a person's age, or an IQ), opt for an unsigned type, thereby doubling the maximum range.

5. Consider how the number will be used. Specific actions, like division and finding the remainder of division, have their own type requirements, as you'll see throughout the rest of this chapter. You'll need to account for this idea when choosing a type as well.

✔ Tips

■ Exponential numbers are represented by the floating point type, as in Table 3.1.

■ Critical financial calculations are best performed using integers that don't have the inexact arithmetic that floats can. This can be accomplished by working in cents (175 cents) instead of dollars (1.75).

■ The `long long int` type is new as of the C99 standard.

■ Unless you specify otherwise, all forms of integers are signed by default.

■ The number ranges indicated in Table 3.1 may vary plus or minus one on different computers.

■ On a more advanced level, you can use other number types if you include the *stdint.h* header file.

■ The `sizeof()` function returns the size, in bytes, taken up by a specific variable or variable type. You can place a variable type within parentheses or precede a variable's name with just `sizeof`:

```
short int temp = 3940;
printf ("Temp: %zd; Int: %zd, Float:
→ %zd\n", sizeof (temp), sizeof(int),
→ sizeof(float));
```

Notice that you use the special `%zd` signifier to print the value, which is of a special type (`sizeof()` returns a value of type `size_t`).

Performing Arithmetic

While the principles of arithmetic in C are exactly like those you learned in school, the actual results are more complex because of how C works with the different number types. For this reason, choosing the appropriate data type depends not only on the possible values it might store but also on how it will be used.

The standard operators for performing arithmetic are

◆ +, for addition

◆ -, for subtraction

◆ *, for multiplication

◆ /, for division

◆ %, for modulus (finding the remainder of a division)

Using these operators, here are some sample calculations:

```
int a = 3;
int b = 2;
int c;
c = a + b; /* 5 */
c = a - b; /* 1 */
c = b - a; /* -1 */
c = a * b; /* 6 */
c = a / b; /* 1, not 1.5! */
c = a % b; /* 1 */
```

When you divide one integer by another integer, the result will always be an integer, meaning that any remainder (fraction) is dropped, as in the previous example. For this reason, you'll pretty much always want to use floats for division. If one of the two numbers involved in a division is a float, a float will automatically be the result:

```
float a = 3.0;
float b = 2.0;
float c;
c = a / b; /* 1.5 */
```

Conversely, the modulus operator (%) can only be used on integers. You cannot return the remainder of a division when one of the two numbers is a float.

To perform some arithmetic, you'll create an example that turns inches into feet. This will also allow you to see how the different types perform within the context of standard arithmetic.

To perform arithmetic:

1. Create a new, blank text document in your editor or integrated development environment (IDE).

2. Being by documenting the file (**Script 3.1**):

   ```
   /* feet_inches.c - Script 3.1 */
   ```

   This simple comment matches the script number to its name. Feel free to add as many other notes as you need to your code.

3. Type the required `include` line:

   ```
   #include <stdio.h>
   ```

4. Begin defining the `main()` function.

   ```
   int main(void) {
   ```

   If you are confused by either this or the previous step, review the two previous chapters.

5. Define the variables to be used:

   ```
   unsigned short int inches = 3435;
   unsigned short int feet_int;
   unsigned short int inches_remainder;
   float feet_float;
   ```

   This application makes use of four variables: three short integers and a standard float. Each of the integers is short, limiting their range, and unsigned, as they can't be negative. One, `inches`, is assigned a value with which calculations will be made.

```
      ⬤ ⬤ ⬤                    Script

 1    /* feet_inches.c - Script 3.1 */
 2
 3    #include <stdio.h>
 4
 5    int main(void) {
 6
 7        unsigned short int inches = 3435;
    → /* Some random value. */
 8        unsigned short int feet_int; /*
    → The integer version of feet. */
 9        unsigned short int
    → inches_remainder; /* The remainder,
    → for working with feet_int. */
10        float feet_float; /* The float
    → version of feet, for comparison. */
11
12        /* Make the calculations. */
13        feet_int = inches/12;
14        inches_remainder = inches % 12;
15        feet_float = inches/12.0; /* Must
    → use 12.0 here to result in a float!
    → */
16
17        /* Print the results. */
18        printf ("%u inches is %u feet, %u
    → inches.\n", inches, feet_int,
    → inches_remainder);
19        printf ("As a float, that's %f
    → feet.\n", feet_float);
20
21        getchar(); /* Pause for the user
    → to press Return or Enter. */
22
23        return 0;
24
25    }
```

Script 3.1 This measurement converter performs arithmetic using different number types.

6. Determine how many feet are in the specified inches:

```
feet_int = inches/12;
```

Dividing 3435 by 12 gives the number 286.25. But, since `feet_int`, `inches` and 12 are all integers, `feet_int` will have a value of just 12, with the remainder being dropped.

7. Calculate how many inches are left over after determining the feet:

```
inches_remainder = inches % 12;
```

To find out how many inches are left (which corresponds to the .25 decimal when dividing 3435 by 12), use the modulus operator. This operator must be applied only to integers and will return an integer as well (`inches_remainder`).

8. Recalculate the division using floats:

```
feet_float = inches/12.0;
```

Even though the `feet_float` variable was defined as a float, to successfully make that calculation, either inches or 12 must also be a float. Here, 12 has been turned into a float by adding a decimal point and a zero. Strange as it may seem, if this line were

```
feet_float = inches/12;
```

the result would be just 286.0 and the remainder would be lost.

9. Print the results of the calculations:

```
printf ("%u inches is %u feet, %u
→ inches.\n", inches, feet_int,
→ inches_remainder);
printf ("As a float, that's %f
→ feet.\n", feet_float);
```

continues on next page

PERFORMING ARITHMETIC

These two lines print all of the values being used, thanks to the `printf()` function and the appropriate signifiers. The `%u` signifier is used to match the unsigned integers, although `%d` (the standard integer marker) would have also worked. If you want, you can change `%f` in the second statement to `%0.2f` to format the result to two decimal places.

10. Add the `getchar()` function to pause execution of the application:

    `getchar();`

    Once again, this function is being used merely to halt execution of the application, waiting for the user to press Return or Enter before closing.

11. Finish the `main()` function:

    ```
        return 0;
    }
    ```

12. Save the file as *feet_inches.c*.

13. Compile the application (**Figure 3.1**).

14. Debug the application, if necessary.

    If your compiler indicated any errors, fix them and recompile.

15. Run the application (**Figure 3.2**).

Figure 3.1 Your compiler (Dev-C++ here) should report on any errors in the code.

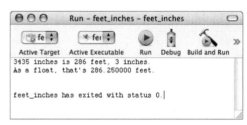

Figure 3.2 Run the executable file to see the results (here the application is being run through Apple's Xcode).

✔ Tips

- If you've forgotten the proper signifiers for the `printf()` function, see Table 2.2 in Chapter 2, "Introduction to Data Types," or see Appendix B, "Resources."

- Do not confuse the addition and subtraction operators with those used to indicate the sign of a number. Spacing makes all the difference:

```
int a = +3; /* Positive 3 */
int b = -2; /* Negative 2 */
int c = a + b; /* 1 */
```

- When using the modulus operator, if the first number (a in the introductory examples) is negative, the resulting remainder will always be negative. Otherwise, the resulting remainder will be positive.

- The float type stores an approximation of values (for example, 2.0 might actually be stored as 1.9999999). For this reason, arithmetic using floats can be tricky and you should never check to see if two floats have the same value.

- Each of the arithmetic operators can be combined with the assignment operator (=) to perform calculations and assign a value in one step. For example:

```
int a = 10;
a += 2; /* 12 */
a -= 3; /* 9 */
a *= 2; /* 18 */
a /= 6; /* 3 */
a %= 2; /* 1 */
```

PERFORMING ARITHMETIC

Increment and Decrement Operators

As you program, you'll often encounter situations in which you need to add or subtract one to or from a number. Quite frequently this occurs within loops, as you'll see in Chapter 6, "Control Structures." For this reason, C has the increment and decrement operators:

```c
int a = 10;
a++; /* 11 */
a++; /* 12 */
a--; /* 11 */
```

These operators come in both the postfix (shown above) and prefix (below) versions, differing only in precedence (see the next section of the chapter for more):

```c
int a = 10;
--a; /* 9 */
++a; /* 10 */
```

When assigning the value of an incremented or decremented variables to another variable, which form you use makes all the difference, as the following example will demonstrate.

To use the increment and decrement operators:

1. Create a new, blank text document in your editor or IDE.

2. Begin by documenting the file (**Script 3.2**):

   ```c
   /* ones.c - Script 3.2 */
   ```

3. Type the required include line and begin defining the main() function:

   ```c
   #include <stdio.h>
   int main(void) {
   ```

```
● ○ ○                    Script
1    /* ones.c - Script 3.2 */
2
3    #include <stdio.h>
4
5    int main(void) {
6
7        int n1, n2; /* Two integers. */
8
9        /* Postfix arithmetic */
10       n1 = 1;
11       n2 = 1;
12       printf ("At first, n1 is %d, n2 is
     → %d.\n", n1, n2);
13       n2 = n1++;
14       printf ("After n2 = n1++, n1 is
     → %d, n2 is %d.\n", n1, n2);
15       n2 = n1--;
16       printf ("After n2 = n1--, n1 is %d,
     → n2 is %d.\n\n", n1, n2);
17
18       /* Reset */
19       n1 = 1;
20       n2 = 1;
21       printf ("After resetting, n1 is
     → %d, n2 is %d.\n", n1, n2);
22
23       /* Prefix arithmetic */
24       n2 = ++n1;
25       printf ("After n2 = ++n1, n1 is
     → %d, n2 is %d.\n", n1, n2);
26       n2 = --n1;
27       printf ("After n2 = --n1, n1 is %d,
     → n2 is %d.\n", n1, n2);
28
29       getchar(); /* Pause for the user
     → to press Return or Enter. */
30
31       return 0;
32
33   }
```

Script 3.2 The results of incrementing and decrementing integers depends on whether you use the postfix or prefix version.

4. Define the variables to be used:

```
int n1, n2;
```

This application makes use of two simple integers, called **n1** and **n2**.

5. Set **n1**'s and **n2**'s initial values and print some introductory text:

```
n1 = 1;
n2 = 1;
printf ("At first, n1 is %d, n2 is
→ %d.\n", n1, n2);
```

The **n1** variable will be incremented and decremented to modify **n2**'s value but both should be initialized before you print them. To give you a sense of what's happening in the application, the initial values of both will be printed.

6. Increment and decrement **n1**, assigning this value to **n2**, and print the results:

```
n2 = n1++;
printf ("After n2 = n1++, n1 is %d,
→ n2 is %d.\n", n1, n2);
n2 = n1--;
printf ("After n2 = n1-, n1 is %d, n2
→ is %d.\n\n", n1, n2);
```

Using the postfix version of incrementation, **n2** is assigned the value of **n1** plus one, then both values are printed for comparison. Next, the process is repeated using decrementation.

7. Reset the value of the variables and add some more descriptive information:

```
n1 = 1;
n2 = 1;
printf ("After resetting, n1 is %d,
→ n2 is %d.\n", n1, n2);
```

To avoid confusion, both variables will be assigned the value of 1 before the prefix operators are used.

continues on next page

INCREMENT AND DECREMENT OPERATORS

8. Use the prefix version of both operators and print those results:

```
n2 = ++n1;
printf ("After n2 = ++n1, n1 is %d,
→ n2 is %d.\n", n1, n2);
n2 = --n1;
printf ("After n2 = -n1, n1 is %d,
→ n2 is %d.\n", n1, n2);
```

   This step is simply a repeat of Step 6, using the prefix (as opposed to the postfix) operators. The print statements will help to demonstrate the differences when the application is run.

9. Add the `getchar()` function to pause execution of the application and finish the `main()` function:

```
    getchar();
    return 0;
}
```

10. Save the file as *ones.c*.

11. Compile and debug the application (**Figure 3.3**).

12. Run the application (**Figure 3.4**).

    As you can see from the results, using the postfix version of each operator, `n2` first is assigned the current value of `n1` and then `n1` is incremented or decremented. Hence, after `n2 = n1++`, `n1` has the value of 2 (1 incremented) but `n2` has the value of 1 (`n1`'s value prior to incrementation). Using the prefix versions, `n1`'s value is first altered and then this value is assigned to `n2`.

C: Visual QuickStart Guide
~ $ cd Documents/Books/C\ VQS/C_code/Ch03
~/Documents/Books/C VQS/C_code/Ch03 $ gcc -g -o ones ones.c
~/Documents/Books/C VQS/C_code/Ch03 $

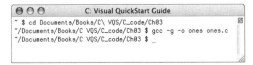

Figure 3.3 Using gcc to compile the application on Mac OS X (this would also work on other Unix-based operating systems).

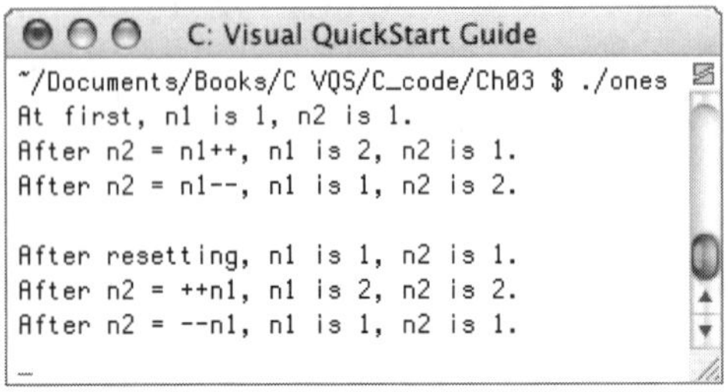

C: Visual QuickStart Guide
~/Documents/Books/C VQS/C_code/Ch03 $ ./ones
At first, n1 is 1, n2 is 1.
After n2 = n1++, n1 is 2, n2 is 1.
After n2 = n1--, n1 is 1, n2 is 2.
After resetting, n1 is 1, n2 is 1.
After n2 = ++n1, n1 is 2, n2 is 2.
After n2 = --n1, n1 is 1, n2 is 1.

Figure 3.4 The results of running the *ones* application, reflecting how the prefix and postfix versions of incrementing and decrementing `n1` affect the value of `n2`.

✔ Tips

- C++ gets its name from the notion that it's one notch above C.
- On the one hand, using the increment and decrement operators creates smaller, faster code. On the other hand, it can make the code harder for a human to follow, so be judicious in its use.

Table 3.2 The precedence of operators from highest to lowest (those listed first will be executed first).

Rules of Precedence
OPERATOR
()
++, --
+, - (Sign operators)
*, /
+, - (Addition and subtraction)
=, +=, -=, *=, /=, %=

Understanding Precedence

As you were probably taught when you first learned arithmetic, operators have a precedence: rules dictating in what order calculations are made. These are important to understand because they can dramatically affect the end result.

Table 3.2 lists the order of precedence in C for the arithmetic operators, but it's probably easiest just to follow these three rules:

1. Multiplication and division take place before addition and subtraction.

2. Operators with the same precedence level are executed from left to right.

3. Use parentheses to guarantee your results.

This last rule is really the most important; if you'd prefer, you can specify all of your arithmetic intentions using parentheses. The second rule means that, for example, if multiplication and division both take place and their order is not mandated by precedence, they'll be executed from left to right.

```
int a;
a = 10 * 2 / 5; /* 4 */
a = 10 / 2 * 5; /* 25 */
```

To show how precedence affects calculations, let's rewrite the temperature conversion example from Chapter 2.

To demonstrate precedence:

1. Create a new C source file (**Script 3.3**):

```
/* temperature2.c - Script 3.3 -
→ remake of Script 2.6
→ (temperature.c) */
#include <stdio.h>
int main(void) {
```

2. Declare the required variables:

```
float temp_f, temp_c;
```

This application will use two variables, both of which are floats.

3. Set the temperature in Celsius and convert this to Fahrenheit:

```
temp_c = 32.0;
temp_f = temp_c * 9.0/5.0 + 32;
```

First, some random value is assigned to the temp_c variable. Because that variable is a float type, a decimal point and zero are added as well.

The formula for making this conversion is to take the temperature in Celsius, multiply it by the result of dividing 9.0 by 5.0 (which is 1.8), and then add 32. Using parentheses to be explicit, this could be written as

```
(temp_c * (9.0/5.0)) + 32
```

However, since multiplication and division automatically take place before addition, it can be simplified by removing the parentheses without affecting its accuracy.

4. Print out the results:

```
printf ("%0.1f degrees Celsius is
→ %0.1f degrees Fahrenheit.\n",
→ temp_c, temp_f);
```

Both the temperature in Celsius and the calculated Fahrenheit will be printed here. Each is formatted to one decimal point (%01.f).

```
1   /* temperature2.c - Script 3.3 -
    → remake of Script 2.6
    → (temperature.c) */
2
3   #include <stdio.h>
4
5   int main(void) {
6
7       float temp_f, temp_c; /*
    → Fahrenheit and Celsius. */
8
9       /* Make the conversion. */
10      temp_c = 32.0;
11      temp_f = temp_c * 9.0/5.0 + 32; /*
    → Or (temp_c * (9.0/5.0)) + 32 */
12
13      /* Print the conversion. */
14      printf ("%0.1f degrees Celsius is
    → %0.1f degrees Fahrenheit.\n",
    → temp_c, temp_f);
15
16      getchar(); /* Pause for the user
    → to press Return or Enter. */
17
18      return 0;
19
20  }
```

Script 3.3 You con control the order in which arithmetic occurs by using parentheses or mastering the rules of precedence.

Figure 3.5 The first conversion of a temperature.

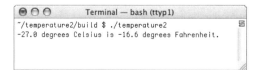

Figure 3.6 Another temperature conversion.

5. Complete the main() function:

```
    getchar();
    return 0;
}
```

6. Save the file as *temperature2.c.*

7. Compile and debug the code.

8. Execute the application (**Figure 3.5**).

9. If desired, change the value of *temp_c* in the code, recompile, and re-execute the application (**Figure 3.6**).

✔ Tips

- Technically, since multiplication and division have the same precedence and are executed from left to right, the temperature conversion formula is first multiplying *temp_c* times 9.0 and then dividing that by 5.0 (as opposed to dividing 9.0 by 5.0 and then multiplying that times *temp_c*). Due to the nature of multiplication and division, this does not affect the end result.

- The conversion formula would not actually work if it were written as temp_c * (9/5) + 32. The division of 9 by 5 would take place, resulting in a value of 1 (because the remainder is dropped when dividing one integer by another). This value (1) would then be multiplied by temp_c. Conversely, the formula temp_c * 9/5 + 32 actually would work, because the float temp_c would first be multiplied by 9 and this resulting float would then be divided by 5, without ever losing a remainder. Rather than confusing yourself with these tedious rules, if you always use floats in division and incorporate parentheses, your arithmetic will stay correct.

- In Chapter 5, "Standard Input and Output," you'll see how to take numbers as keyboard input on which calculations will be made.

Understanding Overflow and Underflow

Another source of potential conflict can arise when the value of a variable becomes too large or too small for its type for the computer running the application. When this occurs, it's called *overflow* and *underflow*. Depending on the computer, this will either cause an error or return alternative results.

This happens most frequently with floats, and it will obviously mess up any calculations made with such a value. When you attempt to print this variable, you'll most likely see either inf or infinity, indicating that the value is out of range.

The best way to avoid these problems is by knowing the limits for a particular type. This information is stored in the *limits.h* (for integers and characters) and *float.h* header files. The following example shows how to use these files to find the maximum and minimum value of a type. Just for fun, it also demonstrates what happens when overflow or underflow occurs.

To cause underflow and overflow:

1. Create a new C source file, beginning with the first include (**Script 3.4**):

   ```
   /* let_it_flow.c - Script 3.4 */
   #include <stdio.h>
   ```

2. Include the two limit files:

   ```
   #include <limits.h>
   #include <float.h>
   ```

   The first line will add the contents of *limits.h* to this application. The second will add the contents of *float.h*. Together, this makes available certain constants that will be used in this application.

```
1    /* let_it_flow.c - Script 3.4 */
2
3    #include <stdio.h>
4    #include <limits.h> // For integer
   → limits.
5    #include <float.h> // For float limits.
6
7    int main(void) {
8
9        short int short_max = SHRT_MAX; //
   → Largest short integer.
10       int integer_min = INT_MIN; //
   → Smallest integer.
11       double double_max = DBL_MAX; //
   → Largest double.
12
13       /* Let it flow! */
14       short_max++; // Add one to
   → short_max.
15       integer_min *= 2; // Double the
   → negative number to make it smaller.
16       double_max *= 10; // Make the
   → double larger.
17
18       /* Print the results. */
19       printf ("The maximum short integer
   → is %d. Overflowed, it looks like
   → %d.\n", SHRT_MAX, short_max);
20       printf ("The minimum integer is
   → %d. Underflowed, it looks like
   → %d.\n", INT_MIN, integer_min);
21       printf ("The maximum double is %f.
   → Overflowed, it looks like %f.\n",
   → DBL_MAX, double_max);
22
23       getchar(); /* Pause for the user to
   → press Return or Enter. */
24
25       return 0;
26
27   }
```

Script 3.4 Using numbers outside the range of possible values results in overflow or underflow. In this application, variables are set to their maximum or minimum value, then increased or decreased.

3. Start defining the main() function:

```
int main(void) {
```

4. Declare and initialize the variables to be used:

```
short int short_max = SHRT_MAX;
int integer_min = INT_MIN;
double double_max = DBL_MAX;
```

Using the constants defined in the two included files, three variables are initialized to maximum and minimum values for different types. SHRT_MAX represents the largest possible value of a short integer; INT_MIN represents the smallest possible value for an integer; and DBL_MAX represents the largest possible value for a double.

5. Cause each variable to over- or underflow:

```
short_max++;
integer_min *= 2;
double_max *= 10;
```

Since short_max already has the value of the maximum possible short integer, increasing it by one will cause that variable to overflow. Conversely, doubling the value of integer_min (the smallest possible integer), will create an even smaller integer, as doubling a negative number makes it twice as small. Finally, the double is multiplied by 10 to create a larger double than the largest possible value.

continues on next page

UNDERSTANDING OVERFLOW AND UNDERFLOW

6. Print out the results:

```
printf ("The maximum short integer is
→ %d. Overflowed, it looks like
→ %d.\n", SHRT_MAX, short_max);

printf ("The minimum integer is %d.
→ Underflowed, it looks like %d.\n",
→ INT_MIN, integer_min);

printf ("The maximum double is %f.
→ Overflowed, it looks like %f.\n",
→ DBL_MAX, double_max);
```

These three print statements will each print the original constant value (the maximum or minimum), followed by the manipulated variable. This way, you'll be able to see the limits—which correspond to the original variable value—and the result of overflow and underflow.

7. Complete the function definition:

```
getchar();
return 0;
}
```

8. Save the file as *let_it_flow.c*.

9. Compile and debug (as necessary) the application.

10. Run the compiled application (**Figures 3.7** and **3.8**).

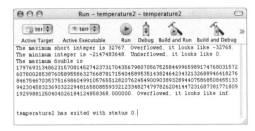

Figure 3.7 Running the application using Xcode on Mac OS X. Notice how each variable type responds differently in terms of the end value.

Figure 3.8 The results using Dev-C++ on Windows. The overflowed double is displayed slightly differently (compare with Figure 3.7).

UNDERSTANDING OVERFLOW AND UNDERFLOW

✔ Tips

- Both *limits.h* and *float.h* are standard C header files, just like *stdio.h,* meaning they should be part of the C distribution that comes with your IDE. You'll learn more about header files and the syntax for including them in Chapter 8, "Using the C Preprocessor."

- You can find all the `limits.h` and `float.h` constants by searching the Internet or by viewing those files on your computer.

- If you see NaN displayed, this means "Not a Number," indicating that the variable either has a non-number value due to over- or underflow.

UNDERSTANDING OVERFLOW AND UNDERFLOW

Variable Conversion

Over the course of this chapter you've seen many ways of working with the various number types. One last technique to be addressed is that of variable conversion: changing the value of a variable from one type (say, float) to another (integer).

C will automatically convert values to match types; for example:

```
int a;
float b = 3.14;
a = b; /* a is 3 */
b = a; /* b is 3.0 */
```

In simplest terms, this means that the decimal value is dropped when converting from a float to an integer and that a 0 is added when going the other way.

You can also manually convert a value from one type to another, a process called *type casting*. To do so, precede the value being converted with the new type in parentheses. For example:

```
int a;
float b = 3.14;
a = (int) b; /* a is 3 */
```

Let's use a quick reworking of the temperature example to demonstrate conversion.

```
⊖ ○ ⊖                    📄 Script
1    /* temperature3.c - Script 3.5 -
   → remake of Script 3.3
   → (temperature2.c) */

2

3    #include <stdio.h>

4

5    int main(void) {

6

7        float temp_f, temp_c; /*
   → Fahrenheit and Celsius. */

8

9        /* Make the conversion. */

10       temp_c = 32.0;

11       temp_f = temp_c * 9.0/5.0 + 32; /*
   → Or (temp_c * (9.0/5.0)) + 32 */

12

13       /* Print the conversion. */

14       printf ("%d degrees Celsius is %d
   degrees Fahrenheit.\n", (int)
   → temp_c, (int) temp_f);

15

16       getchar(); /* Pause for the user
   → to press Return or Enter. */

17

18       return 0;

19

20   }
```

Script 3.5 C allows you to, and can automatically, convert values from one type to another.

To convert variables from one type to another:

1. Open *temperature2.c* (Script 3.3) in your text editor or IDE.

2. Change the `printf()` line to read as follows (**Script 3.5**):

   ```
   printf ("%d degrees Celsius is %d
   → degrees Fahrenheit.\n", (int)
   → temp_c, (int) temp_f);
   ```

   In the original example, the numbers were displayed as decimals. To display them as integers, without having to change the original variable declarations or arithmetic, use type casting when feeding the values to the `printf()` function. Because the types are being changed, the signifiers within the function are also switched (from `%0.1f` to `%d`).

3. Save the file as *temperature3.c*.

4. Compile, debug, and run the application (**Figure 3.9**).

Figure 3.9 To display the numbers as integers rather than floats, type conversion is used (compare with Figure 3.5).

VARIABLE CONVERSION

✔ Tips

■ As you may have already experienced, feeding the printf() function the wrong signifier for a type normally leads to bizarre results. For example (**Figure 3.10**):

```
printf ("Not a float: %f; not an
→ integer: %d", 8, 345.09);
```

■ Type casting has its own rules of precedence, but they're cumbersome and not worth memorization.

■ If the truncation that occurs when converting floats to integers annoys you, you can round the value, like so:

```
printf ("%d degrees Celsius is %d
→ degrees Fahrenheit.\n", (int)
→ (temp_c + 0.5), (int) (temp_f
→ + 0.5));
```

Figure 3.10 Mismatching a printf() signifier to a value type will have unusual consequences.

CONTROL STRUCTURES

While the examples to this point have used variables, performed calculations, and reported on results, they still lack the dynamic nature of true programming. One of the key ingredients in real applications is the flexibility brought about by using control structures: constructs such as conditionals and loops.

The most common control structure is the `if` conditional and its kin: `if-else`, `if-elseif`, `if-elseif-else`, et al. This chapter covers `if` conditionals first; during this discussion you'll also see other operators commonly used in C (you've already come across the arithmetic and assignment operators). Next, you'll use two other conditionals, each with a unique syntax and usage: the ternary operator and the `switch`. Finally, this chapter covers the two most common types of loops: `while` and `for`. Once you've worked your way through this material, you'll be ready to create more fully functioning C applications.

If Statements

Conditionals are a *branching* type of control structure, meaning they dictate the course of an application based on certain parameters. Of the branching control structures, the if conditional is the most common. Its syntax is straightforward:

```
if (condition) {
    statements;
}
```

The condition is placed within parentheses, followed by—within curly braces—the statement or statements to be executed. If the condition is *true*, the statements will be executed. If it is *false*, the statements will not be run.

In C, the simplest representation of false is the number 0 and true is everything else:

```
if (1) {
    printf ("This conditional is always
    → true.");
    printf ("This is another
    → statement.");
}
```

Any quantity or type of statements can be executed as the result of the conditional. If your conditional uses only one statement, you can get away without using the curly braces. For example:

```
if (1) printf ("This conditional is
→ always true.");
```

To get you started programming conditionals, the following example demonstrates how the most basic condition is treated in C.

```
 ○ ○ ○              Script
1     /* if.c - Script 4.1 */

2

3     #include <stdio.h>

4

5     int main (void) {

6

7         int test = 1; // Test variable for
  → conditional purposes.

8

9         // Print introductory text.

10        printf ("Testing the test
  → variable.\n");

11

12        // Check for a test value and print
  → it (if it isn't 0).

13        if (test) {

14            printf ("*** Value of test is
  → %d.\n", test);

15        }

16

17        getchar(); /* Pause for the user to
  → press Return or Enter. */

18

19        return 0;

20

21    }
```

Script 4.1 This basic conditional checks if the test variable has a value other than 0.

To create an if conditional:

1. Create a new, blank C project in your text editor or IDE.

2. Add the initial comments and code (**Script 4.1**):

   ```
   /* if.c - Script 4.1 */
   #include <stdio.h>
   int main (void) {
   ```

3. Declare and initialize an integer variable:

   ```
   int test = 1;
   ```

   The test variable is a simple integer (you could also make it a short unsigned int, if you want to be a minimalist). It will be used as the condition in this application's control structure.

4. Add a message to be printed:

   ```
   printf ("Testing the test
   → variable.\n");
   ```

   This message establishes the context for any forthcoming text. It also guarantees that something will occur when the application is run, regardless of the conditional's truth (if the condition is false, no other text will be printed).

5. Define the if conditional:

   ```
   if (test) {
       printf ("*** Value of test is
       → %d.\n", test);
   }
   ```

   If the condition is true, some text will be printed along with the value of test. This will be the case if test has a value other than 0. If the condition is not true (because test does have a value of 0), the printf() statement will never be executed.

   continues on next page

IF STATEMENTS

6. Complete the `main()` function:

```
    getchar();
    return 0;
}
```

7. Save the project as *if.c*.

8. Compile and debug, as necessary.

9. Run the executable application (**Figure 4.1**).

10. For comparison, change the value of `test` to 0, recompile, and rerun the application (**Figure 4.2**).

In this case, the condition is false, because 0 (`test`'s value) is false in C.

Figure 4.1 If the `test` variable has a value other than 0, the condition is true and the variable's value is printed.

Figure 4.2 If the `test` variable's value is 0, the condition is false and only the print statement before the conditional is executed.

✔ Tips

- Creating single-statement conditionals without curly braces, while perfectly legal, can make your code harder to follow and possibly lead to errors if you make future changes to that conditional. That being said, you may like the terseness of this format or encounter it in other people's work. In this book, you'll see almost every conditional using curly braces.

- The C99 standard includes a new data type called `_Bool`, short for *boolean*. Variables of this type can have a value of either 0 (representing false) or 1 (true). In fact, assigning any value other than 0 to it results in a value of 1. Note that version 4 of Dev-C++ does not support `_Bool` but version 5 does.

- Available in the C99 standard is the *stdbool.h* file, which defines three related keywords: `bool`, which is an alias for the `_Bool` data type; `true`, which is an alias for 1; and `false`, which is an alias for 0. The purpose of this file and these aliases is to help make your C code more portable to C++, which uses those terms.

Table 4.1 These comparison and logical operators are frequently used in conditionals and other control structures.

Comparison and Logical Operators	
OPERATOR	MEANING
>	Greater than
<	Less than
>=	Greater than or equal to
>=	Less than or equal to
==	Equal to
!=	Not equal to
&&	and
||	or
!	not

Comparison and Logical Operators

Using a simple variable (as in the previous example) as a condition won't take you very far in your programming. In order to make more complex, real-world if statements, you'll want to utilize the various comparison and logical operators (**Table 4.1**).

The comparison operators are used with mathematical values, for example, to tell if one value is greater than, equal to, or less than another. Using these, the true/false status of a conditional can be based on more elaborate formulas:

```
if (age >= 18) {
    printf ("You are old enough to vote.");
}
```

The logical operators are used, often in conjunction with parentheses, to create compound conditions, such as a range:

```
if ( (age > 12) && (age < 20)) {
    printf ("Teenager alert!");
}
```

Special attention should be given to the equality operator (==). One of the most common mistakes programmers make—even the most seasoned ones—is to inadvertently use the assignment operator (=) in a condition:

```
if (var = 190) {...
```

The real intent of the conditional is to check if the value of var is *equal* to 190 (written as var == 190), which may or may not be true. The above, miswritten conditional, will always be true (as var can be assigned the value of 190).

One simple use of these operators is to print a message based on the value of a grade point average.

To use comparison and logical operators:

1. Create a new, blank C project in your text editor or IDE.

2. Add the initial comments and code (**Script 4.2**):

```
/* gpa.c - Script 4.2 */
#include <stdio.h>
int main (void) {
```

3. Declare and initialize a float variable:

```
float gpa = 3.8;
```

The *gpa* variable will store the value of a person's grade point average. For the initial run, it will be set to 3.8.

4. Determine if the grade point average qualifies for graduating summa cum laude (with highest honors):

```
if (gpa >= 3.9) {
    printf ("You're graduating summa
→ cum laude with a %0.2f GPA!\n", gpa);
}
```

If the value of **gpa** is greater than or equal to 3.9 (a standard mark for summa cum laude), this print statement will be executed. If the value is less than 3.9, this print statement will be skipped.

5. Determine if the grade point average qualifies for graduating magna cum laude (with great honors):

```
if ( (gpa >= 3.75) && (gpa < 3.9) ) {
    printf ("You're graduating magna
→ cum laude with a %0.2f GPA!\n", gpa);
}
```

```
 1    /* gpa.c - Script 4.2 */
 2
 3    #include <stdio.h>
 4
 5    int main (void) {
 6
 7        float gpa = 3.8; // Grade Point
   → Average
 8
 9        // Check for summa cum laude (3.9
   → to 4.0).
10        if (gpa >= 3.9) {
11            printf ("You're graduating
   → summa cum laude with a %0.2f
   → GPA!\n", gpa);
12        }
13
14        // Check for magna cum laude (3.75
   → to 3.89).
15        if ( (gpa >= 3.75) && (gpa < 3.9)
   → ) {
16            printf ("You're graduating
   → magna cum laude with a %0.2f
   → GPA!\n", gpa);
17        }
18
19        // Check for cum laude (3.5 to 3.74).
20        if ( (gpa >= 3.50) && (gpa < 3.75)
   → ) {
21            printf ("You're graduating cum
   → laude with a %0.2f GPA!\n", gpa);
22        }
23
24        getchar(); /* Pause for the user
   → to press Return or Enter. */
25
26        return 0;
27
28    }
```

Script 4.2 Thanks to the comparison and logical operators, a variable can be tested against several possible conditions.

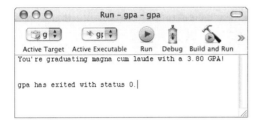

Figure 4.3 Different messages are printed based on the value of the gpa variable (compare with Figure 4.4).

Using the logical operator and parentheses, this conditional tests if gpa has a value greater than or equal to 3.75 but less than 3.9 (which is the start of summa cum laude). Because of the *and* (&&) operator, both conditions must be true in order for the entire condition to be true. If gpa is less than 3.75 or greater than or equal to 3.9, this conditional is false.

6. Determine if the grade point average qualifies for graduating cum laude (with honors):

```
if ( (gpa >= 3.50) && (gpa < 3.75) ) {
→ printf ("You're graduating cum
→ laude with a %0.2f GPA!\n", gpa);
}
```

The final conditional is like the one in Step 5, but uses different number values.

7. Complete the main() function:

```
getchar();
return 0;
}
```

8. Save the project as *gpa.c*.

9. Compile and debug, as necessary.

10. Run the executable application (**Figure 4.3**).

11. For comparison, change the value of gpa, recompile, and rerun the application (**Figure 4.4**).

continues on next page

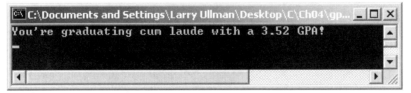

Figure 4.4 Running the *gpa* application using a different value for the main variable.

COMPARISON AND LOGICAL OPERATORS

✔ Tips

- As the example is written, if *gpa* is not greater than 3.5, no message is printed at all. This will be rectified in the next example, or you could add a fourth conditional, printing a message if *gpa* is less than 3.5.

- Remember never to compare the equality of floats. Due to the way computers represent this data type, two seemingly equal values may be off by the merest fraction. Similarly, the integer 2 and the float 2.0 may not equate!

- Some programmers recommend reversing the values in a conditional when one literal value is used. For example:

  `if (24 == hours) {...`

  The benefit of this is that if you inadvertently use only one equals sign, an error message will be reported upon compilation (as you cannot assign the value of a variable to a number).

- To determine if two strings are the same, you would use the `strcmp()` function. This function, which is short for *string compare*, returns a number indicating the difference between two strings. If the returned value is 0, they are the same:

  `if (strcmp(var1, var2) == 0) {...`

  You'll learn more about this data type in Chapter 11, "Working with Strings."

The Perils of Precedence

Just as you learned that the assignment and arithmetic operators have a precedence to them, so do the comparison and logical operators. Specifically, <, >, <=, and >= rank higher than either == or !=.

In the greater scheme of things, the comparison operators have a higher precedence than the assignment operator (=) but a lower precedence than the arithmetic operators.

Conversely, not (!) is above multiplication and division, whereas and (&&) and or (||) have a higher precedence than the assignment operators but a lower one than the relational operators. And && is higher than ||.

Confusing? Yet bet. You can either memorize all of this—replicated in a table in Appendix B, "Resources"—or just use parentheses to enforce precedence: the easiest, most foolproof method.

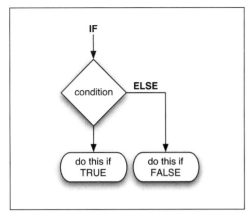

Figure 4.5 This diagram shows how an application flows through an if-else conditional.

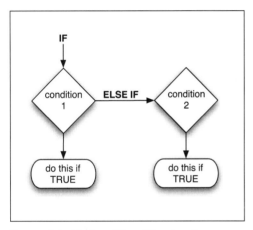

Figure 4.6 An if-else if conditional can have multiple, separate conditions to test against.

Using Else and Else If

The if conditional is useful in its own right, but it can be greatly expanded on by using the additional else and else if clauses. The syntax of the if-else conditional is

```
if (condition) {
    /* Do whatever. */
} else {
    /* Do this instead. */
}
```

Note that the else statements take place if the main condition is not true. In other words, the else acts as the default response (**Figure 4.5**).

The else if clause takes this a step further by letting you set a secondary condition to check for if the initial one turns out to be false (**Figure 4.6**):

```
if (condition 1) {
    /* Do whatever. */
} else if (condition 2) {
    /* Do something else. */
}
```

You can have as many else if clauses as you want. You can even, and often do, combine else and else if clauses together, so long as the else is the final part of the conditional (because it's the default case). The following example rewrites the *gpa.c* application more professionally.

To use else and else if:

1. Open *gpa.c* (Script 4.2) in your text editor or IDE.

2. Delete all of the existing conditionals (**Script 4.3**):

   The three separate if conditionals will be rewritten as one if-else if-else if-else conditional and is therefore no longer needed.

3. Create the main conditional:

   ```
   if (gpa >= 3.9) {
       printf ("You're graduating summa
   → cum laude with a %0.2f GPA!\n", gpa);
   } else if (gpa >= 3.75) {
       printf ("You're graduating magna
   → cum laude with a %0.2f GPA!\n", gpa);
   } else if (gpa >= 3.5) {
       printf ("You're graduating cum
   → laude with a %0.2f GPA!\n", gpa);
   } else {
       printf ("There's more to life
   → than grades.\n");
    }
   ```

   The conditions themselves are similar to those in the previous version of this code, but now they have all been tied into one conditional. The application will continue through the conditional until a condition is met. If none of the if or else if conditions are true, the else statement will be run.

```
1    /* gpa2.c - Script 4.3 - rewrite of
   → Script 4.2 (gpa.c) */
2
3    #include <stdio.h>
4
5    int main (void) {
6
7        float gpa = 3.8; // Grade Point
   → Average
8
9        // Report on the GPA.
10       if (gpa >= 3.9) {
11           printf ("You're graduating
   → summa cum laude with a %0.2f
   → GPA!\n", gpa);
12       } else if (gpa >= 3.75) {
13           printf ("You're graduating
   → magna cum laude with a %0.2f
   → GPA!\n", gpa);
14       } else if (gpa >= 3.5) {
15           printf ("You're graduating cum
   → laude with a %0.2f GPA!\n", gpa);
16       } else `{
17           printf ("There's more to life
   → than grades.\n");
18       }
19
20       getchar(); /* Pause for the user
   → to press Return or Enter. */
21
22       return 0;
23
24   }
```

Script 4.3 By using else and else if clauses, *gpa.c* (Script 4.2) can be rewritten using one complex control structure.

Notice that the second and third conditions do not need to check if a value is less than a certain value. For example, if *gpa* is equal to 3.8, the first condition is false and the second is true. In this second condition, you no longer need to check if *gpa* is less than 3.9 (as in the previous version of this application) as that's already been determined by the first condition. The same notion applies to the third condition (you already know that *gpa* is less than 3.75).

4. Save the file as *gpa2.c*, compile, and run (**Figure 4.7**).

5. Change the value of *gpa*, recompile, and rerun the application (**Figure 4.8**).

✔ Tips

■ Although it's not required, indenting statements four spaces from their associated `if`, `else`, or `else if` clause (as in *gpa2.c*) makes it easier to see which statements are associated with which clauses.

■ Like a simple `if` statement, the `if-else` and `if-else if` don't require curly braces if each has only one resulting statement. Again, it's good practice to always use the curly braces, though.

Figure 4.7 For the most part, the application behaves as it previously had (see Figures 4.3 and 4.4) even though the main conditional has been rewritten.

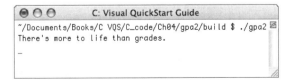

Figure 4.8 Now a response is printed if the grade point average is below 3.5.

The Ternary Operator

C has an alternative syntax for the `if-else` conditional, referred to as the *ternary* (or *trinary*) operator. The name stems from the fact that there are three parts to using the operator. The basic syntax of it is

```
(condition) ? true_result :
→ false_result;
```

What is notable about this operator is that it returns one of two values based on a condition. This returned value is normally assigned to a variable or printed. For example, the following will return a value indicating whether a number is even or odd (it uses the modulus operator to see if there's a remainder when the number is divided by 2):

```
char even_odd;
even_odd = ( (number % 2) == 0) ? 'e' :
'o';
```

Rewritten as a conditional, it would be

```
char even_odd;
if ( (number % 2) == 0) {
    even_odd = 'e';
} else {
    even_odd = 'o';
}
```

In this next example, the ternary operator will be used to print an appropriate message depending on the temperature.

To use the ternary operator:

1. Create a new, blank C project in your text editor or IDE.

2. Add the initial comments and code (**Script 4.4**):

```
/* weather.c - Script 4.4 */
#include <stdio.h>
int main (void) {
```

```
 1    /* weather.c - Script 4.4 */
 2
 3    #include <stdio.h>
 4
 5    int main (void) {
 6
 7        int temperature = 102; //
   → Temperature in degrees Fahrenheit.
 8
 9        if (temperature > 90) { // Check to
   → see if it's hot.
10
11            printf ("At %d degrees, it's
   → hot, hot, hot outside!\n",
   → temperature);
12
13        } else if (temperature < 40) {  //
   → Print 'freezing' or 'cold' depending
   → upon the temperature.
14
15            printf ("At %d degrees, it's %s
   → outside!\n", temperature,
   → (temperature < 20) ? "freezing" :
   → "cold" );
16
17        } else { // Not too hot, not too cold.
18
19            printf ("At %d degrees, it's a
   → relatively temperate day.\n",
   → temperature);
20
21        }
22
23
24        getchar(); /* Pause for the user to
   → press Return or Enter. */
25
26        return 0;
27
28    }
```

Script 4.4 The ternary operator can often be used as shorthand for `if-else` conditionals, returning one of two values depending on the truth of its condition.

3. Declare and initialize an integer variable:

```
int temperature = 102;
```

This variable will store the current temperature as degrees Fahrenheit in an integer value.

4. Begin the main if conditional:

```
if (temperature > 90) {
    printf ("At %d degrees, it's
→ hot, hot, hot outside!\n",
→ temperature);
```

The first clause of the conditional checks to see if it's over 90 degrees. If so, the printf() statement prints the temperature and states that it's hot outside (for those who like applications that point out the obvious).

5. Add an else if clause with a ternary operator as part of its print statement:

```
} else if (temperature < 40) {
→ printf ("At %d degrees, it's %s
→ outside!\n", temperature,
→ (temperature < 20) ? "freezing" :
→ "cold" );
```

If the temperature is below 40 degrees, the application will print that it's either *freezing* or *cold* outside. Rather than having another else if clause, this is accomplished using the ternary operator within the printf() statement.

The %s marker in the printf() statement is the placeholder for a string to be determined by the ternary operator, which is the third argument (after temperature, which corresponds to %d in the quote). The condition of the ternary operator checks if the temperature is below 20 degrees. If it is, the word *freezing* is returned. If that conditional is false, the word *cold* is returned. Note that both returned words are in double quotes, as they are strings.

continues on next page

THE TERNARY OPERATOR

6. Complete the conditional:

```
} else {
    printf ("At %d degrees, it's a
→ relatively temperate day.\n",
→ temperature);
}
```

Finally, if it's not over 90 degrees (the first condition) or under 40 (the second), it's assumed to be a temperate day.

7. Complete the main() function:

```
    getchar();
    return 0;
}
```

8. Save the project as *weather.c*.

9. Compile and debug, as necessary.

10. Run the executable application (**Figure 4.9**).

11. For comparison, change the value of temperature, recompile, and rerun the application (**Figure 4.10**).

Figure 4.9 If the temperature is above 90 degrees, the first printf() statement is executed (see Script 4.4).

✔ Tips

■ As a variation on the weather application, you could change the first conditional to check if it's over 70 degrees, then add a printf() with a ternary operator as its statement, reporting on weather it's *warm* or *hot*.

■ The main benefit of using the ternary operator instead of an if-else conditional is that it makes for shorter code. This is at the expense of some legibility. If you find the format to be too confusing, stick with the if structure.

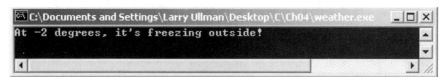

Figure 4.10 If the temperature is below 40 degrees, it will be described as either *freezing* or *cold*, thanks to the ternary operator.

The Switch Conditional

Along with the ternary operator, the `switch` is a useful variation on an `if` conditional. This conditional takes an integer variable as its condition and checks its value against several possibilities:

```
switch (year) {
    case 2005:
        /* Do something. */
        break;
    case 2004:
        /* Do something else. */
        break;
    default:
        /* Do this. */
        break;
}
```

The **break** statement is critical to the operation of the conditional. Upon hitting a **break**, the application will leave the switch. If you omit a **break**, then every subsequent statement—even those that fall under other cases—will be executed.

The default case is an optional one but, if included, is normally placed last. If none of the other cases are matched, the default case will be applied (like an `else` clause).

The following example uses a `switch` conditional to respond differently based on the value of a **gender** variable. The variable will be of type **char**, which is technically a form of integer, and is therefore a candidate for using in a `switch`.

To use the switch conditional:

1. Create a new, blank C project in your text editor or IDE.

2. Add the initial comments and code (**Script 4.5**):

```
/* gender.c - Script 4.5 */
#include <stdio.h>
int main (void) {
```

3. Declare and initialize a character variable:

```
char gender = 'M';
```

This variable will store a person's gender as a single character.

4. Begin the switch conditional:

```
switch (gender) {
```

The proper syntax of the switch conditional begins with the word *switch*, followed by the name of the variable to be referenced (in parentheses). The opening curly brace marks the beginning of the switch's contents.

5. Add the first case:

```
case 'M':
    printf ("Dear Sir,\n");
    break;
```

The first case in the switch will check if gender has the value of *M*. If it does, the *Dear Sir,* salutation will be printed. The break then ensures that the switch is exited, so that the remaining printf() statements aren't executed.

6. Add the second case:

```
case 'F':
    printf ("Dear Madam,\n");
    break;
```

The structure of this case is the same as that in Step 5, but uses a different test value.

```
 1    /* gender.c - Script 4.5 */
 2
 3    #include <stdio.h>
 4
 5    int main (void) {
 6
 7        char gender = 'M'; // Gender as a
    → single character.
 8
 9        switch (gender) { // Change the
    → salutation for the gender.
10
11            case 'M':
12                printf ("Dear Sir,\n");
13                break;
14
15            case 'F':
16                printf ("Dear Madam,\n");
17                break;
18
19            default:
20                printf ("To whom it may
    → concern,\n");
21                break;
22
23        } // End of switch.
24
25        getchar(); /* Pause for the user to
    → press Return or Enter. */
26
27        return 0;
28
29    }
```

Script 4.5 Switch conditionals can be used to respond to different integer and character values.

Figure 4.11 The result of the switch conditional if gender has a value of *M*.

Figure 4.12 If gender is not equal to either *M* or *F*, this salutation is created.

7. Add the default case and complete the switch:

```
default:
    printf ("To whom it may
→ concern,\n");
    break;
}
```

If gender is not equal to either *M* or *F* (unusual as that may be), this default, non-gender-specific message is printed.

8. Complete the main() function:

```
    getchar();
    return 0;
}
```

9. Save the project as *gender.c*.

10. Compile and debug, as necessary.

11. Run the executable application (**Figure 4.11**).

12. For comparison, change the value of gender to another letter or a blank space, recompile, and rerun the application (**Figure 4.12**).

✔ Tips

- It is acceptable to have multiple cases in a switch that use the same statements. The syntax for that would be

```
switch (gender) {
    case 'M':
    case 'm':
            /* Do whatever. */
            break;
    case 'F':
    case 'f':
            /* And so on... */
            break;
}
```

- The main downside to using switch is that it can only be used with integer and character data types. This greatly restricts when you can use it, but if it's a possibility, it's often a faster, cleaner method (as opposed to a long if conditional).

- Another control structure exists in C that we do not discuss in this book: goto. People coming from other languages, like Basic and Pascal, will be familiar with it, but it's not really necessary in C.

THE SWITCH CONDITIONAL

The While Loop

Conditionals are one broad type of control structure and loops are the other. The C language supports two loop formats: `while` (and its sibling `do…while`) and `for`. Each loop type accomplishes the same thing—repeatedly performing some statements for a certain duration—but in slightly different ways.

The `while` loop is like an `if` conditional in that it checks a condition and then executes some statements if it's true:

```
while (condition) {
    /* Do whatever. */
}
```

Once the loop has successfully executed its statements, it will then recheck the condition. If the condition is still true, the process will be repeated. If the condition is false, the execution of the loop is over and the program will continue running (**Figure 4.13**).

A common enough mistake programmers make is to create a loop whose condition will never be false. This creates an *infinite loop*, resulting in an application that will just run and run. Therefore, you should ensure that something occurs within the loop so that the condition will eventually be false.

This example will use a `while` loop to help calculate the factorial of a number. In simplest terms, the factorial (represented in math by the exclamation mark) is the sum of the multiplication of every number between 1 and the number. So,

```
5! = 1 * 2 * 3 * 4 * 5; // 120
3! = 1 * 2 * 3; // 6
```

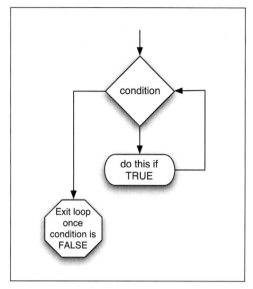

Figure 4.13 This flowchart represents how loops function in C, repeatedly performing certain tasks as long as a condition is true.

```
000                  Script
1     /* factorial.c - Script 4.6 */
2
3     #include <stdio.h>
4
5     int main (void) {
6
7          // Only using positive numbers in
      → this example!
8
9          unsigned int num = 5; // Number to
      → get the factorial of.
10         unsigned int sum = 1; // Factorial
      → sum.
11         unsigned int multiplier = 1; //
      → Multiplier to be used in
      → calculating factorial.
12
13         // Loop through every multiplier
      → up to and including num.
14         while (multiplier <= num) {
15
16             sum *= multiplier; // Multiply
      → the current sum by the multiplier.
17             ++multiplier; // Increase the
      → multiplier by one.
18
19         } // End of loop.
20
21         // Print the results.
22         printf ("The factorial of %u is
      → %u.\n", num, sum);
23
24         getchar(); /* Pause for the user
      → to press Return or Enter. */
25
26         return 0;
27
28     }
```

Script 4.6 A while loop is used to help calculate the factorial of a number. The loop continues to execute as long as the multiplier variable is less than or equal to the num variable.

To use the while loop:

1. Create a new, blank C project in your text editor or IDE.

2. Add the initial comments and code (**Script 4.6**):

   ```
   /* factorial.c - Script 4.6 */
   #include <stdio.h>
   int main (void) {
   ```

3. Establish the required variables:

   ```
   unsigned int num = 5;
   unsigned int sum = 1;
   unsigned int multiplier = 1;
   ```

   This application makes use of three unsigned integers, each of which is initialized to a set value. The first, num, represents the number whose factorial is being determined (for example, 5). The second, sum, will be the total of that factorial (eventually reaching 120 if num is 5). The third, multiplier, will be used in calculating the factorial.

4. Start the while loop:

   ```
   while (multiplier <= num) {
   ```

   The factorial will be calculated by multiplying every number from 1 to num. The calculation itself will take place within the loop, so all the loop's condition has to do is check that the multiplier, which starts at 1, is still less than or equal to the number. If it is, the calculation should take place. Once the multiplier is greater than the value of num, no more calculations should be done.

continues on next page

THE WHILE LOOP

5. Perform the calculation:

```
sum *= multiplier;
```

Using the multiplication assignment operator, the sum variable is set to be the value of sum times multiplier. On the first iteration of the loop, sum will be equal to 1 (1 * 1). On the second iteration, it will be equal to 2 (1 * 2). On the third, it will be six (2 * 3); on the fourth, 24 (6 * 4); and on the fifth and final iteration (if num is 5), 120 (24 * 5).

6. Increase the value of multiplier by 1:

```
++multiplier;
```

In a way, this is the most critical line in the loop. If you fail to increase the value of multiplier, then the initial condition will never be false and the loop will run endlessly.

7. Complete the while loop:

```
} // End of loop.
```

As your code becomes more complex, commenting the end of conditionals and other control structures improves legibility.

8. Print the results of the calculations:

```
printf ("The factorial of %u is
→ %u.\n", num, sum);
```

The printf() statement prints both the initial number and the result of the calculations.

9. Complete the main() function:

```
    getchar();
    return 0;
}
```

10. Save the project as *factorial.c*.

11. Compile and debug, as necessary.

Using break, continue, and exit

The break statement—which you saw within the switch conditional—is just one of the language constructs C uses within control structures. As a reminder, break is used to exit out of the current loop or switch. Here is how it would work within a loop:

```
while (condition1) {
    /* Do whatever. */
    if (condition2) {
        break; /* Leave the loop. */
    }
}
```

Conversely, the continue statement will exit the current iteration of a loop. The loop's condition will then be tested again and the loop may or may not continue to be executed:

```
while (condition1) {
    /* Do whatever. */
    if (condition2) {
        continue; /* Back to the
    → beginning of the loop. */
    }
}
```

Again, both of these language constructs only work within loops and the switch conditional. They have no effect on if conditionals.

Another language construct is exit, which terminates the whole application. Towards the end of the book you'll see how it is used to stop the execution of a program when a significant problem occurs.

Figure 4.14 Running the application shows the calculated factorial of the number 5.

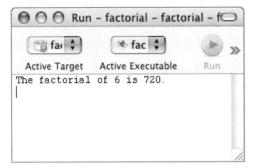

Figure 4.15 By changing only the num value, the application will continue to accurately determine the factorials.

12. Run the executable application (**Figure 4.14**).

13. For comparison, change the value of num, recompile, and rerun the application (**Figure 4.15**).

✔ Tips

- There is a variation on the while loop, called the do...while loop. The main difference is that the condition is tested after the loop has already been run once, so this control structure will always be executed at least once. The syntax is

```
do {
    /* statements */
} while (condition);
```

- In Chapter 6, "Working with Input and Output," you'll learn how to use the while loop to continually take keyboard input.

- The factorial application can also be a good demonstration of the problems with variable overflow (see Chapter 3, "Working with Numbers"). When creating factorials you can quickly and easily eclipse the possible range of a number type.

The For Loop

The final control structure we discuss in this chapter (and in the book) is the for loop. Much like while, it will perform an operation for a certain number of iterations. The syntax, though, is vastly different:

```
for (initial expression; conditional;
concluding expression) {
    /* Do whatever. */
}
```

The first time the application encounters the loop, the initial expression will be executed. Then the conditional will be checked. If true, the statements (marked by *Do whatever.* earlier) are run. Then, the concluding expression is executed. Finally, the condition is checked again and the process is repeated (except that the initial expression is only run the first time; see **Figure 4.16**). With the for loop, the *concluding expression* is usually responsible for ensuring that the condition becomes false at some point.

A rewrite of the *factorial.c* example will better demonstrate this syntax and how similar for and while can be in usage.

To use the for loop:

1. Open *factorial.c* (Script 4.6) in your text editor or IDE.

2. Change the name of the multiplier variable to be just i and do not set its initial value (**Script 4.7**):

   ```
   unsigned int i;
   ```

   It's standard practice in C to use the letter i as a counter in for loops. Although that's not required, this example will abide by that norm. You no longer have to initialize it (set a value) as that will happen in the for loop.

```
1   /* factorial2.c - Script 4.7 - rewrite
    → of Script 4.6 (factorial.c) */
2
3   #include <stdio.h>
4
5   int main (void) {
6
7       // Only using positive numbers in
    → this example!
8
9       unsigned int num = 5; // Number to
    → get the factorial of.
10      unsigned int sum = 1; // Factorial
    → sum.
11      unsigned int i; // Multiplier to
    → be used in calculating factorial.
12
13      // Loop through every multiplier
    → up to and including num.
14      for (i = 1; i <= num; ++i) {
15
16          sum *= i; // Multiply the
    → current sum by the multiplier.
17
18      } // End of loop.
19
20      // Print the results.
21      printf ("The factorial of %u is
    → %u.\n", num, sum);
22
23      getchar(); /* Pause for the user
    → to press Return or Enter. */
24
25      return 0;
26
27  }
```

Script 4.7 This revision of the *factorial.c* application (Script 4.6) replaces the while loop with a for loop.

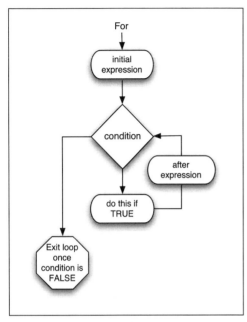

Figure 4.16 How a for loop functions is significantly different than a while loop, considering the addition of the initial and post-expressions.

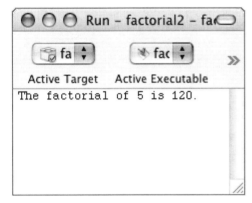

Figure 4.17 The factorial is now calculated using a for loop, which can be just as effective as a while loop.

3. Delete the entire while loop.

4. Begin defining the for loop:

```
for (i = 1; i <= num; ++i) {
```

Upon first encountering this loop, the application will set the i variable to the value of 1. Then, if i is less than or equal to num, the loop's statements (Step 5) will be executed. After the loop's statements are executed, the i variable will be incremented by 1.

5. Add the loop's single statement:

```
sum *= i;
```

Since the multiplier is now named i, the calculation is changed slightly. More important, though, is that the multiplier no longer has to be incremented as part of the loop's statements, since that is now part of the loop's definition (Step 4).

6. Close the for loop:

```
} // End of loop.
```

7. Save the file as *factorial2.c*.

8. Compile, debug (as necessary), and run the application (**Figure 4.17**).

9. If you want, change the value of num, recompile, and rerun the application.

continues on next page

THE FOR LOOP

✔ Tips

- Although the `for` loop often only uses three separate expressions, it's not limited to that. The first and last part of the `for` syntax (the initial and concluding expressions) can have multiple expressions if they are separated by commas:

  ```
  for (sum = 1, i = 1; i <= num; ++i) {...
  ```

- Conversely, each of the three `for` loop sections is optional. The code

  ```
  for (;;) {…
  ```

  is perfectly valid, although it does create an infinite loop.

- The `for` loop is often used with arrays to do something with each of the array's elements. This will be demonstrated in Chapter 6, "Working with Arrays."

- When nesting `for` loops (see the sidebar), it's quite common to use a variable called i for the first, outermost loop; j for the inner one; k for one inside of that; and so forth.

Nesting Conditionals and Loops

C allows you to nest the different control structures: place one conditional within another; put a loop within another loop; have a conditional within a loop; and so forth. When doing this, maintaining the proper syntax is crucial. Follow these suggestions when nesting any control structures:

- ♦ Always use opening and closing curly braces to mark where control structures begin and end.

- ♦ Indent subordinate control structures in their entirety.

- ♦ Use comments to mark the purpose of control structures and where they conclude.

With nested control structures, improperly balancing your curly braces is a common cause of errors. You'll see many examples of nested control structures throughout the course of this book, and every one abides by those suggestions in order to help avoid errors.

STANDARD
INPUT AND OUTPUT

Working with standard input and output (I/O) is often a requirement for any real-world C application. Although practically all the examples in this book so far have had output (in other words, they printed messages), they have also relied entirely on set values within the code. This is not only boring (apologies for that) but impractical. In this chapter you'll see how to make your applications interactive by taking and responding to user input.

You'll first learn and practice taking a single character input and reacting to that. Next, you'll see how to read in an entire word at a time. Afterwards, the chapter moves on to handling numeric and then multiple inputs. Finally, validating input and more advanced output techniques are covered.

Inputting a Single Character

A simple interactive application will make a request (for a number or a *Yes/No* answer) and respond accordingly. Doing so can be described as a four-step process:

1. Prompting the user, indicating the type of information requested (**Figure 5.1**)

2. Reading the input typed into the keyboard

3. Validating that the input is of the proper format

4. Reacting based on the value of the input

This chapter will teach all of these steps from the ground up.

The simplest type of input to be read (Step 2) is a single character. This is accomplished using the getchar() function, which you've already seen (you've been using it to pause applications until the Enter or Return key is pressed). The getchar() function reads a single inputted character and assigns that to a variable:

```
char gender;
gender = getchar();
```

As a demonstration of this idea, the following example will ask the user to respond to a *Yes* or *No* question.

To read a single character:

1. Create a new file or project in your text editor or IDE.

2. Type the standard beginning lines of code (**Script 5.1**):

```
/* Script 5.1 - donut.c */
#include <stdio.h>
int main (void) {
```

```
1   /* Script 5.1 - donut.c */
2
3   #include <stdio.h>
4
5   int main (void) {
6
7       char answer; // Single character
→   to store Yes (Y) or No (N) answer.
8
9       // Prompt the user and read their
→   reply.
10      printf("Would you like a donut?
→   [Y/N] ");
11      answer = getchar ();
12
13      // Respond to the answer.
14      switch (answer) {
15
16          case 'Y':
17          case 'y':
18              printf
→   ("Mmmm...donuts.\n");
19              break;
20
21          case 'N':
22          case 'n':
23              printf ("You don't want a
→   donut!?! But they're so sweet and
→   tasty!\n");
24              break;
25
26          default:
27              printf ("Um...you were
→   supposed to enter either 'Y' or
→   'N'.\n");
28              break;
29
30      } // End of switch.
31
32      getchar(); /* Pause for the user to
→   press Return or Enter. */
33      getchar(); /* Extra call may be
→   necessary. */
34
35      return 0;
36  }
```

Script 5.1 Single-character input can be read from the keyboard using the getchar() function.

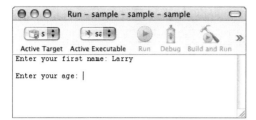

Figure 5.1 Letting the user know what type (and often, which format) of information is requested is an important facet of your applications.

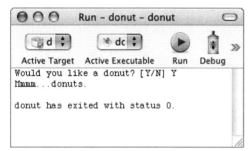

Figure 5.2 The donut application prompts the user to answer a simple question.

3. Create a character variable:

```
char answer;
```

The char data type was briefly introduced in Chapter 2, "Introduction to Data Types." In this case, the variable answer will be able to hold a single character. Comments are added (see the corresponding script) to indicate what type and format of data is expected to be stored in this variable.

4. Prompt the user and read in the reply:

```
printf("Would you like a donut?
→ [Y/N] ");
```

This line prints the question being asked and indicates within square brackets the type and format the answer is expected to be in. Using square brackets like this is a common technique, giving a visual cue to the user as to how the application should be used.

Notice that, unlike previous examples, no newline character (\n) is added to the end of the printf(). Because of this, the cursor—and therefore the user's answer—will appear on the same line as the prompt. Similar to using the square brackets, this is in no way a requirement but instead provides a nicer interface (**Figure 5.2**).

5. Read in the typed reply:

```
answer = getchar();
```

This line reads in the first character typed and assigns this to the answer variable. It will read in whatever character is first typed, including numbers or white space.

continues on next page

6. Begin a conditional that prints different messages based on what the user entered.

```
switch (answer) {
```

Since `answer` is a single-character variable, a `switch` conditional can be used here (`switch` works only on `char` and integer values). You could also use an `if-else if-else` conditional here, but a `switch` will work better.

7. Add the first two cases:

```
case 'Y':
case 'y':
        printf ("Mmmm...donuts.\n");
        break;
```

Since the `switch` will perform a case-sensitive comparison, two cases are added to see if *Yes* (in the form of *Y* or *y*) was typed. If either of these cases is true, then the print statement is executed and the `switch` is exited, thanks to the `break`.

8. Add two more cases to handles *No*'s:

```
case 'N':
case 'n':
        printf ("You don't want a
→ donut!?! But they're so sweet
→ and tasty!\n");
        break;
```

This is a repeat of Step 7, using different values for the cases and a different message to be printed. As a reminder, normally you want a `break` for every case in a `switch` statement. In this example, there are *fall-through* cases (*Y* and *N*), allowing multiple cases to have the same result.

Understanding Input and Output

The C language provides the *stdio.h* library file to assist in the handling of input and output (*stdio* refers to *standard input/output*). By including this file in an application, you have access to such common functions as `printf()`.

The *standard input* for an application is the keyboard, where input is typed. The *standard output* is the screen, where text is displayed within a console or terminal window. These aren't the only options, though. For example, input can be read from a text file, and output can be sent to a system or error log.

In this chapter you'll be working with the standard input and output, but many of the same processes apply in other situations, such as reading and writing to files. You'll see this in Chapter 12, "File Input and Output."

9. Add a default case and complete the switch:

```
default:
        printf ("Um...you were
→ supposed to enter either 'Y'
→ or 'N'.\n");
        break;
}
```

The default case will be called if the typed answer is not one of the accepted values (*Y*, *y*, *N*, or *n*). The break isn't required at the end of this case, but it's a good idea to include it.

10. Type two more calls to the getchar() function:

```
getchar();
getchar();
```

In previous applications the getchar() function was called once to pause execution until the user presses Return or Enter. This is necessary on some platforms (in particular, Windows) so that the console window does not close before you have the chance to view the results.

In this and the following examples, an extra call to the same function may be required. This would be because, for example, the first character typed in (*Y*, *y*, *N*, or *n*) would be read by the first getchar() and the Return or Enter pressed after that would be read by the second getchar(). Once again, this would close the console window before you had the opportunity to see the results.

If you are not having problems with the console or terminal window closing too quickly, you may omit these lines.

continues on next page

INPUTTING A SINGLE CHARACTER

11. Complete the main function:

```
    return 0;
}
```

12. Save the file as *donut.c*, compile, and debug as necessary.

13. Run the application, entering different values (**Figure 5.3**) to see the results.

✔ Tips

■ Because the getchar() function reads in only a single character, if the user types *Y5089ljj* in response to the *donut* application, that will still be treated as just Y (**Figure 5.4**).

■ The opposite of getchar() is putchar(), which sends a single character to the output. This line will print the value of the gender variable (assuming it's a single character):

```
putchar (gender);
```

■ Whenever you need to read only a single character, getchar() is definitely the way to go. Other methods covered in this chapter will also work on single characters, but they aren't as fast and require more complex code.

Figure 5.3 The application responds differently based on the answer submitted by the user.

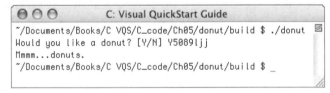

Figure 5.4 The getchar() function literally records only the first character, so *Y5089ljj* is the same as just *Y* (Figure 5.2) in this example.

Table 5.1 Use these special characters to tell scanf() what kind of value is being assigned to a variable.

scanf() Signifiers

SIGNIFIER	MEANING
%c	Single character
%d	Signed integer
%f	Float
%s	String
%u	Unsigned integer

Retrieving Whole Word Input

To read in more than a single character requires the scanf() function. This function reads what has been typed into the keyboard and converts it to a particular data type, based on the formatting code given to it (just as the printf() function prints values based on formatting codes).

To use this function to read in a word, you must first define a character string, which was also briefly mentioned in Chapter 2. For example:

```
char word[20];
```

This creates a character string called word that can be up to 20 characters in length.

Next, you would prompt the user and tell the scanf() function what type of data to expect and to which variable that data should be assigned:

```
printf ("Please enter a word: ");
scanf ("%s", word);
```

Just as with the printf() function, the %s signifier indicates that scanf() should store a string value in word. **Table 5.1** lists the most popular scanf() signifiers.

There are some tricks to using this function. For starters, when using %s to read in a string, it will only read up until the first whitespace character (a space, a tab, or a newline). In other words, it can read only a single word at a time.

Second, if the function encounters input that does not match the formatting signifier, scanf() will not work. The scanf() function returns a value, namely the number of items it read in (not the number of characters or digits). If nothing was read, it will return a value of 0 or EOF (short for *end of file*) or -1 (the numeric equivalent to EOF).

Third, you should definitely add the *maximum field width* parameter to your signifier. This value, which should match the length of the variable to which the input is assigned, dictates the maximum number of characters to be read. So, with the word example, the better syntax is

```
scanf ("%19s", word);
```

By using this, you avoid possible input buffer overruns, where C tries to read in more characters than it can handle. The number 19 is used (instead of 20) because strings include a terminating \0 character. So a word can contain 19 typed characters plus this \0.

The last thing you should know about using scanf() is that the syntax differs if reading in anything other than a string. To read in an integer or other nonstring value, you must pass the address of the variable to the scanf() function by preceding the variable name with the ampersand:

```
scanf ("%d", &number);
```

You'll learn about variables and their addresses in Chapter 9, "Working with Pointers," but for now, follow that syntax for nonstring variables.

To retrieve string input:

1. Create a new file or project in your text editor or IDE.

2. Type the standard beginning lines of code (**Script 5.2**):

```
/* Script 5.2 - name.c */
#include <stdio.h>
int main (void) {
```

3. Create a character string variable:

```
char first_name[10];
```

The first_name variable will be a character string, holding up to 10 characters.

```
1    /* Script 5.2 - name.c */
2
3    #include <stdio.h>
4
5    int main (void) {
6
7        char first_name[10]; // Character
  →  string.
8
9        // Get their first name and then
  →  use it in a sentence.
10       printf("Enter your first name: ");
11       scanf ("%9s", first_name);
12       printf ("Thanks, %s.\n",
  →  first_name);
13
14       /* Pause for the user to press
  →  Return or Enter. */
15       getchar();
16       getchar();
17
18       return 0;
19   }
```

Script 5.2 A whole word can be read using the scanf() function.

4. Prompt for, and read in, the user's first name:

```
printf("Enter your first name: ");
scanf ("%9s", first_name);
```

First, the user is prompted. As with the previous example, a space but no newline concludes the statement so that the answer is entered immediately after the prompt.

The scanf() function then reads in up to 9 characters of the typed text, which should be a string. This value is assigned to the first_name variable.

5. Use the submitted name in a simple sentence:

```
printf ("Thanks, %s.\n", first_name);
```

To print the string, again use the %s formatter, but within the printf() function.

6. Type two more calls to the getchar() function:

```
getchar();
getchar();
```

While using these two functions to temporarily halt execution is a nice technique, it becomes more and more unreliable as more input is read or as the user mistypes input. Adjust your use of them accordingly.

Later in this chapter you'll learn a technique for automatically discarding unnecessary input.

7. Complete the main function:

```
    return 0;
}
```

8. Save the file as *name.c*, compile, and debug as necessary.

continues on next page

9. Run the application, entering different values (**Figures 5.5** and **5.6**) to see the results.

✔ Tips

- The %c signifier will read the next character, even if it's a blank space, tab, or newline. However, if you're reading in only a single character, you're better off using getchar().

- The scanf() function is like printf() in that it can take a variable number of arguments. You'll see an example of this later in the chapter.

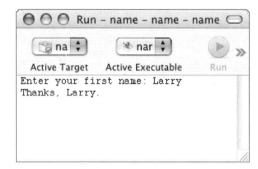

Figure 5.5 This simple yet responsive application reads and then prints a person's name.

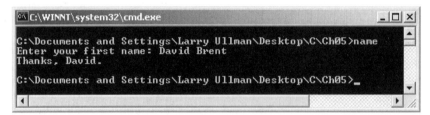

Figure 5.6 If the submitted text contains a space, only those characters up to the space will be assigned to the first_name variable.

Reading Numeric Input

The previous two examples read in a single character and then an entire string. But what if you want to read in numeric input? For this, you can again use the scanf() function:

```
int age;
printf ("Enter your age: ");
scanf ("%d", &age);
```

This method generally works and has the added benefit of familiarity. Unfortunately, this function can be unreliable in properly handling numeric input (although it's still commonly used). A better solution—which is really a kludge (an inelegant solution)— uses the fgets() and sscanf() functions:

```
int age;
char input[10];
printf ("Enter your age: ");
fgets (input, sizeof(input)-1, stdin);
sscanf (input, "%d", &age)
```

With the fgets() function, the first argument (input) tells C to which variable the inputted text should be assigned. The second argument dictates how many characters should be read, as a maximum value. The most flexible way to set this is to use the sizeof() function, which returns the length of a variable. So if input is set to be up to 10 characters long, fgets() should read up to 9 characters from the keyboard (the tenth character will be the terminating \0). The third argument (stdin) tells fgets() from which file the string should be read. In this case, the file is stdin, the standard input (the keyboard).

The second function in this code—sscanf()—converts a string to another data type. It uses the same signifiers as printf() and scanf(). The first argument is the existing string (input), the second is the formatting, and the third is the variable to which the value should be assigned. The variable's name is preceded by the ampersand so that the address of the variable is referenced. Again, you'll better understand this concept in Chapter 9.

To demonstrate reading in numeric input, let's write another temperature-conversion application, this time converting a user-submitted temperature from Celsius to Fahrenheit.

To read in numeric input:

1. Create a new file or project in your text editor or IDE.

2. Type the standard beginning lines of code (**Script 5.3**):

```
/* c_to_f.c - Script 5.3 */
#include <stdio.h>
int main (void) {
```

3. Declare the required variables:

```
float temp_f, temp_c;
char input[10];
```

This application has three variables. The first two are floats, for the temperature in degrees Fahrenheit and Celsius. The third is a character string that will store the inputted text (that the user types into the keyboard).

4. Prompt the user and read in the input:

```
printf ("Enter a temperature in
→ degrees Celsius: ");
fgets (input, sizeof(input)-1, stdin);
sscanf (input, "%f", &temp_c);
```

```
                                    Script
1    /* c_to_f.c - Script 5.3 */
2
3    #include <stdio.h>
4
5    int main(void) {
6
7        float temp_f, temp_c; //
  → Fahrenheit and Celsius
8        char input[10]; // Input to be read.
9
10       // Prompt the user.
11       printf ("Enter a temperature in
  → degrees Celsius: ");
12
13       // Read in the input and assign
  → this to temp_c.
14       fgets (input, sizeof(input)-1,
  → stdin);
15       sscanf (input, "%f", &temp_c);
16
17       // Make the conversion.
18       temp_f = temp_c * 9.0/5.0 + 32; //
  → Or (temp_c * (9.0/5.0)) + 32)
19
20       // Print the conversion.
21       printf ("%0.1f degrees Celsius is
  → %0.1f degrees Fahrenheit.\n",
  → temp_c, temp_f);
22
23       // Pause for the user to press
  → Return or Enter.
24       getchar();
25       getchar();
26
27       return 0;
28
29   }
```

Script 5.3 Two functions are used to read in numeric input, which will then be used in a calculation.

Following the syntax outlined earlier, the fgets() function will read in up to 9 characters (which is the value of sizeof(input) minus the one required for the \0) from the standard input (the keyboard). The sscanf() function will then convert this to a float, which is assigned to the temp_c variable.

5. Convert the temperature:

```
temp_f = temp_c * 9.0/5.0 + 32;
```

This is the same formula that has been used earlier in the book.

6. Print the results:

```
printf ("%0.1f degrees Celsius is
→ %0.1f degrees Fahrenheit.\n",
→ temp_c, temp_f);
```

Both the initial and calculated temperatures will be printed. The formatting specifies that they are printed with one decimal point.

7. Complete the main function:

```
        getchar();
        getchar();
        return 0;
}
```

8. Save the file as c_to_f.c, compile, and debug as necessary.

9. Run the application to see the results (**Figure 5.7**).

continues on next page

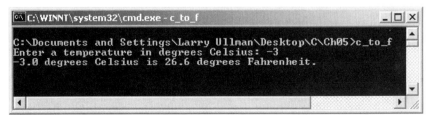

Figure 5.7 The submitted temperature in degrees Celsius is converted into Fahrenheit and then both values are printed.

✔ Tips

■ If a non-numeric value is entered
(**Figure 5.8**), you'll see different results
based on your development environment. The "Validating Keyboard Input"
section of this chapter will show how to
first validate data before using it in calculations.

■ The fgets() function will read either
sizeof(input)-1 characters or until a
newline (\n) character, whichever comes
first. If it does read in a newline, that will
also be assigned to the input variable.

■ The fgets() with sscanf() method can
be used to read in any variable type,
although getchar() works just fine for
characters and scanf() is good with
strings.

■ The fgets() function is also used for
reading from files, as you'll see in
Chapter 12.

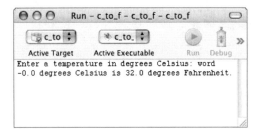

Figure 5.8 If you enter characters instead of a number
value, you'll see odd results as the sscanf() function
will not be able to create a float value from a character
string.

Reading Multiple Inputs

```
1    /* temp_conversion.c - Script 5.4 */
2
3    #include <stdio.h>
4
5    int main(void) {
6
7        float temp_i, temp_o; // Two
→ temperatures: inputted and outputted
8        char which_i, which_o; // F or C:
→ inputted and outputted
9
10       // Prompt the user.
11       printf ("Enter a temperature and
→ indicate if it's Fahrenheit or
→ Celsius [##.# C/F]: ");
12
13       // Read the input.
14       scanf ("%f %c", &temp_i,
→ &which_i);
15
16       // Make the conversion based upon
→ which_i.
17       switch (which_i) {
18
19           // Celsius, convert to
→ Fahrenheit.
20           case 'C':
21           case 'c':
22               temp_o = (temp_i *
→ (9.0/5.0)) + 32;
23               which_o = 'F';
24               break;
25
26           // Fahrenheit, convert to
→ Celsius.
27           case 'F':
28           case 'f':
29               temp_o = (temp_i - 32)
→ * (5.0/9.0);
```

continues on next page

Script 5.4 This well-rounded application takes both a numeric temperature and the letter *C* or *F*, and then converts the temperature accordingly.

Reading in single chunks of input is great, but being able to read in multiple pieces of input at once would be better. This can be accomplished using the scanf() function, which can read multiple inputs. For example:

```
int num1, num2;
scanf("%d %d", &num1, &num2);
```

That line of code will read in two integer values, separated by a space, and assign them to the num1 and num2 variables.

To demonstrate this, the following example will take both a number (the temperature) and the letter *F* or *C* (which determines whether that value is in degrees Fahrenheit or degrees Celsius). The application will then convert that number to the other format.

To read in multiple inputs at once:

1. Create a new file or project in your text editor or IDE.

2. Type the standard beginning lines of code (**Script 5.4**):

```
/* temp_conversion.c - Script 5.4 */
#include <stdio.h>
int main (void) {
```

3. Declare the required variables:

```
float temp_i, temp_o;
char which_i, which_o;
```

There are four variables in this application. Two are floats representing the inputted temperature (in degrees Celsius or Fahrenheit) and the outputted temperature (converted from the input). The other two variables are single characters, storing *C* or *F*. Again, one is to record the inputted value and the other stores the outputted format.

continues on next page

4. Prompt the user for the required information:

```
printf ("Enter a temperature and
→ indicate if it's Fahrenheit or
→ Celsius [##.# C/F]: ");
```

When taking multiple inputs—particularly when they are of different types—it's very important to adequately indicate to the user how the information should be keyed. Again, the square brackets are used to suggest the formatting.

5. Read the input and store this in the appropriate variables:

```
scanf ("%f %c", &temp_i, &which_i);
```

This function will look for a float and store that in `temp_i`. Next it will look for a character, which will be stored in `which_i`.

6. Create the `switch` statement, wherein conversion will take place:

```
switch (which_i) {
```

If the entered value is in degrees Fahrenheit, then degrees Celsius must be determined, and vice versa. This `switch` will use the value of `which_i` (which should be *C*, *F*, *c*, or *f*) to decide the action that should take place.

7. Add the first two cases:

```
case 'C':
case 'c':
    temp_o = (temp_i * (9.0/5.0)) + 32;
    which_o = 'F';
    break;
```

The first two cases perform the same calculation if the user entered either *C* or *c*. The applicable case statements will take the entered degrees in Celsius and convert this to Fahrenheit, assigned to `temp_o`. The `which_o` variable is assigned the value of *F*, to mark the format of the output.

```
○ ○ ○                    Script
30              which_o = 'C';
31              break;
32
33          // Problem: neither C nor
    → F entered, set which_o to FALSE.
34          default:
35              which_o = 0;
36              break;
37
38      } // End of switch.
39
40      // Print the results, using
    → which_o to indicate if it worked.
41      if (which_o) {
42          printf ("%0.1f %c is %0.1f
    → %c.\n", temp_i, which_i, temp_o,
    → which_o);
43      } else {
44          printf ("You failed to enter
    → 'C' or 'F' to indicate the current
    → temperature.\n");
45      }
46
47      // Pause for the user to
    → press Return or Enter.
48      getchar();
49      getchar();
50
51      return 0;
52
53 }
```

Script 5.4 *continued*

8. Repeat the cases for Fahrenheit:

```
case 'F':
case 'f':
    temp_o = (temp_i - 32) * (5.0/9.0);
    which_o = 'C';
    break;
```

9. Set the default case and close the `switch`:

```
default:
        which_o = 0;
        break;
} // End of switch.
```

If `which_i` is not equal to one of the four allowed values, the conversion shouldn't take place. In this case, `which_o` is set to 0. This value will let the conditional at the end of the application know there was a problem.

10. Print the results of the conversion, assuming that it took place:

```
if (which_o) {
    printf ("%0.1f %c is %0.1f
→ %c.\n", temp_i, which_i, temp_o,
→ which_o);
} else {
    printf ("You failed to enter 'C'
→ or 'F' to indicate the current
→ temperature.\n");
}
```

If `which_o` is true (because it has a value other than 0), the results of the conversion will be printed. The print statement outputs both the starting values and the converted ones. If `which_o` is false (because it has a value of 0, assigned within the `switch`'s default case), a message stating that the input was not of the proper format is sent.

continues on next page

READING MULTIPLE INPUTS

11. Complete the main function:

```
getchar();
getchar();
return 0;
}
```

12. Save the file as *temp_conversion.c*, compile, and debug as necessary.

13. Run the application, entering different values (**Figures 5.9** and **5.10**) to see the results.

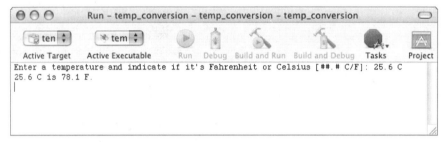

Figure 5.9 Converting Celsius to Fahrenheit.

Figure 5.10 Converting Fahrenheit to Celsius.

✔ Tips

- If the user doesn't input the right number and type of arguments, the user will most likely see results like those in **Figure 5.11**. The next section of this chapter will demonstrate how to better react in such a case.

- If the submitted temperature is 32 degrees Fahrenheit, the outputted temperature will be 0.0 degrees Celsius. This still passes through the if (which_o) conditional because while 0 is false, 0.0 is not.

- Although the previous example suggested that scanf() isn't the best way to read in single numeric values, it is the best way to read in multiple values, if even those multiple values may include numbers.

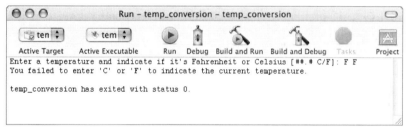

Figure 5.11 The application doesn't register that an *F* or *C* was entered because the first argument (which should have been a float) could not be properly read.

Validating Keyboard Input

The biggest problem when working with standard input is that it's reliant on the user properly responding. If the user does not type the right number or format of input, the application cannot be expected to perform properly. This is the old *garbage in, garbage out* maxim and the reason you'll want to validate input before working with it.

The validity of many answers can be checked with relative ease. For example:

◆ Seeing if an age variable is greater than 0 but less than, say, 120

◆ Checking that an answer is equal to *Yes* or *No* (or *Y, y, N, n*)

◆ Comparing an input against the logical values (like *C* and *F* in the temperature-conversion application)

In other cases—such as a temperature conversion where the inputted number can be any value—validation is trickier. One technique you can use involves the scanf() function itself. Because that function returns the number of items it read in, you can use that returned value to determine if the input matched the assumed type. To explain more clearly, let's rewrite the *temp_conversion* application. This new version will also make use of a technique for ignoring extraneous input (see the sidebar).

To validate user input:

1. Open *temp_conversion.c* (Script 5.4) in your text editor or IDE.

2. Declare a third char variable (**Script 5.5**):

   char junk;

   The junk variable will be used within a while loop to help read in and discard extraneous input (see the sidebar, "Ignoring Input").

```
1   /* temp_conversion2.c - Script 5.5 -
    → revision of Script 5.4
    → (temp_conversion.c) */

2

3   #include <stdio.h>

4

5   int main(void) {

6

7       float temp_i, temp_o; // Two
    → temperatures: inputted and outputted.

8       char which_i, which_o; // F or C:
    → inputted and outputted.

9       char junk; // For discarding extra input.

10

11      // Prompt the user.

12      printf ("Enter a temperature and
    → indicate if it's Fahrenheit or
    → Celsius [##.# C/F]: ");

13

14      // Read the input as a conditional.

15      if (scanf ("%f %c", &temp_i,
    → &which_i) == 2) {

16

17          // Make the conversion based
    → upon which_i.

18          switch (which_i) {

19

20              // Celsius, convert to
    → Fahrenheit.

21              case 'C':

22              case 'c':

23                  temp_o = (temp_i *
    → (9.0/5.0)) + 32;

24                  which_o = 'F';

25                  break;

26

27              // Fahrenheit, convert
    → to Celsius.

28              case 'F':

29              case 'f':

30                  temp_o = (temp_i - 32) *
    → (5.0/9.0);
```

continues on next page

Script 5.5 Input validation requires thought and testing but is crucial to reliable, professional applications. Here, the act of reading input is written as the tested condition before any calculations are made.

VALIDATING KEYBOARD INPUT

```
31              which_o = 'C';
32              break;
33
34              // Problem: neither C
   → nor F entered, set which_o to FALSE.
35          default:
36              which_o = 0;
37              break;
38
39          } // End of switch.
40
41          // Print the results, using
   → which_o to indicate if it worked.
42          if (which_o) {
43              printf ("%0.1f %c is %0.1f
   → %c.\n", temp_i, which_i, temp_o,
   → which_o);
44          } else {
45              printf ("You failed to
   → enter C or F to indicate the current
   → temperature.\n");
46          }
47
48      } else { // Didn't enter the right
   → input.
49
50          printf ("You failed to use the
   → proper syntax.\n");
51
52      } // End of main IF.
53
54      // Discard any extra input.
55      do {
56          junk = getchar();
57      } while (junk != '\n');
58
59      // Pause for the user to press
   → Return or Enter.
60      getchar();
61
62      return 0;
63
64  }
```

Script 5.5 *continued*

3. Rewrite the `scanf()` line so that it's part of a conditional:

```
if (scanf ("%f %c", &temp_i,
→ &which_i) == 2) {
```

The `scanf()` function will return the number of items it successfully read in. As it has been formatted in this example to receive a float followed by a character, if the keyed input was correct, `scanf()` should return the number 2 as two values were read and assigned to variables.

That knowledge allows you to place the entire `scanf()` code within a conditional. The condition specifically checks if the `scanf()` function returns a value that is equal to 2. If this condition is true, you know that one float and one character were successfully read in and you can proceed with the calculations.

If you find this syntax to be too complicated, you can rewrite it like so:

```
int n;
n = scanf ("%f %c", &temp_i,
→ &which_i);
if (n == 2) {
```

4. Make all of the functionality of the original program part of the `if` conditional.

The `switch` and `if-else` conditionals that were at the heart of the original application are now the resulting code for the `if` part of the main (`scanf()`) conditional.

5. Complete the main conditional:

```
} else {
    printf ("You failed to use the
→ proper syntax.\n");
}
```

If the `scanf()` function does not return the number 2, a problem occurred and this message is printed.

continues on next page

6. Add a while loop to read in any more input:

```
do {
    junk = getchar();
} while (junk != '\n' );
```

Following the syntax outlined in the sidebar, this while loop reads in everything after the last read character (which should be *C* or *F*).

7. Delete the second getchar() function at the end of the application.

Since the do...while loop should take care of any extraneous stuff, only one getchar() call is required on Windows.

8. Save the file as *temp_conversion2.c*, compile, and debug as necessary.

9. Run the application, keying in both valid (**Figure 5.12**) and invalid (**Figure 5.13**) input.

VALIDATING KEYBOARD INPUT

Figure 5.12 After adding more input validation, the application works as it had before if the input is entered correctly.

```
C:\Documents and Settings\Larry Ullman\Desktop\C\Ch05\temp_conversion2.exe
Enter a temperature and indicate if it's Fahrenheit or Celsius [##.# C/F]: This
is entered incorrectly.
You failed to use the proper syntax.
```

Figure 5.13 The input is now validated so that no conversions are attempted using improper input.

Ignoring Input

As you may have experienced when using some of the examples in this chapter, improper input can throw off an application. For example, if you enter *Yes* instead of just *Y*, two extra characters are present (plus the newline created by pressing Return or Enter). These extra characters can throw off your application if further input is read later on. For example, if one use of `getchar()` expects either *Y* or *N* and a later use of `getchar()` expects another *Y* or *N* and the user types in *Yes* to the first prompt, the second prompt will read in the *e* following the *Y*. This was obviously not the intent.

To ignore and discard input, you can use the `getchar()` function within a `while` loop to read until the end of a line. The syntax is

```
char var;
do {
   var = getchar();
} while ( var != '\n' );
```

In short, this loop continues to read a single character from the standard input, assigning this value to `var`, until it encounters a newline (created when the user presses Return or Enter). At that time, the loop will be exited and the rest of the application will continue to execute.

✔ Tips

- There are many ways to validate input; which you use depends on the type, number, and format of the input expected. In this chapter you've seen a couple of options (using `scanf()` and checking values against a `switch`). The most important thing to know is that you should not assume people will always properly use an application.

- Some validation can be accomplished using the *ctype.h* library. It adds several functions, such as `isalpha()`, `isdigit()`, and `isspace()`, that check if a single character is of a certain type. The *ctype.h* file also adds conversion functions to your applications. These functions include `tolower()` and `toupper()`, for converting the cases of single characters .

Advanced printf() Usage

Through most of this chapter and the book, the printf() function has been used in a rather minimal way. We have used it to print simple messages or even those with variables, thanks to special placeholders. But the function can be customized in far more ways. Just one example is using %0.1f to format a float to a single decimal point (as in the temperature-conversion examples).

Each placeholder in a printf() statement can use many formatting parameters, each of which is placed between the initial percent sign and the final signifying character (*c* for character, *s* for string, *d* for integer, *f* for float, etc.). There are basically three extra formatting options.

First, there is a flag. This can be any one of the values in **Table 5.2**.

Second, you can indicate the minimum width to be used. So %5d would ensure that an integer value is printed using at least 5 characters (more would be used if the integer was longer). By default, spaces are used for padding, unless you add 0 as a flag.

Finally, a signifier can use a decimal point and a precision indicator. You've already seen this for floats. The precision indicator formats a float to that many decimal places. It has different effects on strings and integers but is less commonly used on those.

The easiest way to appreciate how different formatting parameters affect the end result is to create examples that print out values in different ways (**Figure 5.14**). However, in the following example, padding will be used to produce a more legible table for three columns of numbers.

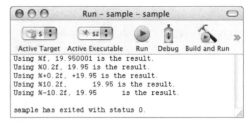

Figure 5.14 Using the same value each time *(19.95)*, different formatting parameters create different results.

Table 5.2 These flags affect the formatting of values when using printf().

printf() Flags	
CHARACTER	EFFECT
–	Left-justify the printed value
+	Always mark signed numeric values (+ for positive, – for negative)
(space)	Use a space for positive signed values (– for negative signed values)
0	Pad to the minimum width using zeros instead of spaces (ignored if using the – flag)

```
1    /* tips.c - Script 5.6 */
2
3    #include <stdio.h>
4
5    int main(void) {
6
7        float i; // Variable for a loop.
8
9        // Print the header.
10       printf ("Total with tip calculator
→ for various amounts:\n\n");
11       printf ("%10s %9d%% %9d%%\n",
→ "Bill", 15, 20);
12
13       // Loop through several iterations,
→ printing the calcuations for each.
14       for (i = 10.00; i <= 100.00; i
→ += 5) {
15
16           // Print the original amount,
→ the amount with 15% tip added, and
→ the amount with 20% tip added.
17           printf ("%10.2f %10.2f
→ %10.2f\n", i, (i * 1.15),
→ (i * 1.20));
18
19       }
20
21       // Pause for the user to press
→ Return or Enter.
22       getchar();
23
24       return 0;
25
26   }
```

Script 5.6 The printf() function is highly flexible and can be customized to format the output.

To use printf():

1. Create a new file or project in your text editor or IDE.

2. Type the standard beginning lines of code (**Script 5.6**):

   ```
   /* tips.c - Script 5.6 */
   #include <stdio.h>
   int main (void) {
   ```

3. Declare the required variable:

   ```
   float i;
   ```

   This application will use only one variable, a float called i. It will be used within a for loop.

4. Print a title message and then a table heading:

   ```
   printf ("Total with tip calculator
   → for various amounts:\n\n");
   printf ("%10s %9d%% %9d%%\n", "Bill",
   → 15, 20);
   ```

   The first line merely prints a statement indicating the purpose of the following numbers. This purpose is to print a total with tip for several different bill amounts, using both a 15% and a 20% gratuity.

   The second line creates the heading for the table columns. First, the word *Bill* will be printed, using at least 10 spaces (%10s). Then two integers are printed, each using at least 9 spaces (%9d). Each of these integers will be followed by a percent sign, created by using two percent signs together (%%). The end result will be a table heading of *Bill 15% 20%*, spaced out appropriately.

5. Create a for loop:
   ```
   for (i = 10.00; i <= 100.00;
   → i += 5) {
   ```

continues on next page

Advanced printf() Usage

The loop initially sets the i variable to a value of *10.00*. Then it will check if i is less than or equal to *100.00*. If so, the contents of the loop (Step 6) will be executed. After each iteration, the value of i is increased by 5. In short, this loop will go from 10 to 100 in five-dollar increments.

6. Define the print statement, formatting the results accordingly:

```
printf ("%10.2f %10.2f %10.2f\n", i,
→ (i * 1.15),(i * 1.20));
```

This print statement creates three formatted numbers. Each is a float with two decimal places (.2f) and will be padded so that they take up at least 10 spaces.

The values themselves are the value of i (10.00, 15.00, and so on), the value of i including a 15% gratuity, and the value of i plus a 20% gratuity.

7. Close the for loop and complete the rest of the main function:

```
        }
    getchar();
    return 0;
}
```

8. Save the file as *tips.c*, compile, and debug as necessary.

9. Run the application to see the results (**Figure 5.15**).

✔ Tips

■ As you might guess, many of the formatting parameters for printf() also apply to scanf().

■ Although we haven't used this feature in this book, the printf() function returns the number of characters it printed.

■ **Figure 5.16** shows this result using tabs instead of printf() padding. Even with tabs, the layout can become muddled.

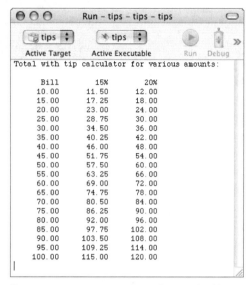

Figure 5.15 More exact spacing and a more legible result can be accomplished by padding the printed values (compare with Figure 5.16).

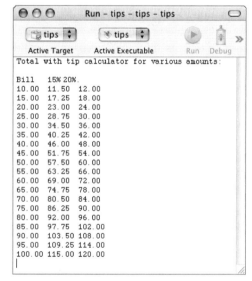

Figure 5.16 A table heading plus three columns of numbers printed out, each separated by tabs. The end result is not as clear as when spaces were used for padding (Figure 5.15).

Working with Arrays

Most of the examples in this book have dealt with two general data types: numbers and characters. These are useful, common variables but nowhere near as potent as arrays, the type you'll learn about in this chapter.

Before we start working with arrays, we'll introduce the concept, the syntax, and how to go about defining arrays. After that, we'll run through two methods of assigning values to your arrays. Then, we'll access the assigned values and print them out. Finally, we'll examine four key array-related ideas: using constants to define arrays, using loops with arrays, working with character arrays, and working with multidimensional arrays.

Introduction to Arrays

Whereas numbers and characters are scalar variables—meaning they contain only a single value at a time—arrays are a more complex structure. An array allows you to store a series of values, all under the heading of one variable. It's perhaps easiest to think of arrays as a two-column table (**Table 6.1**).

Arrays consist of *key-value* pairs, each pair constituting an *element*. By referencing a specific key (also called its *index*), you can obtain that corresponding value.

You create an array much like any other variable: by giving it a type and a name. The type will apply to every element in the array. In other words, an array contains values that are all integers, or all floats, or all characters.

When you define an array, you must identify its *dimension*, or the number of elements it has. The whole syntax is

```
type variable_name[size];
```

For example

```
int months[12];
```

Before working with arrays in the context of an application, let's go through the mental steps for establishing an array.

To create a simple array:

1. Determine the maximum number of values the array must store.

   Arrays in C are of a fixed size (set when you declare the variable). Once this length has been defined, you cannot put more than that number of elements in the array. Even if you store fewer values in the array than the set limit, the array will still take up the full limit's length. So if you define an array as having 10 elements but you store only 5 in it, the array will still require as much memory as if it had 10 stored values.

Table 6.1 Arrays are like tables with two columns: a numeric index (or key) and its associated value.

A Simple Array	
KEY	VALUE
0	98.5
1	74.3
2	82.0

2. Analyze the types of values being stored.

Arrays can store integers, floats, or characters but not a combination of them. Hence, if you'll need to work with decimal points, your array must be of type `float`. If you need more precision, then use a `double`. If you'll never need decimal points, work with `int`.

3. Give the array an appropriate name.

The rules for array names are the same as they are for any other variable. Beyond the standard syntax, be certain that your name is appropriate and descriptive.

One suggestion is to make your array names plural forms of a word (*grades*, *answers*, etc.) to indicate that the variable is storing a list of data.

4. Note the final syntax for declaring the array.

The final syntax will look something like this:

```
int ages[100];
float gpas[20];
char answers[10];
```

✔ Tips

- Arrays of variable size can be created in C by using a technique discussed in Chapter 10, "Managing Memory."

- Later in the chapter, you'll learn about *multidimensional* arrays—arrays whose values are also arrays.

- It may help you when working with arrays to understand how the computer treats them. When you define an array of 10 integers, the application will set aside 10 contiguous blocks of memory for that array (each block will be big enough to store one of the integer values). If you assign values to only 5 array elements, those other 5 memory blocks are still tied up. Or—and this will make more sense later—if you try to refer to the array's eleventh element, you'll actually be referring to a separate, unrelated memory block.

Assigning Values to Arrays

You can *initialize* arrays (assign values to them) in one of two ways. First, you can do it one element at a time. Second, you can assign all of the values when declaring the array (just as you can assign values to any variable when you declare it). Let's go over both approaches in more detail.

Assigning values to one element

Assigning values to array elements is similar to assigning values to any other variable: you use the assignment operator. The one distinct difference is that you must indicate the index to which the assigned value should apply. But first, a quick word about indexes in C.

Strange as it may seem, arrays in C are indexed beginning at 0. So the first element in an array called answers is answers[0]. The twentieth element would be found at answers[19]. Therefore, to assign a value to an array's first element, you would code something like

```
int answers[20];
answers[0] = 32;
```

Programmers commonly make one of two mistakes when using this syntax. The first is to refer to an index that does not exist:

```
int answers[20];
answers[20] = 32;
```

Although answers has 20 elements in it, the final element can be found at answers[19]. This is called an *Off-By-One-Bug* (*OB1B*) and can happen to the best of us.

The second common error is to inadvertently refer to the same index multiple times:

```
answers[4] = 100;
answers[4] = 212;
```

```
        Script
1    /* quiz.c - Script 6.1 */
2
3    #include <stdio.h>
4
5    int main (void) {
6
7        unsigned int answers[3]; // Array
  →  to store three correct answers.
8
9        // Assign values to the array.
10       answers[0] = 6; // Number of Bulls
  →  championships.
11       answers[1] = 1908; // Last year the
  →  Cubs won the World Series.
12       answers[2] = 1985; // Year the
  →  Bears won the Super Bowl.
13
14       return 0;
15
16   }
```

Script 6.1 In this first incarnation, the application creates an array with three elements and assigns values to each of them.

The end result of those two lines is that answers[4] now has the value of *212*, because the second assignment overwrites the value assigned the first time. In the following example, an array will be populated, although nothing will be done with that array quite yet.

To assign a value to an array element:

1. Create a new file or project in your text editor or IDE.

2. Type the standard beginning lines of code (**Script 6.1**):

   ```
   /* quiz.c  - Script 6.1 */
   #include <stdio.h>
   int main (void) {
   ```

3. Create an array variable:

   ```
   unsigned int answers[3];
   ```

   This variable, called answers, will store three values. The values will each be a non-negative (which is to say, *unsigned*) integer. The values correspond to the right answers for three questions that this application will eventually ask the user.

4. Assign the value to the first array element:

   ```
   answers[0] = 6;
   ```

   The first element in the array—which is the right answer to the first question—should have a value of *6*. This is assigned using the assignment operator and by referring to the array's index. Because it's the first element, 0 is used as the index.

continues on next page

5. Assign values to the remaining two array elements:

```
answers[1] = 1908;
answers[2] = 1985;
```

The process (Step 4) is repeated, assigning values to the second and third elements of the array.

6. Complete the main function:

```
    return 0;
}
```

7. Save the file as *quiz.c*, compile, and debug as necessary (**Figure 6.1**).

This application doesn't do anything yet, so there's no reason to execute it.

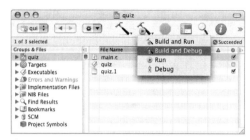

Figure 6.1 Compile the code as you would any C application, checking for errors. In this figure, the *Build and Debug* option is being selected in Xcode.

✔ Tips

- Array elements may have some random value until you formally initialize them. Thinking in terms of arrays and your computer's memory, keep in mind that whatever was stored in that memory block previously will be the value of an element until you assign it something else.

- Referring to an array element that does not exist (like answers[20] when the array only goes up to answers[19]) will normally cause unfortunate results during the program's execution. These results could range from simply using values from adjacent memory blocks to crashing the application.

```
000                    Script
1      /* quiz2.c - Script 6.2 - remake of
    → Script 6.1 (quiz.c) */

2

3      #include <stdio.h>

4

5      int main (void) {

6

7          unsigned int answers[] = {6, 1908,
    → 1985}; // Array to store three
    → correct answers (number of Bulls
    → championships, last Cubs World
    → Series victory, year the Bears won
    → the Super Bowl).

8

9          return 0;

10

11     }
```

Script 6.2 It's very easy to create and populate an array in one step, provided you use the proper syntax.

Assigning values to an entire array

If you want to populate an array all at once, the easiest way is to do so when you declare it. This technique still uses the assignment operator, but you need to separate the values by commas within curly braces:

```
int grades[3] = {94, 82, 87};
```

In such a case, you don't even have to specify the length of the array as that will be determined by how many values it is assigned:

```
int grades[] = {94, 82, 87};
```

Let's rewrite the *quiz* example, populating the array when it's defined.

To populate an array in one step:

1. Open *quiz.c* (Script 6.1) in your text editor or IDE, if it is not already open.

2. Change the array definition line to read as follows (**Script 6.2**):

   ```
   unsigned int answers[] = {6, 1908,
   → 1985};
   ```

   This one-line command has the same effect of defining and assigning values to the array over the course of four lines (the declaration plus one line for each array element). This format is more concise, and you don't need to muck around with setting the array's size or referring to specific indexes.

3. Delete the later lines where the array was previously populated.

   Obviously, you no longer have to set values for each element. There is some merit, however, to retaining the comments (which indicate what each numeric value means) so that you don't have mysterious numbers in your code.

   continues on next page

4. Save the file as *quiz2.c*, compile, and debug as necessary (**Figure 6.2**).

Again, there's no reason to run the application but you should still compile it to check for errors.

✔ Tips

■ You can specify a starting index when populating an array. For example,

```
ratings[20] = {[10] = 8.9};
```

assigns the value of *8.9* to the eleventh item in the array. This is new as of the C99 standard and is referred to as a *designated initializer*.

■ If for some reason you decide to use the syntax for indicating a starting point when assigning array values, subsequent values will be assigned to elements in order thereafter:

```
ratings[20] = {[10] = 8.9, 23.4,
→ 54.2}
```

This code assigns values to `ratings[10]`, `ratings[11]`, and `ratings[12]`.

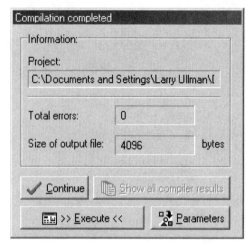

Figure 6.2 Again, assuming that your compiler is up to standards and that you typed the code properly, you should not see compilation errors. This is the view using Dev-C++.

ASSIGNING VALUES TO ARRAYS

```
         ╔══════════════════════════╗
  ⊙ ⊙ ⊙  ║        📄 Script         ║
 1    /* quiz3.c - Script 6.3 - remake of
   →  Scripts 6.1 and 6.2 (quiz.c and
   →  quiz2.c) */

 2

 3    #include <stdio.h>

 4

 5    int main (void) {

 6

 7       unsigned int answers[] = {6, 1908,
   →  1985}; // Array to store three
   →  correct answers.

 8       char input[10]; // For keyed input.

 9       int user_answer; // Store the
   →  user's answer.

10       char junk; // To get rid of extra
   →  input.

11

12       // Ask the first question and
   →  check the answer.

13       printf ("How many NBA
   →  championships have the Chicago Bulls
   →  won? ");

14

15       // Read in the input and assign
   →  this to user_answer.

16       fgets (input, sizeof(input), stdin);

17       sscanf (input, "%d", &user_answer);

18

19       // Check for correctness.

20       if (user_answer == answers[0]) {

21          printf ("You are correct!\n");

22       } else {

23          printf ("You are incorrect!
   →  The Bulls have won a total of %d NBA
   →  championships.\n", answers[0]);

24       }

25

26       // Discard any extra input and
   →  make the user press Return or Enter
   →  once more.
```

continues on next page

Script 6.3 The (mostly) completed quiz application reads in user input and compares that to the correct answers stored in an array.

Accessing Array Values

Once you've declared and initialized an array, you'll want to be able to access those array values. For the most part, doing so is much like referring to any other variable except that now you must use the square brackets and indicate to which element you are referring:

```
int num;
int grades[] = {94, 82, 87};
num = grades[0]; // num is 94.
printf ("The third element in grades has
a value of %d.", grades[2]);
```

To demonstrate this, let's flesh out the *quiz* application so that it compares a user-submitted answer to the correct one.

To access array values:

1. Open *quiz2.c* (Script 6.2) in your text editor or IDE, if it is not already open.

2. Add three new variables (**Script 6.3**):

   ```
   char input[10];
   int user_answer;
   char junk;
   ```

   These three variables will be used to handle all of the standard input. What the user types will first be read into the input character string (which happens to be a character array). This will then be assigned to the user_answer variable. Finally, the junk variable will be used to discard extraneous user input.

3. After the variable declarations, prompt the user with the first question:

   ```
   printf ("How many NBA championships
   → have the Chicago Bulls won? ");
   ```

   This is the first question; the correct answer is stored as the first element in the answers array.

continues on next page

4. Retrieve the user's answer:

```
fgets (input, sizeof(input), stdin);
sscanf (input, "%d", &user_answer);
```

Using the techniques covered in Chapter 5, "Standard Input and Ouput," what the user types in after the prompt is first read and then an integer value from that input is assigned to the user_answer variable. See Chapter 5 for a detailed discussion of this syntax.

5. Compare the user's answer to the right answer:

```
if (user_answer == answers[0]) {
    printf ("You are correct!\n");
} else {
    printf ("You are incorrect! The
→ Bulls have won a total of %d NBA
→ championships.\n", answers[0]);
}
```

The right answer is stored in answers[0]. The user's answer is in user_answer. By seeing if these two values are equal, this conditional indicates whether the user provided the correct answer. The array value is also used in the context of a printf() statement, which has the %d signifier for an integer, because the array is an integer type.

6. Discard any extra input using a do... while loop:

```
do {
    junk = getchar();
} while (junk != '\n' );
```

Again, this structure was introduced at the end of the previous chapter. It reads in and does nothing with all extra input until it reaches a newline (\n). While not obligatory, this feature keeps the execution of this application tidy.

7. Repeat Steps 3 through 6 for the next two questions.

```
27      do {
28          junk = getchar();
29      } while (junk != '\n');
30
31      /* -- Repeat process for other
→ questions. -- */
32
33      /* Wait for user to press Enter
→ or Return. */
34      getchar();
35
36      return 0;
37
38  }
```

Script 6.3 *continued*

Figure 6.3 Answering the first question correctly gives this result.

✔ Tips

- The *quiz* example could be improved in many ways, including adding the ability to track the number of correct answers. You could accomplish this by incrementing an integer variable for each correct response.

- There is no `printf()` signifier for printing an array in its entirety. Therefore, you cannot do something like

```
printf ("This is an array: %d.",
→ my_array);
```

In order to save space and time, the next two questions are not part of the listed code. But you can repeat Steps 3 through 6 (prompt the user, read in the input, compare against the right answer, delete extraneous input) for them if you want. The proper questions (corresponding to the right answers) would be: *What was the last year in which the Chicago Cubs won the World Series?* and *When did the Chicago Bears win the Super Bowl?* Of course, you can use your own questions and answers as you see fit.

8. Call the `getchar()` function to halt the execution of the application until the user presses Return or Enter.

   This is only required on Windows and other environments where the console window will automatically close after successful execution.

9. Save the file as *quiz3.c*, compile, and debug as necessary.

10. Run the application, entering different values (**Figures 6.3** and **6.4**) to see the results.

Figure 6.4 Answering the first question with anything other than *6* (including words, decimals, or letters) gives this result.

Defining Arrays Using Constants

In the *quiz* example, the number of array elements has been set by either using a literal value (answers[3]) or by letting C make that determination when values are assigned. Each method works, but it's allowed—even recommended—that you simplify this process by using a constant to represent the number of array elements.

Constants were introduced in Chapter 2, "Introduction to Data Types." You'll recall that C supports two formats for constant definitions. The first is to use the **const** keyword before defining the variable:

```
const int NUM = 10;
float gpas[NUM];
```

The second method is to define the constant using a preprocessor directive outside of the main function:

```
#define NUM 10
```

You'll learn more about preprocessor directives in Chapter 8, "Using the C Preprocessor."

Using constants to set the number of array elements makes sense in situations where you might access that value (the array's dimension) multiple times—for example, once when declaring the array and again when processing through all of the array elements in a loop. In this and the next section of the chapter you'll create such an example. By using constants for the array's size, if you later need to change the size, you will need to edit just this one value.

To use constants with arrays:

1. Create a new file or project in your text editor or IDE.

2. Type the standard beginning lines of code (**Script 6.4**):

```
                              Script
1    /* exchange.c - Script 6.4 */
2
3    #include <stdio.h>
4
5    int main (void) {
6
7        const int NUM = 10; // Constant
     for number of array elements.
8        float amounts[NUM]; // Holds
     different currency amounts.
9
10       /* Wait for user to press Enter
     or Return. */
11       getchar();
12
13       return 0;
14
15   }
```

Script 6.4 A good use of a constant is as a placeholder for the number of elements in an array.

Figure 6.5 Successful compilation of the exchange application, using the gcc compiler.

✔ Tips

- You could use a variable instead of a constant in this example:

  ```
  int NUM = 10;
  int amounts[NUM];
  ```

  This is referred to as a *variable-length array* (VLA), because the length of the array is determined by a variable. The benefit of using a constant is that you know the value will not be changed as the application runs.

- Do not confuse a variable-length array (VLA) with an array that has a varying length. The former uses a variable to set the array's size but has a fixed size. The latter does not have a fixed size but requires memory management (see Chapter 10).

```
/* exchange.c - Script 6.4 */
#include <stdio.h>
int main (void) {
```

3. Create a constant:

```
const int NUM = 10;
```

This constant is an integer named NUM. You don't have to use all uppercase letters for constant names, but that is a standard convention. The constant is given an initial value of *10*, which means that the array that uses this value in its declaration will have 10 elements.

If you'd like to assign more descriptive names, you could call this constant something like ARRAY_SIZE.

4. Define an array, using the constant to dictate the number of elements:

```
float amounts[NUM];
```

Instead of using a literal value (like *10*), this array has NUM elements in it. When the application is compiled, NUM will be replaced by NUM's value (*10*). The array itself is a float type, as it will be holding dollar amounts. You could define amounts as a double, if you want to be more precise.

5. Complete the main function:

```
    getchar();
    return 0;
}
```

6. Save the file as *exchange.c*, compile, and debug as necessary (Figure 6.5).

Yet again, this application doesn't do anything in its current form, so there's no reason to execute it.

DEFINING ARRAYS USING CONSTANTS

Looping through Arrays

Obviously if you have an array of any substantial size, then working with its individual elements—as in the previous examples—quickly becomes tedious. This is even truer if the same process is used on each value (printing it, performing calculations with it, and so forth). The easiest way to access every array element is to use a for loop.

You can review Chapter 4, "Control Structures," for the syntax of a for loop, but normally there are four parts (**Figure 6.6**). The loop first initializes a variable to a value, and then checks that variable against another value as its condition. If that condition is true, certain statements are executed. Finally, the variable is incremented.

When working with an array, you'll want to use the variable to represent all of the array's indexes, from 0 (the first element) to NUM - 1, where NUM is the number of elements in the array. You'll need to subtract 1 because if an array has NUM elements, there is no element indexed at NUM (because counting starts at 0).

The basic code, then, is

```c
int i;
const int NUM = 10;
int my_array[NUM];
for (i = 0; i < NUM; i++) {
    /* Do something with my_array[i]. */
}
```

With this in mind, the *exchange* application will be modified so that it creates an array of dollar amounts using a loop.

To loop through an array:

1. Open *exchange.c* (Script 6.4) in your text editor or IDE, if it is not already open.

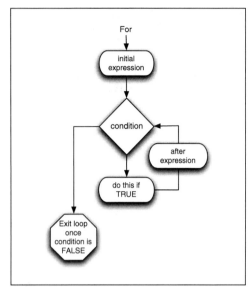

Figure 6.6 This flowchart reflects how for loops function.

```
 ○ ○ ○              📄 Script
1    /* exchange2.c - Script 6.5 - rewrite
  → of Script 6.4 (exchange.c)*/
2
3    #include <stdio.h>
4
5    int main (void) {
6
7        const int NUM = 10; // Constant for
  → number of array elements.
8        float amounts[NUM]; // Holds
  → different currency amounts.
9        unsigned int i; // Index variable.
10
11       // Print the header.
12       printf ("US Dollar to Mexican Pesos
  → converter:\n\n");
13       printf ("%10s %10s\n", "Dollars",
  → "Pesos");
14
15       // Loop through the array.
16       for (i = 0; i < NUM; i++) {
17
18           // Array values are in $5
  → increments.
19           amounts[i] = (i + 1) * 5.00;
20
21           // Print original amounts and
  → peso conversion (1 dollar = 11.317466
  → pesos).
22           printf ("%10.2f %10.2f\n",
  → amounts[i], (amounts[i] *
  → 11.317466));
23
24       } // End of for loop.
25
26       /* Wait for user to press Enter or
  → Return. */
27       getchar();
28
29       return 0;
30
31   }
```

Script 6.5 This for loop, along with the NUM constant and the i index variable, accesses every array element.

2. Add a new variable for the loop (**Script 6.5**):

```
unsigned int i;
```

The i variable is a simple unsigned integer. It will be used as the array index variable within the for loop.

3. Print two header lines that will describe the forthcoming table:

```
printf ("US Dollar to Mexican Pesos
→ converter:\n\n");
printf ("%10s %10s\n", "Dollars",
→ "Pesos");
```

Like the tips calculator in the last chapter, this application will print a table of values. To help it lay out nicely, some padding in the printf() statement creates spacing. Here, two strings are printed (*Dollars* and *Pesos*), each using a total of 10 spaces.

4. Begin defining the for loop:

```
for (i = 0; i < NUM; i++) {
```

This loop begins by setting the i variable to a value of *0*. That number corresponds to the first index in the array. Then the conditional checks to see if i is less than NUM, which was defined earlier as a constant. As there are NUM elements in the array, the last element is indexed at NUM - 1. Therefore, as long as i is less than NUM, amounts[i] is a valid reference. The third part of the loop increments i by 1.

5. Set the value of the array for each element:

```
amounts[i] = (i + 1) * 5.00;
```

The first statement within the loop assigns a value to the array element. Since the loop iterates through the entire array using i, this line will populate the entire array. The value itself is calculated as the sum of i + 1 multiplied by 5.00. The end result will be an array of five-dollar increments, from 5.00 to NUM * 5.

continues on next page

LOOPING THROUGH ARRAYS

6. Print the original amount and the converted amount:

```
printf ("%10.2f %10.2f\n",
→ amounts[i], (amounts[i] *
→ 11.317466));
```

This conversion turns U.S. dollars (the original array values) into Mexican pesos, using the current exchange rate at the time of this writing. Again, formatting is used within the `printf()` statement so that the table is more legible.

7. Complete the `for` loop syntax:

```
} // End of for loop.
```

8. Save the file as *exchange2.c*, compile, and debug as necessary.

9. Run the application to see the results (**Figure 6.7**).

10. Change the value of NUM, recompile, and rerun the application (**Figure 6.8**).

✔ Tips

■ The exchange example as written does not need an array at all, since nothing is done with amounts after its values are set. But if you wanted to, for example, create a separate table showing exchange rates for a different currency, you could add another for loop that performs and displays that calculation using the same amounts array.

■ When using loops to work with arrays, it's easy to create an Off-By-One-Bug. Remember that the highest index in an array is 1 less than the number of elements in the array (because arrays are indexed starting at 0). For this reason, the condition in the loop is i < NUM and not i <= NUM.

Figure 6.7 An array and a loop helps to create this table of numbers.

Figure 6.8 Changing just one simple value—the NUM constant in Script 6.5—creates different results (compare with Figure 6.7).

Table 6.2 A string stored in a character array is actually multiple individual characters terminated by the NULL character.

The name Array	
INDEX	VALUE
0	A
1	u
2	b
3	r
4	e
5	y
6	\0

Using Character Arrays

All of the examples in this chapter have used numeric arrays, but arrays can also store characters (which, yes, are technically integers). By creating an array of characters, you can create a string. This concept was introduced back in Chapter 2 but merits a review.

There are two important differences between character arrays and other array types. First, storing a string in a character array always requires an extra element. This extra, final element stores the terminating NULL character (\0), which marks the end of a string. **Table 6.2** lists the elements for a character array called name with a value of *Aubrey*.

The second difference is that character arrays must be assigned a value using double quotation marks:

```
name[7] = "Aubrey";
```

Whereas number values do not use quotation marks and single-character values use single quotation marks, strings use double quotation marks. Notice that this syntax implies the NULL character, which does not need to be explicitly stated within double quotation marks.

Of course, you could assign strings to character arrays in a more tedious way, like this:

```
char name[7] = {'A', 'u', 'b', 'r', 'e',
→ 'y', '\0'};
```

But the double quotation technique is a handy feature to use.

This next example will take a user-submitted word and print it backwards by using the array indexes.

To use character arrays:

1. Create a new file or project in your text editor or IDE.

2. Type the standard beginning lines of code (**Script 6.6**):

```
/* backwards.c - Script 6.6 */
#include <stdio.h>
```

3. Include the *ctype.h* library file:

```
#include <ctype.h>
```

This standard header file defines several functions that can be useful in validating single characters. In this particular example, the isalpha() function will be required. When we include *ctype.h*, that function becomes available to this application.

4. Begin defining the main function:

```
int main (void) {
```

5. Declare the required variables:

```
char input[11];
int i;
char junk;
```

The first variable, input, will be the character array used to store the keyed characters. The second variable, i, is the index variable, which will be used to help loop through the character array. Finally, junk is a single character used to help discard extraneous input.

```
 1   /* backwards.c - Script 6.6 */
 2
 3   #include <stdio.h>
 4   #include <ctype.h> // Need in order to
     → use isalpha().
 5
 6   int main (void) {
 7
 8       char input[11]; // For keyed input.
 9       int i; // Index variable.
10       char junk; // To get rid of extra
     → input.
11
12       // Prompt the user.
13       printf ("Enter a word up to ten
     → characters long: ");
14
15       // Read the input.
16       scanf ("%10s", input);
17
18       // Print it backwards.
19       printf ("The word '%s' is '",
     → input);
20
21       // Loop through the input in
     → reverse.
22       for (i = 9; i >= 0; i--) {
23
24           // Only print letters.
25           if (isalpha(input[i])) {
26               printf ("%c", input[i]);
27           }
28
29       } // End of for loop.
30
31       printf ("' spelled backwards.\n");
32
```

continues on next page

Script 6.6 This simple application reads in a word from the standard input and then prints it in reverse order.

```
33        // Discard any extra input and make
   → the user press Return or Enter once
   → more
34        do {
35            junk = getchar();
36        } while (junk != '\n');
37
38        /* Wait for user to press Enter or
   → Return. */
39        getchar();
40
41        return 0;
42
43    }
```

Script 6.6 *continued*

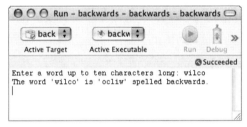

Enter a word up to ten characters long: wilco
The word 'wilco' is 'ocliw' spelled backwards.

Figure 6.9 A short word is printed backwards by the application.

6. Prompt the user and read in the keyboard input:

```
printf ("Enter a word up to ten
 → characters long: ");
scanf ("%10s", input);
```

The prompt itself is quite simple and self-explanatory. After it, the scanf() function is used to read up to a 10-character string (%10s). This will be assigned to the input variable (along with the eleventh character, which is the \0). Because input is a string, you can refer directly to the variable rather than its address (&input). This concept and all of the important syntax was discussed in Chapter 5.

7. Reprint the entered word:

```
printf ("The word '%s' is '", input);
```

The end result of the application (**Figure 6.9**) will be a prompt, followed by a line of text where the inputted word is printed both forwards and backwards. This print statement creates all of the text up until the word is printed backwards.

8. Define the for loop:

```
for (i = 10; i >= 0; i--) {
```

Unlike the previous loop, this one will iterate through an array in reverse order. Instead of going from 0 to 10 in increments of 1, it counts down from 10 to 0 in decrements of 1. The consequence of this reverse structure is that the input array will be accessed in the opposite order it was entered.

continues on next page

USING CHARACTER ARRAYS

9. Print every character:

```
if (isalpha(input[i])) {
    printf ("%c", input[i]);
}
```

If the user enters a string only 5 characters long, there will be 5 unused spaces in the input array. Rather than include these in the backwards printout, the isalpha() function is used to verify that the element value is an alphabetical character. If the current array value passes this test, that character is printed.

Notice that the syntax for accessing array elements—input[i]—is the same even though the loop is working backwards through the array. In other words, you don't have to always loop through arrays in ascending order from 0.

10. Complete the for loop and finish the feedback statement:

```
}
printf ("' spelled backwards.\n");
```

This printf() statement completes the one begun in Step 7, including the closing single quotation mark that helps surround the backwards version of the word (Figure 6.9).

Figure 6.10 Only 10 letters of a long word are read in and printed in reverse.

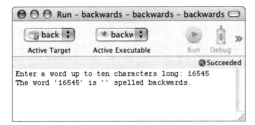

Figure 6.11 Improper input is more or less ignored by the application.

- The integer version of the `name` array could be created using this code:

```
char name[7] = {65, 117, 98, 114,
  101, 121, 0};
```

where each letter in *Aubrey* is represented by its numeric equivalent. See the character table in Appendix B, "Resources," for the complete list of characters and their associated numeric values.

11. Read in and discard any extraneous input:

```
do {
    junk = getchar();
} while (junk != '\n');
```

Since this application makes use of user input, it's a good idea to remove all extraneous input (for instance, if the user enters a word longer than 10 characters) using this trick.

12. Complete the `main` function:

```
    getchar();
    return 0;
}
```

13. Save the file as *backwards.c*, compile, and debug as necessary.

14. Run the application, entering different values at the prompt (**Figures 6.10** and **6.11**).

✔ Tips

- It's possible that this example would print some garbage if a shorter word was entered. For example, if all eleven blocks of memory aren't used by the submitted word, whatever was present in those unused memory blocks would still be part of the `input` array. To correct for this, you could initialize the entire array by setting each value to `NULL` before assigning the user's input to it.

- In Chapter 11, "Working with Strings," you'll learn about another method of creating and using strings in C.

- Alternatively, you can assign a value to a character array using the `strncpy()` function:

```
char name[12];
strncpy (name, "David Brent", 11);
```

Using Multidimensional Arrays

The power of an array can be greatly increased by creating multidimensional arrays: an array whose element values are also arrays. This concept is tough to visualize (it's roughly equivalent to a stack of two-column tables) but not that hard to use.

All of the same rules for arrays apply to multidimensional arrays. Once again you'll use the square brackets to indicate the number of elements. This time you'll do so twice:

```
float grades[3][20];
```

The first number indicates the number of subarrays (or tables, in layman's terms) the main array contains. The second number specifies the number of rows each subarray (table) contains.

Populating multidimensional arrays is also tricky. You first refer to the subarray index and then the index for that subarray. So the first element in the first subarray would be at grades[0][0]. The tenth element in the third subarray is at grades[2][9].

Again, you can populate an entire multidimensional array in one step using the curly braces. With a multidimensional array, you'll need to use one set of curly braces for each subarray, with each separated by a comma and the entire construct within another pair of curly braces (for the main array):

```
int grades [][] {
{84, 72, 91, 88},
{65, 68, 94, 96},
{75, 91, 82, 82},
}
```

USING MULTIDIMENSIONAL ARRAYS

```
1    /* exchange3.c - Script 6.7 - rewrite
     → of Scripts 6.4 and 6.5 (exchange.c
     → and exchange2.c) */
2
3    #include <stdio.h>
4
5    int main (void) {
6
7        const int NUM = 10; // Constant
     → for number of array elements.
8        double amounts[2][NUM]; // Holds
     → different currency amounts.
9
10       // titles stores the table headers.
11       char titles[2][6] = {
12           {"Pesos"},
13           {"Euros"}
14       };
15
16       double rates[] = {11.317466,
     → 0.823859}; // Pesos and Euros,
     → respectively.
17
18       unsigned int i, j; // Index
     → variables.
19
20       // Print the header.
21       printf ("US Dollar amounts
     → converted to Mexican Pesos and
     → Euros:\n\n");
22
23       for (i = 0; i < 2; i++) {
24           printf ("%10s %10s\n",
     → "Dollars", titles[i]);
25
26           // Loop through the array.
27           for (j = 0; j < NUM; j++) {
28
29               // Array values are in $5
     → increments.
30               amounts[i][j] = (j + 1) *
     → 5.00;
```

continues on next page

Script 6.7 This final version of the exchange rate conversion application uses three different multidimensional arrays.

```
31
32              // Print original amounts
     → and conversion.
33                 printf ("%10.2f %10.2f\n",
     → amounts[i][j], (amounts[i][j] *
     → rates[i]));
34
35          } // End of inner for loop.
36
37          printf ("\n\n");
38
39       } // End of outer for loop.
40
41       /* Wait for user to press Enter or
     → Return. */
42       getchar();
43
44       return 0;
45
46  }
```

Script 6.7 *continued*

```
US Dollar amounts converted to Mexican Pesos and Euros:

    Dollars       Pesos
      5.00         56.59
     10.00        113.17
     15.00        169.76
     20.00        226.35
     25.00        282.94
     30.00        339.52
     35.00        396.11
     40.00        452.70
     45.00        509.29
     50.00        565.87


    Dollars       Euros
      5.00          4.12
     10.00          8.24
     15.00         12.36
     20.00         16.48
     25.00         20.60
     30.00         24.72
     35.00         28.84
     40.00         32.95
     45.00         37.07
     50.00         41.19
```

Figure 6.12 Two tables of currency conversions are created using three multidimensional arrays.

The preceding code creates a multidimensional array containing three subarrays, each of which has four elements. Notice that by spacing the assignment out over several lines it's more legible.

You can use loops with multidimensional arrays, but to access every element, you'll need two loops: an outer loop to access the main array's elements (which are also arrays), and an inner loop to access every element of each subarray. Let's rewrite the exchange application using a multidimensional array.

To use multidimensional arrays:

1. Open *exchange2.c* (Script 6.5) in your text editor or IDE, if it is not already open.

2. Turn the amounts array into a multidimensional double (**Script 6.7**):

   ```
   double amounts[2][NUM];
   ```

   In its previous incarnation, amounts was a simple array of floats. Now it will contain two subarrays, each of which is NUM elements long. Every value stored in the array will be a double.

3. Store the data table column headers as a multidimensional array:

   ```
   char titles[2][6] = {
       {"Pesos"},
       {"Euros"}
   };
   ```

   This application uses a second multidimensional array, called titles. This array contains essentially two strings—*Pesos* and *Euros*—but creating strings requires a character array. The titles array will be used to create the table column headings for the output (**Figure 6.12**).

continues on next page

4. Store the conversion rates in a simple array:

```
double rates[] = {11.317466,
→ 0.823859};
```

Rather than hardcoding these numbers in the code, we will store them in a variable as well. Maintaining the same structure created in Step 3, the array's first element corresponds to pesos and the second to euros.

5. Add a second loop variable:

```
unsigned int i, j;
```

Because multidimensional arrays often require two loops, two separate index variables are needed for these loops. Keeping with standard C practices, i will be used in the outermost loop and j in the inner loop.

6. Alter the main application statement:

```
printf ("US Dollar amounts converted
→ to Mexican Pesos and Euros:\n\n");
```

The caption should now indicate that the output reflects conversion into both pesos and euros.

7. Create the first loop:

```
for (i = 0; i < 2; i++) {
```

This first loop will be used to access the primary arrays: amounts, titles, and rates. Each of those was defined with two elements, so this loop counts from 0 to 1 (i < 2).

8. Add the table header print statement:

```
printf ("%10s %10s\n", "Dollars",
→ titles[i]);
```

This header text is exactly like it was in the previous examples except that now the second column heading (*pesos* or *euros*) will be pulled from the titles array.

9. Add another loop that prints every calculation:

```
for (j = 0; j < NUM; j++) {
    amounts[i][j] = (j + 1) * 5.00;
    printf ("%10.2f %10.2f\n",
    → amounts[i][j], (amounts[i][j]
    → * rates[i]));
}
```

This loop is almost exactly like the original loop in the previous version of the exchange application. The first key difference is that this loop refers to amounts[i][j] instead of just amounts[i] in order to access the scalar values of the multidimensional array.

A second difference here is that the rates array is used for determining the conversion rate for the respective currency.

Aside from those two changes, the functionality remains the same. Again, the initial dollar value is calculated in increments of 5 and assigned to the array. This then is used in making calculations and printing the amounts.

10. Complete the formatting and the outer loop:

```
    printf ("\n\n");
} // End of outer for loop.
```

When using complex, nested loops, it's increasingly important to comment on where they end so that you understand what braces in your code are doing.

11. Save the file as *exchange3.c*, compile, and debug as necessary.

12. Run the application to see the results (Figure 6.12).

continues on next page

USING MULTIDIMENSIONAL ARRAYS

13. Change the value of NUM, recompile, and rerun the application (**Figure 6.13**).

✔ Tips

■ Once again, the amounts array is under-utilized here, having been assigned values that are never later used. Still, the example demonstrates a concept well, and you could add to the application so that amounts is used again.

■ Through C libraries you can use different array-related functions, like qsort(), a common and powerful sorting algorithm. See Appendix B, "Resources," to learn where you can find out more.

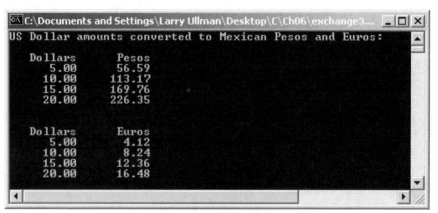

Figure 6.13 Despite the more complex nature of the application—relying heavily on multidimensional arrays—changing the value of NUM creates different-length lists of data.

CREATING YOUR OWN FUNCTIONS

The bulk of programming involves using functions: performing set tasks by calling established procedures. C, like any language, has defined hundreds of functions used to simplify common steps. These range from the standard input/output ones like `scanf()` and `printf()` to specialized mathematical functions for trigonometry.

C also provides syntax for you to define your own functions. By doing so, you can encapsulate blocks of code under one name. This allows you to repeatedly execute that code through a simple function call. This move toward more modular programming is a key aspect to developing real-world applications.

In this chapter you'll learn everything you need to know about creating and using your own functions. For starters, you'll create simple functions, ones that take arguments, and ones that return values. Then you'll work your way into more complex subjects like inline and recursive functions. Finally, you'll learn about variable scope: understanding where variables exist.

Creating Simple Functions

Writing your own functions requires following the proper syntax. First, you must create a function *prototype*—a declaration of a function's name, arguments, and what type of value it returns. This prototype helps the compiler check that the function is properly used in an application. The syntax for the prototype is

```
type_returned function_name (arguments);
```

The `type_returned` section refers to what sort of value the function will return. For example, the `main` function returns an integer (0 in all of the book's examples so far). If the function returns no value, its `type_returned` will be `void`.

Naming functions follows the same rules as naming variables: you use alphanumeric characters plus the underscore. Also, function names are case-sensitive in C, so you should stick to a consistent capitalization strategy. More important, though, is that you cannot use an existing function name for your functions (or any keyword, like `int` or `break`).

The arguments a function takes is a more complicated subject, which will be covered later in this chapter. For now, keep in mind that if a function takes no arguments, again `void` is used.

The function prototype is normally placed after any include lines but before the `main` function definition. So the bare-bones syntax is

```
#include <stdio.h>
void my_func (void); /* prototype */
int main (void) {
```

You can call your own functions as you would any standard library function in C:

```
my_func();
```

```
        Script
1    /* discard_function.c - Script 7.1 */
2
3    #include <stdio.h>
4
5    void discard_input (void); /* Function
  →  prototype. */
6
7    int main (void) {
8
9        // Prompt the user.
10       printf ("Enter some text and watch me
  →  do nothing with it: ");
11
12       // Read the input.
13       getchar();
14
15       // Discard everything else.
16       discard_input();
17
18       // Wait for user to press Enter or
  →  Return.
19       getchar();
20
21       return 0;
22
23   } /* End of main() function. */
24
25
26   /* This function discards all of the
  →  input until a newline. */
27   void discard_input (void) {
28
29       char junk; // To get rid of extra
  →  input.
30
31       // Loop through the input and
  →  ignore it.
```

continues on next page

Script 7.1 In this application, a user-defined function is created and called.

The final step in defining and using your own functions is the function definition itself. Normally this is placed after the `main` function in your code. The beginning of the function definition looks like the function prototype. Then you place the function's content (what code is executed when the function is called) between opening and closing curly braces. Let's finish the function definition we began earlier:

```
void my_func (void) {
    printf ("This is a silly function.\n");
}
```

In our first example, you will take the code for discarding extraneous input and turn that into a function.

To define and use your own functions:

1. Create a new file or project in your text editor or IDE.

2. Type the standard beginning lines of code (**Script 7.1**):

   ```
   /* discard_function.c - Script 7.1 */
   #include <stdio.h>
   ```

3. Add the function prototype:

   ```
   void discard_input (void);
   ```
   The function being defined in this file is called `discard_input`. It takes no arguments and returns no value.

4. Begin the `main` function:

   ```
   int main (void) {
   ```
   Even though this application has a user-defined function, it still requires a `main` function. Remember that the `main` function is automatically called when an application is executed, so the core of any application must still go here.

continues on next page

5. Prompt the user and read in a single character:

```
printf ("Enter some text and watch me
→ do nothing with it: ");
getchar();
```

This application will do very little; its main purpose is to highlight the process of defining and using your own functions. Since the user-defined function helps ignore extraneous input, the user must be prompted for some input first. This first getchar() call creates that prompt, even though nothing is done with the read-in character.

6. Call the user-defined function:

```
discard_input();
```

To call the function, simply type its name followed by empty parentheses. The line concludes with a semicolon, as does every statement in C.

7. Add another getchar() call to pause execution on Windows:

```
getchar();
```

8. Complete the main function:

```
    return 0;
} /* End of main() function. */
```

When your applications contain multiple functions, you may find it useful to comment on where each function terminates.

9. After the main function, begin defining the discard_input() function:

```
void discard_input (void) {
```

This definition line is very similar to the main definition line, except that this function returns no value (hence the initial void). The curly braces mark the start of the function's contents.

```
32      do {
33          junk = getchar();
34      } while (junk != '\n');
35
36  } /* End of discard_input() function. */
```

Script 7.1 *continued*

10. Define any necessary variables:

```
char junk;
```

Your own functions can, and often will, have their own variables. As you'll see at the end of the chapter (in the section "Understanding Variable Scope"), these are separate variables, pertaining only to this function.

The `discard_input()` function makes use of a single character called `junk`.

11. Add the function's content:

```
do {
    junk = getchar();
while (junk != '\n');
```

You've seen this structure before and should recognize it as a handy way to read in and ignore standard input.

12. Complete the `discard_input()` function:

```
} /* End of discard_input()
→ function. */
```

This closing brace marks the end of the function definition. We've added a comment so that it's clear where the function begins and ends. Notice as well that there's no `return` statement here, as this function returns nothing.

13. Save the file as *discard_function.c*, compile, and debug as necessary.

14. Run the application (**Figure 7.1**).

✔ Tips

■ Technically, you could define your own functions before the `main` function and therefore you would not have to use a function prototype. Or you could define your own functions within the `main` function. But it is standard procedure to code the `main` function first, as this example demonstrates.

■ If a large application makes use of the same function several times, or if you have a function or set of functions that you use in many applications, you'll want to place these in their own library file. You'll learn more about this in Chapter 8, "Using the C Preprocessor."

Figure 7.1 While it's not the most exciting application, it does make use of your own user-defined function, creating a more modular code structure.

Creating Functions That Take Arguments

The next logical evolution of your user-defined functions is to have them take arguments. Most C functions take arguments, like isalpha(), which expects a character to be passed to it. To have your functions take arguments, you need to define them—both in the prototype and in the formal definition—with the type of arguments expected:

```
void my_func (int age, int year);
int main (void) {
    // Call my_func().
}
void my_func (int age, int year) { …
```

When calling a function that takes arguments, you need to then pass it the appropriate values. As you've already seen, there are many ways of doing this, from passing literal values to variable values to the results of calculations. Each of these function calls are valid:

```
int my_var = 100;
my_func (my_var, 8);
my_func (my_var * 2, my_var + 1);
```

It's important to remember that the values passed to the function must be of the right type and order. In other words, the first value passed to a function will be assigned to the function's first argument variable and the second to the second. There's no way to pass a value to the second function argument without passing one to the first.

In our next example, the ability to display a list of currency conversions will be turned into its own function. This function will take two arguments: the exchange rate and the column title (e.g., *Euro* or *Peso*).

```
                        Script
1    /* exchange_function.c - Script 7.2 */
2
3    #include <stdio.h>
4
5    void make_exchange_table(float rate, char
  →  title[]); /* Function prototype. */
6
7    int main (void) {
8
9        // Show Pesos.
10       make_exchange_table (11.317466,
  →  "Pesos");
11
12       // Show Euros.
13       make_exchange_table (0.823859,
  →  "Euros");
14
15       // Wait for user to press Enter or
  →  Return.
16       getchar();
17
18       return 0;
19
20   } /* End of main() function. */
21
22   /* This function displays a list of
  →  currency conversions. */
23   void make_exchange_table(float rate,
  →  char title[]) {
24
25       float i; // Loop variable.
26
27       // Print the header.
28       printf ("%10s %10s\n", "Dollars",
  →  title);
29
30       // Loop through several increments.
```
continues on next page

Script 7.2 The make_exchange_table() function takes two arguments—a conversion rate and a column heading—and creates a list of currency conversions.

```
 ● ● ●              Script
31        for (i = 10.00; i <= 100.00; i +=
     → 10.00) {

32

33           // Print original amounts and
     → conversion.

34             printf ("%10.2f %10.2f\n", i,
     → i * rate);

35

36        }

37

38        printf ("\n\n");

39

40    } /* End of make_exchange_table()
     → function. */
```

Script 7.2 *continued*

```
 ● ● ●    Run - exchange_fun ⬭
    Dollars        Pesos
     10.00        113.17
     20.00        226.35
     30.00        339.52
     40.00        452.70
     50.00        565.87
     60.00        679.05
     70.00        792.22
     80.00        905.40
     90.00       1018.57
    100.00       1131.75


    Dollars        Euros
     10.00          8.24
     20.00         16.48
     30.00         24.72
     40.00         32.95
     50.00         41.19
     60.00         49.43
     70.00         57.67
     80.00         65.91
     90.00         74.15
    100.00         82.39
```

Figure 7.2 The make_exchange_table()
function uses the second argument it
receives as the column heading for the table.

To define and use functions that take arguments:

1. Create a new file or project in your text editor or IDE.

2. Type the standard beginning lines of code (**Script 7.2**):

```
/* exchange_function.c - Script 7.2
→ */
#include <stdio.h>
```

3. Add the function prototype:

```
void make_exchange_table(float rate,
→ char title[]);
```

The function being defined in this file is called make_exchange_table. It's a long name, but descriptive. This function takes two arguments. The first will be a float, and the second will be a character array. When passing arrays of any type to your function, do not include their dimension (the number of elements in the array) in the definition. In other words, prototype the function with array_name[] instead of array_name[6] or array_name[600].

4. Begin the main function:

```
int main (void) {
```

5. Call the make_exchange_table() function:

```
make_exchange_table (11.317466,
→ "Pesos");
```

This first call will convert dollars to pesos. The two proper arguments are passed to the function. The first is a float, corresponding to the conversion rate. This will be assigned to the rate variable within the make_exchange_table() function.

The second argument will be used for the column heading in the displayed table (**Figure 7.2**).

continues on next page

CREATING FUNCTIONS THAT TAKE ARGUMENTS

6. Make another call to the function, using different values:

```
make_exchange_table (0.823859,
→ "Euros");
```

This step calls the same function again, passing different parameters, which will generate different results (see the bottom table in Figure 7.2).

7. Complete the `main` function:

```
    getchar();
    return 0;
}
```

8. After the `main` function, begin defining the `make_exchange_table()` function:

```
void make_exchange_table(float rate,
→ char title[]) {
```

As the prototype indicates, this function takes two arguments: a float and a character string. With the first function call (Step 5), *11.317466* is assigned to **rate** and *Pesos* to **title**. In the second function call (Step 6), **rate** and **title** are *0.823859* and *Euros*, respectively.

9. Define the required variable:

```
float i;
```

This function will make use of a loop, which therefore requires a counter variable, called i. The other two variables used by the function have already been declared in the function definition.

10. Print a table heading:

```
printf ("%10s %10s\n", "Dollars",
→ title);
```

Like the similar examples in previous chapters, this application creates a spaced-out header. The heading for the second column comes from the passed **title** value.

```
●  ○  ○     Run - exchange_func⊂⊃
    Dollars          Yen
     10.00        1073.54
     20.00        2147.07
     30.00        3220.61
     40.00        4294.15
     50.00        5367.69
     60.00        6441.22
     70.00        7514.76
     80.00        8588.30
     90.00        9661.84
    100.00       10735.37


    Dollars       Canada $
     10.00          13.49
     20.00          26.97
     30.00          40.46
     40.00          53.95
     50.00          67.44
     60.00          80.92
     70.00          94.41
     80.00         107.90
     90.00         121.38
    100.00         134.87

|
```

Figure 7.3 Changing the function call lines creates different conversion tables.

11. Define the loop:

```
for (i = 10.00; i <= 100.00; i +=
⇢ 10.00) {
```

This loop will iterate from 10.00 to 100.00 in $10 increments.

12. Print each dollar amount and the respective conversion:

```
printf ("%10.2f %10.2f\n", i, i *
⇢ rate);
```

This line will print the original value of i, representing U.S. dollars, along with the value of i times the conversion rate. This second calculated number will represent the other currency value.

13. Complete the function definition:

```
    }
    printf ("\n\n");
}
```

The first curly brace closes the for loop. Then, two blank lines are printed for a better appearance in the standard output. Finally, the function itself is closed.

14. Save the file as *exchange_function.c*, compile, and debug as necessary.

15. Run the application (Figure 7.2).

16. If desired, change the function call lines, recompile, and run the application again (**Figure 7.3**).

continues on next page

CREATING FUNCTIONS THAT TAKE ARGUMENTS

✔ Tips

- You can even pass values to a function by calling a separate function and using its returned value as the argument. In this example, the sscanf() function will return the number of items it read in, which will be an integer passed to my_func():

  ```
  my_func (4, sscanf ("%s", input));
  ```

- If your function takes several arguments of the same type, you cannot use the variable declaration shortcut of separating each by a comma. This is invalid:

  ```
  void function_name (int num1,
  → num2) { …
  ```

  This is valid:

  ```
  void function_name (int num1, int
  → num2) {…
  ```

- You cannot set default values for function arguments in C.

- The make_exchange_table() function could be altered to take a third parameter, indicating the dollar increments you want to use or the dollar range (**Figure 7.4**):

  ```
  void make_exchange_table(float rate,
  → char title[], float limit);
  ```

- You aren't required to include the variable name in a function's prototype (just its type), but it's a good idea.

- C99 technically calls variables in the function definition *parameters*; *arguments* are passed to the function when it's called.

```
⊙ ⊙ ⊙   Run – exchange_fu⊂⊃
 Dollars          Yen
   10.00      1073.54
   20.00      2147.07
   30.00      3220.61
   40.00      4294.15
   50.00      5367.69


 Dollars      Canada $
   10.00         13.49
   20.00         26.97
   30.00         40.46
   40.00         53.95
   50.00         67.44
   60.00         80.92
   70.00         94.41
   80.00        107.90
   90.00        121.38
  100.00        134.87
  110.00        148.36
  120.00        161.84
  130.00        175.33
  140.00        188.82
  150.00        202.31
```

Figure 7.4 Minor modifications to the function definition can make it easy to generate different results. Here, the upper limit for each conversion is sent as an argument.

Creating Functions That Return a Value

The final addition to making your functions as practical as the standard C library functions is to have them return values. This is accomplished using the return statement, which you've already been using in the main function. You can return any single value from your function:

```
return 1;
```

The returned value can even be based on a variable's value:

```
int num = 8;
return num;
```

Any function that returns a value must have a proper prototype and definition, both of which must indicate the type of value returned. You've already seen this with the main function (which returns an int). Here's another sample function definition:

```
int my_func (void) {
    return 27;
}
```

You can assign the returned values to variables when the function is called, use them in calculations, or even use them as the argument to another function:

```
number = my_func();
sum = num + my_func();
printf("A number: %d", my_func());
```

This next example will take an integer and return its factorial. In case you don't remember from the previous factorial example in Chapter 4, "Control Structures," the factorial is represented in math as *n!* and is equal to every number from 1 to n multiplied together (so 4! is equal to 1 * 2 * 3 * 4).

To define and use your own functions that return values:

1. Create a new file or project in your text editor or IDE.

2. Type the standard beginning lines of code (**Script 7.3**):

   ```
   /* return_factorial.c - Script 7.3 */
   #include <stdio.h>
   ```

3. Add the function prototype:

   ```
   unsigned long long int
   → return_factorial (unsigned int
   → num);
   ```

   The function being defined in this file is called `return_factorial`. This function takes one argument, an unsigned integer that will be assigned to `num`. The function also returns an integer value, as indicated by the initial `int` in the function prototype. Because factorials can quickly become quite large, an `unsigned long long int` will be returned, which is acceptable in the C99 standard.

4. Begin the `main` function:

   ```
   int main (void) {
   ```

5. Declare the required variables:

   ```
   char input[3];
   int number;
   ```

   The application will take a user-submitted number and calculate the factorial of that. Therefore, one integer variable is necessary and a character string will be used to read in the input.

6. Prompt the user:

   ```
   printf ("Enter a positive integer
   → for which the factorial will be
   → calculated: ");
   ```

```
                               Script
1    /* return_factorial.c - Script 7.3 */

2

3    #include <stdio.h>

4

5    unsigned long long int return_factorial
     → (unsigned int num); /* Function
     → prototype. */

6

7    int main (void) {

8

9        char input[3]; // Keyboard input.

10       int number; // Number to work with.

11

12       // Prompt the user.

13       printf ("Enter a positive integer
     → for which the factorial will be
     → calculated: ");

14

15       fgets (input, sizeof(input), stdin);
     → // Read in the input.

16       sscanf (input, "%d", &number);

17

18       // Check the input as a conditional.

19       if (number > 0 ) {

20

21           // Input is okay, print the
     → input and the factorial.

22           printf ("The factorial of %d is
     → %lu.\n", number, return_factorial
     → (number));

23

24       } else { // Input not okay.

25           printf ("You must enter a
     → positive integer!\n");

26       }

27

28       getchar(); /* Pause for the user to
     → press Return or Enter. */

29

30       return 0;
                         continues on next page
```

Script 7.3 The `return_factorial()` function returns the factorial value of a submitted integer.

```
⊖ ○ ⊖              📄 Script
31
32    }
33
34    /* This function takes a number and
      → returns its factorial. */
35    unsigned long long int return_factorial
      → (unsigned int num) {
36
37        unsigned long long int sum = 1; //
      → Factorial sum.
38        unsigned int i; // Multiplier to be
      → used in calculating factorial.
39
40        // Loop through every multiplier up
      → to and including num.
41        for (sum = 1, i = 1; i <= num; ++i) {
42
43            sum *= i; // Multiply the current
      → sum by the multiplier.
44
45        }
46
47        return sum;
48
49    } /* End of return_factorial() function.
      → */
```

Script 7.3 *continued*

Be certain in your prompts to indicate to the user what type of information is expected (**Figure 7.5**). It doesn't guarantee that the user will submit that type, but it helps.

7. Read in the input and assign it to the number variable:

   ```
   fgets (input, sizeof(input), stdin);
   sscanf (input, "%d", &number);
   ```

   The fgets()-sscanf() method of reading in numbers was introduced in Chapter 5, "Standard Input and Output," as a safe technique. You can review the instructions there if you are confused about the syntax.

8. Validate the number:

   ```
   if (number > 0 ) {
   ```

   To ensure that the number is a positive integer, a conditional is used before calling the return_factorial() function. If this condition is true, the factorial can be calculated. If it is false, the user will be notified of the error.

9. Call the return_factorial() function and print the result:

   ```
   printf ("The factorial of %d is
   → %lu.\n", number, return_factorial
   → (number));
   ```

   This print statement prints the original value and the factorial value. Instead of calling the return_factorial() function and assigning this to another variable, the value is returned as an argument to the printf() function.

continues on next page

Figure 7.5 The application first prompts the user to indicate what kind of input is expected.

CREATING FUNCTIONS THAT RETURN A VALUE

In the print statement, the %lu signifier is used for the factorial value, because this is an unsigned long long integer.

10. Complete the conditional:

```
} else {
    printf ("You must enter
➝ a positive integer!\n");
}
```

This statement is executed if the number is not greater than 0. The error message (**Figure 7.6**) lets the user know a problem occurred.

11. Complete the main function:

```
    getchar();
    return 0;
}
```

12. After the main function, begin defining the return_factorial() function:

```
unsigned long long int
➝ return_factorial (unsigned int
➝ num) {
```

This definition mirrors the function prototype, indicating that one unsigned integer value is expected and another is returned.

Figure 7.6 If the user does not enter an integer greater than 0, an error message is printed.

13. Define the required variables:

```
unsigned long long int sum = 1;
unsigned int i;
```

Along with the number submitted to the function, this function needs two more integers: sum, which will total up the factorial, and, i, a counter for the loop.

14. Calculate the factorial:

```
for (sum = 1, i = 1; i <= num; ++i) {
    sum *= i;
}
```

This code comes from the factorial example in Chapter 4. It creates a sum by multiplying every number up to and including num (the submitted number) together.

15. Return the calculated value and complete the function definition:

```
    return sum;
}
```

The final step in this function is to use the **return** statement to return the calculated sum.

16. Save the file as *return_factorial.c*, compile, and debug as necessary.

17. Run the application (**Figure 7.7**).

continues on next page

Figure 7.7 The factorial of a user-entered number is calculated and returned using a user-defined function.

CREATING FUNCTIONS THAT RETURN A VALUE

✔ Tips

■ The `return_factorial` example primarily focuses on demonstrating how to return values from functions. There are several improvements you could make to polish it, such as discarding extraneous input, confirming that the submitted value is a number (the application will calculate the factorial of *S*, if given the chance), and checking that the factorial value does not go out of range.

■ Some programmers think it's best to have only one `return` statement within a function, but C allows you to have multiple statements. Only one `return` statement will ever be executed, though. A common example is something like

```
if (condition) {
    return 1;
} else {
    return 0;
}
```

■ The `return` statement stops the execution of a function so if you have any code after an executed `return`, it will never be executed. This applies within a specific code block, like this:

```
if (condition) {
    return 1;
    /* This line won't be executed
→ if the condition is true. */
} else {
    return 0;
    /* This line won't be executed
→ if the condition is false. */
}
```

■ To be really formal, you can use

```
return;
```
as a line in a function that returns no values.

■ You cannot return multiple values from a function in C. You can simulate this effect using pointers, however. You'll learn about pointers in Chapter 9, "Working with Pointers."

Creating Inline Functions

```
   ○ ○ ○              📄 Script
1    /* inline.c - Script 7.4- rewrite of
   → return_factorial.c (Script 7.3) */

2

3    #include <stdio.h>

4

5    unsigned long long int return_factorial
   → (unsigned int num); /* Function
   → prototype. */

6

7     /* This function discards all of the
   → input until a newline. */

8    inline void discard_input (void) {

9

10       char junk; // To get rid of extra input.

11

12       // Loop through the input and
   → ignore it.

13       do {

14           junk = getchar();

15       } while (junk != '\n');

16

17   } /* End of discard_input() function. */

18

19   int main (void) {

20

21       char input[3]; // Keyboard input.

22       int number; // Number to work with.

23

24       // Prompt the user.

25       printf ("Enter a positive integer
   → for which the factorial will be
   → calculated: ");

26

27       fgets (input, sizeof(input), stdin);
   → // Read in the input.

28       sscanf (input, "%d", &number);

29

30       //  Check the input as a conditional.

31       if (number > 0 ) {

32

33           // Input is okay, print the input
   → and the factorial.
```

continues on next page

Script 7.4 Rewritten as an inline function, discard_input() may work slightly faster.

New to C99 is the ability to create *inline* functions: user-defined functions that will, theoretically, perform faster. Inline functions are normally defined before the main function and are preceded with the keyword inline. For example:

```
#include <stdio.h>
inline int my_func() {
    // Function content.
}
int main (void) {...
```

Inline functions do not require the prototype, because they are defined before the main function.

These types of function definitions have the potential to be faster because the compiler treats them differently. Instead of setting aside the resources necessary for defining a new function, the compiler will go through an application's code, replacing calls to the inline function with the function code itself. This way, you have the benefit of managing repeated tasks in one space without the overhead of an extra function.

The catch to inline functions is that they must be relatively simple in order for there to truly be a benefit. As an example of this, you'll now rewrite the factorial example, adding the discard_input() function created earlier as an inline function.

To define and use inline functions:

1. Open *return_factorial.c* (Script 7.3) in your text editor or IDE.

2. After the function prototype for return_factorial(), define discard_input() as an inline function (**Script 7.4**):

continues on next page

CREATING INLINE FUNCTIONS

```
inline void discard_input (void) {
    char junk;
    do {
        junk = getchar();
    { while (junk != '\n');
}
```

The bulk of the code is taken directly from the earlier example where the `discard_input()` function was first defined. The significant addition here is the use of the word `inline`, at the beginning of the function definition.

3. After the program's primary conditional, call the `discard_input()` function.

Calling inline functions is no different than calling any other functions. Here, the `discard_input()` will get rid of any extraneous input before the user has to press Return or Enter to finish executing the application.

```
                                    Script

34        printf ("The factorial of %d is
    → %lu.\n", number, return_factorial
    → (number));

35

36     } else { // Input not okay.

37        printf ("You must enter a
    → positive integer!\n");

38     }

39

40     discard_input(); /* Get rid of other
    → input. */

41

42     getchar(); /* Pause for the user to
    → press Return or Enter. */

43

44     return 0;

45

46 }

47

48 /* This function takes a number and
    → returns its factorial. */

49 unsigned long long int return_factorial
    → (unsigned int num) {

50

51     unsigned long long int sum = 1; //
    → Factorial sum.

52     unsigned int i; // Multiplier to be
    → used in calculating factorial.

53

54     // Loop through every multiplier up
    → to and including num.

55     for (sum = 1, i = 1; i <= num; ++i) {

56

57        sum *= i; // Multiply the current
    → sum by the multiplier.

58

59     }

60

61     return sum;

62

63 } /* End of return_factorial() function.
    → */
```

Script 7.4 *continued*

4. Save the file as *inline.c*.

5. Compile, debug, and run (**Figure 7.8**).

✔ Tip

■ Whether or not inline functions are faster than standard user-defined ones depends on the environment in question. The best way to test their effectiveness is by benchmarking—timing the execution speed—of your application with and without using a function inline.

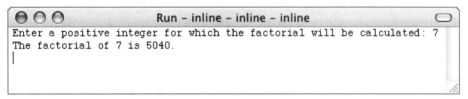

Figure 7.8 Inline functions shouldn't change the functionality of your applications, but they may improve their performance.

Using Recursion

Recursion is the act of a function calling itself. The concept is very theoretical, so it's best understood by working with concrete examples. Say you want to create an application that determines the next highest prime number after a submitted value. The process would work like this:

1. Increase the submitted number by 1 (because you want to find the next highest number).

2. Check if this new number is prime (by checking the remainder when dividing that number by every prime that comes before it).

3. If the number is not prime, go back to Step 1.

4. If the number is prime, return it.

As a recursive function, this process could be written like so:

```
int find_prime(int num) {
    short int is_prime = 0; // Flag
    ++num;
    // Calculations to see if num is
    → prime.
    if (is_prime) {
        return num;
    } else {
        find_prime(num);
    }
}
```

This structure creates a loop, continuing to call itself until the is_prime variable is true. With each new call to the find_prime() function, the next highest number is tested.

As when using any loop, one of the most important considerations is that you establish context for recursion to stop. If you don't, you'll have an infinite loop on your hands.

```
         ● ● ●              📄 Script
1     /* counter.c - Script 7.5 */

2

3     #include <stdio.h>

4

5     void countdown (int start, int end); /*
      → Function prototype. */

6

7     int main (void) {

8

9         // Call the countdown() function.

10        countdown (50, 40);

11

12        getchar();

13

14        return 0;

15

16    }

17

18    /* This function counts down from start
      → to end using recursion. */

19    void countdown (int start, int end) {

20

21        printf ("Before: %d\n", start); //
      → Print initial value.

22

23        --start; // Decrement.

24

25        // If the end point hasn't been
      → reached, call the function again.

26        if (start > end) {

27            countdown (start, end);

28        }

29

30        printf ("After: %d\n", start); //
      → Print values after recursion, for effect.

31

32    }
```

Script 7.5 Using recursion, this function counts down from a starting number to an ending one. The second printf() statement helps demonstrate that where recursion occurs in a function affects the end result.

Recursive functions that call themselves as the final act use what is referred to as *tail* or *end* recursion. These are the easiest to comprehend because the function's entire code will be executed before the function is called again. If, however, recursion occurs in the middle of a function, this has a unique impact because subsequent statements will be executed in reverse order. Our next example, predicated upon a simple countdown, will better demonstrate this concept.

To use recursion:

1. Create a new file or project in your text editor or IDE.

2. Type the standard beginning lines of code (**Script 7.5**):

   ```
   /* counter.c - Script 7.5 */
   #include <stdio.h>
   ```

3. Add the function prototype:

   ```
   void countdown (int start, int end);
   ```
   This function takes two integers: a starting number and an ending one. It does not return any values.

4. Begin the main function:

   ```
   int main (void) {
   ```

5. Call the countdown() function:

   ```
   countdown (50, 40);
   ```
   For recursion to occur at all, the function must be called once. Here the function is called while being passed a starting value of 50 and an ending value of 40.

6. Complete the main function:

   ```
       getchar();
       return 0;
   }
   ```

continues on next page

USING RECURSION

7. After the main function, begin defining the countdown() function:

```
void countdown (int start, int end) {
```

8. Print the initial value of the start variable:

```
printf ("Before: %d\n", start);
```

To best demonstrate how where recursion occurs in a function—at the beginning, middle, or end—affects its results, this function will print the start value both before and after the recursive call.

9. Decrease the value of start:

```
--start;
```

Since this function is counting down, it needs to use the decremental operator. If you wanted to count up, switch this to the incremental operator.

10. If the end point has not yet been reached, call this function again:

```
if (start > end) {
    countdown (start, end);
}
```

As long as the start variable is greater than the end variable, this function will continue to call itself. Each time the function is called, start will be worth 1 less but end always stays the same.

This conditional is a crucial part of the function definition because it gives the looping structure a stopping point (namely, when start becomes equal to end).

11. Reprint the value of start and complete the function:

```
printf ("After: %d\n", start);
```

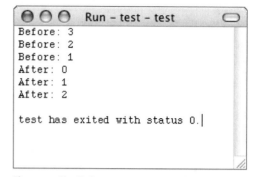

Figure 7.9 The *Before* statements occur immediately each time the function is called. The *After* statements are only executed after recursion is stopped (when start is no longer greater than end).

Figure 7.10 Running the application using the original values (counting down from 50 to 40).

This print statement reprints the value of start. As you'll see in the end result, this line will not be executed until after start is equal to end, because recursion always occurs up until that point.

So if the function were to count down from 3 to 0 (**Figure 7.9**), *Before: 3* is printed, then the function is called again. *Before: 2* is printed, the function is called again, and then *Before: 1* is printed. start is now equal to 0 (because it's decremented after being printed), so the function is not called again.

Now that recursion is over, *After: 0* is printed, which completes the innermost function call. The function returns up one level and *After: 1* is called. The function returns back to the initial call and *After: 2* is printed.

12. Save the file as *counter.c*, compile, and debug as necessary.

13. Run the application (**Figure 7.10**).

Why Use Recursion?

There's an argument to be made that understanding and effectively using recursion may be outside the scope of a beginner's programming book. Conceptually, the idea can be difficult to grasp, but there is merit to being familiar with the technique.

Part of the art of programming is the ability to recognize what kind of problem you're facing, and then being able to pick the best tool to solve that problem. Recursion is just one utility you have at your disposal.

Although the counter example in this section could be rewritten as a loop, some kinds of problems are best solved with recursive functions. Typically, the problems involve hierarchies, like the hierarchy present in a file system, where directories can contain subdirectories. To browse through the entire structure, you would need to create a function that browses a single directory. If in that directory the function encounters another directory, the function would need to call itself to browse through that subdirectory.

Experience will help you understand when loops are adequate and when recursion is the answer. So, even if this example doesn't bring the concept home for you, remember in the back of your mind that recursive functions are available when the time comes.

USING RECURSION

Understanding Variable Scope

The final topic we'll discuss in this chapter is variable scope—in other words, where variables exist. This is pertinent to functions because variables within a function are not accessible by code outside a function. And, for that matter, variables outside a function are not necessarily accessible inside the function.

There are two realms of scope to deal with: *global*, which means that a variable is available inside and outside any function (it's available everywhere); and, *local*, which refers to the area inside a particular function. Note that this means each function has its own local scope. A variable existing within one function does not exist inside another.

To create a global variable, you just need to define it—as you would any other variable—outside of any function definition, including `main`. The following (rather trivial) example will demonstrate this.

To work with variable scope:

1. Create a new file or project in your text editor or IDE.

2. Type the standard beginning lines of code (**Script 7.6**):

   ```
   /* global.c - Script 7.6 */
   #include <stdio.h>
   ```

3. Add a function prototype:

   ```
   void other_function (void);
   ```

   As you can tell, this `other_function()` won't do too much: it takes no arguments and returns no values.

4. Define a global variable:

   ```
   int g_num = 100;
   ```

Understanding Static Variables

Variables within functions are different not only because of variable scope but also because they can be *static*. Let's start with this example:

```
void up_one (void) {
    int num = 0;
    printf ("%d\n", ++num);
}
```

Even though `num` is incremented with each `up_one()` call, its ending value will only be 1 because it's reinitialized to 0 each time the function is called. In other words, the `num` variable does not retain any changes.

This behavior can be altered by using the `static` keyword:

```
void up_one (void) {
    static int num = 0;
    printf ("%d\n", ++num);
}
```

Each call to this function will now increase the value of `num` by 1. So instead of continually printing 1s, you would see 1, 2, 3, and so on, with each call to the function.

Global variables are automatically static, and whatever changes they experience will be retained, inside or outside a function.

```
 1    /* global.c - Script 7.6 */
 2
 3    #include <stdio.h>
 4
 5    int g_num = 100; // Global variable.
 6
 7    void other_function (void); /* Function
      → prototype. */
 8
 9    int main (void) {
10
11        int num = 20; // Local variable.
12
13        // Print the local and global
      → variables.
14        printf ("Inside of the main
      → function, the global g_num is %d.
      → The local num is %d.\n", g_num, num);
15
16        // Call the other function.
17        other_function();
18
19        // Print the local and global
      → variables again.
20        printf ("After calling the
      → other_function, the global g_num is
      → %d. The local num is %d.\n", g_num,
      → num);
21
22        getchar();
23
24        return 0;
25
26    }
27
28    /* This function prints two variables.
      → */
29    void other_function (void) {
```

continues on next page

Script 7.6 Unless special steps are taken, variables within a function are separate entities than those outside the function, even if they have the same name.

The variable, called g_num, is an integer with a value of 100. Because it has been defined outside any function, it has global scope.

5. Begin the main function:

   ```
   int main (void) {
   ```

6. Define a local variable:

   ```
   int num = 20;
   ```
   This variable will be local to the main function, meaning it only exists within the confines of main.

7. Print both the local and global variables:

   ```
   printf ("Inside of the main function,
   → the global g_num is %d. The local
   → num is %d.\n", g_num, num);
   ```
   This print statement shows the current value of both the local (num) and global (g_num) variables.

8. Call the other_function():

   ```
   other_function();
   ```
   This statement will execute the code within the other_function() definition.

9. Print the values of the local and global variables once again:

   ```
   printf ("After calling the
   → other_function, the global g_num is
   → %d. The local num is %d.\n", g_num,
   → num);
   ```
   So that you can track how each variable changes, their values are printed both before and after calling the second function.

10. Complete the main function:

    ```
    getchar();
    return 0;
    }
    ```

continues on next page

11. Begin defining the second function:

```
void other_function (void) {
```

12. Create a new variable, local to this function:

```
int num = 600;
```

Although it has the same name as the num variable found in the main function, this is an entirely separate variable with a separate value.

13. Change the value of the global variable:

```
g_num = 0;
```

Unlike the two num variables, g_num's scope pervades all functions. So changing its value within any one function has the effect of changing its value everywhere.

14. Print both variable values:

```
printf ("Inside of the other_function
→ function, the global g_num is %d.
→ The local num is %d.\n", g_num,
→ num);
```

15. Complete the second function:

```
    return;
}
```

Because this function returns no values, an empty return statement is used.

16. Save the file as *global.c*, compile, and debug as necessary.

17. Run the executable application (**Figure 7.11**).

```
30
31      int num = 600; // Local variable.
32      g_num = 0;
33
34      // Print local and global variables.
35      printf ("Inside of the other_function
   → function, the global g_num is %d. The
   → local num is %d.\n", g_num, num);
36
37      return;
38
39  }
```

Script 7.6 *continued*

The Black Box Theory of Programming

When making more modular code by defining your own functions, you should try to follow the *black box* theory of programming, which is to say that what happens inside a function should be irrelevant to the code calling it. Or, to put another way: when creating your own functions, they should be written so that they take certain arguments, return a certain value, and have no other contingencies outside the function.

With respect to variable scope, programs are more stable when they are divided into functions that don't exchange data using global variables but rather through their clearly defined arguments and return values. Such code is much easier to understand and maintain. Thus, the limited scope of variables is a good thing.

✔ Tips

- Even when you use a variable in a function call, like this:

```
int my_var = 20;
some_function (my_var);
```

you are not truly passing that variable to the second function but rather that variable's value. In the above code, the my_var variable still doesn't exist within the some_function() function.

- You might think that since global variables exist everywhere, it would be best to use nothing but global variables. Although this makes it easier for you, the programmer, it's poor form. If a variable is only necessary within a single function, there's no reason for it to have global scope.

- Be extra careful not to give global and local variables the same name. If you do, the local variable will take precedence within that function and the global variable will not exist for all practical purposes. Some programmers avoid this by starting global variable names with a small *g*, to indicate their global status.

- Global variables are only truly global to functions defined after they have been declared. But since it's standard to define global variables before any functions (or to place them in a header file), this is rarely an issue.

- Another confusing aspect of recursion is that each iteration of the function has its own variables local to that function call. This means that the compiler and system must store and track these variables, associated with each level of recursion.

- One way to work around variable scope is to pass values to a function by reference (passing its address instead of its value). This requires pointers, which you'll learn about in Chapter 9.

- Variables also have a *class* status: either *permanent* or *temporary*. Global and static variables are always permanent, meaning that memory is set aside for them during the entire execution of an application. Memory is used for temporary variables as needed, such as within the execution of a single function.

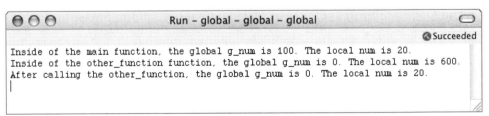

```
● ● ●            Run – global – global – global              ⬭
                                                    🔵 Succeeded
Inside of the main function, the global g_num is 100. The local num is 20.
Inside of the other_function function, the global g_num is 0. The local num is 600.
After calling the other_function, the global g_num is 0. The local num is 20.
```

Figure 7.11 Notice that local variables return their value within each function while global variables can exist and be altered within any function.

USING THE C PREPROCESSOR

As your applications grow in complexity, they become harder and more time consuming to manage, program, and edit. Furthermore, as you begin using modular coding methods, such as defining your own functions and working with multiple files, you need easier ways to manage and use all that code. This is where the C preprocessor—an essential tool developed to assist the C programmer—comes in.

This chapter begins by discussing the basic syntax for using the preprocessor and how it relates to C. We'll then show you a common, practical example for using the C preprocessor to define array sizes. You can also create pseudo-functions using the C preprocessor, and you'll learn how, both with and without arguments. Finally, we provide a recap on including header files—which is technically a C preprocessor event—and cover the syntax for writing conditionals for the C preprocessor.

Introduction to the C Preprocessor

The C preprocessor is a special tool created to facilitate the programming of C applications and expedite their execution. This is an important and, at the same time, confusing thing: the C preprocessor is a wholly separate entity from the C language itself. That being said, most C compilers will manage preprocessing for you, so as long as you abide by the proper syntax and understand how the preprocessor functions, working with it can be a relatively seamless process.

The C preprocessor helps you organize your code by providing utilities for

◆ Creating reusable snippets of code, called *macros*

◆ Including the contents of one source file during another source file's compilation

◆ Providing additional direction to the compiler for how to compile your code

Over the next several pages you'll learn how to use the C preprocessor to accomplish the first two tasks. The last feature—providing additional direction—is beyond the scope of this book and tends to be compiler-specific and platform-specific.

But before we delve into the details of using the C preprocessor, you must understand its syntax and methodology.

The basic syntax

You invoke the C preprocessor by including special markers in your source file. Each of these markers is called a *directive* and begins with the *hash mark* (#). It is very important that you include the hash mark as the first character in a line: no spaces should come immediately before or after it.

The C preprocessor provides many kinds of directives. The most commonly used are #include and #define. You've already seen both of these: #include is used to include other files like *stdio.h*:

```
#include <stdio.h>
```

The #define directive creates *macros*. These macros can be used to represent functions or simple constant values. The syntax for creating a constant is

```
#define CONSTANT_NAME VALUE
```

So, you might have

```
#define NUM_ELEMENTS 20
```

Beyond the syntax above, there aren't too many rules involved in using the C preprocessor. Like C variables, macro names are limited to letters, numbers, and the underscore, and the first character cannot be a number. It is standard practice to put macro names in all uppercase letters, but that's not required. Also, the C preprocessor accepts old-school C comments, such as

```
#define START 1000  /* Start number. */
```

Our first example will define and use a simple directive. Between executing this code and peeking behind the scenes in the next section of this chapter, you should gain an understanding of how the C preprocessor works.

INTRODUCTION TO THE C PREPROCESSOR

To create a C preprocessor directive:

1. Create a new text file in your IDE or text editor.

2. Begin with your standard comment for the file (**Script 8.1**):

   ```
   /* test.c - Script 8.1 */
   ```

3. Add an #include directive to include the standard input/output header file:

   ```
   #include <stdio.h>
   ```

   You've already seen this code dozens of times by now, but this chapter should help you understand its greater meaning. The effect of this directive is that the contents of the *stdio.h* (standard input/output) file will be inserted into this application at this location.

4. Add a #define directive to create a constant macro:

   ```
   #define MY_NAME "Larry"
   ```

   This directive associates the value *"Larry"* (including the quotation marks) to MY_NAME. Notice that you do not use the assignment operator here (=), because this is not C code.

5. Define the main function:

   ```
   int main (void) {
   ```

   This is normal C code, not a preprocessor directive (it doesn't begin with the hash mark).

6. Use MY_NAME in a print statement:

   ```
   printf ("Hey %s.", MY_NAME);
   ```

   The end result, as you might expect, will be the text *Hey Larry.* sent to the standard output. The %s signifier is used since MY_NAME has a string value.

```
 ● ● ●                    Script
1      /* test.c - Script 8.1 */
2
3      #include <stdio.h> /* Include directive.
       → */
4
5      #define MY_NAME "Larry" /* Macro
       → directive. */
6
7      int main (void) {
8
9          /* Refer to the defined macro. */
10         printf ("Hey %s.", MY_NAME);
11
12         getchar(); /* Wait for the user to
       → press Enter or Return. */
13         return 0;
14
15     }
```

Script 8.1 This rudimentary application makes use of two C preprocessor directives.

7. Complete the main function:

```
        getchar();
        return 0;
}
```

8. Save the file as *test.c*, compile, and debug.

9. Run the executable (**Figure 8.1**).

All of these steps should be very familiar to you; even the use of the #define directive was mentioned back in Chapter 2, "Introduction to Data Types." In the next section, you'll gain a better understanding of what goes on behind the scenes.

✔ Tips

■ Because C preprocessor instructions are not part of the C language, they do not share the C syntax. Among the many implications of this is the fact that you do not end C preprocessor directives with a semicolon as you do C expressions.

■ Many current systems will let you get away with not starting a directive first thing on a line (in other words, you would be able to put a space before the hash mark). Still, it's best to abide by tradition here and ensure backwards compatibility.

■ The #undef directive *undefines* (deletes) an existing macro definition:

```
#define TEN 10
#undef TEN
```

Figure 8.1 When seeing the results of an application you will most likely be oblivious to the use of the C preprocessor.

How the C preprocessor works

As the `test.c` file shows, to use a preprocessor directive such as `#define`, you'll invoke it at the top of your code and then reference that directive within the C code itself. Here's another example:

```
#define MY_NUM 8
int main (void) {
    printf ("%d", MY_NUM);
    // Rest of main function.
```

During the preprocessing stage each occurrence of `MY_NUM` within the C code will be replaced with the value of `MY_NUM` as it was defined in the directive (the value 8 in this case).

Understanding Tokens

Spacing in your C preprocessor directives in more important than you might initially think. When a macro is defined, the preprocessor breaks that definition into pieces using spaces as the delimiter. So a macro definition first has the macro name, followed by a space, and then the first character after that space begins the definition for that macro.

A macro can be further broken down into *tokens*, where each token is defined by spaces.

Consider the following:

```
#define NUM 24
```

There is one token present in the macro definition: *24*.

In this more complex example:

```
#define ZERO 1 - 1
```

there are three tokens in the definition: *1*, *-*, and *1*. However, this next expression contains only one token because it does not contain the extra spaces:

```
#define ZERO 1-1
```

The C preprocessor relies heavily on tokens when making substitutions. Without getting into the nitty-gritty of what goes on behind the scenes, you should understand that the spacing of your directives can have dire, unexpected consequences on the processed C code. For that reason, you'll see many explicit statements in this chapter dealing with how to space (or not space) your directives. Do not treat those recommendations lightly!

For the record, the C compiler treats tokens differently than the C preprocessor, but those details are irrelevant to this chapter's content.

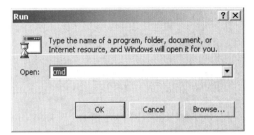

Figure 8.2 Access the command line on Windows by using the Start menu's Run option.

Figure 8.3 When working from the command line, it's easiest to do so within the same directory as the file you're addressing.

If the macro defines a function, each reference to that macro is replaced with the definition (i.e., contents or specific actions) of that function.

With #include directives, during preprocessing the #include directive is replaced by the contents of that included file.

Although preprocessing is handled by the compiler, the preprocessing occurs *before* compilation. Each file to be compiled is first run through the preprocessor, which makes substitutions in the source code using the preprocessor rules. Then, this processed code is formally compiled. Most compilers will let you see the results of preprocessing, which may help you better comprehend the inner workings. This next sequence will show you how to view the results of preprocessing using the gcc compiler from a command-line interface.

To view the preprocessor result:

1. Open a terminal or console window.

   Depending on your operating system, this might entail

   ▲ Double-clicking on the Terminal application icon (Mac OS X and Unix)

   ▲ Clicking on the Start button, selecting Run, entering cmd at the prompt (**Figure 8.2**), and pressing Return (Windows).

2. Move to the directory containing the test.c file (**Figure 8.3**):

   cd /path/to/directory

   The change directory command will move you to the proper directory so that you can more easily run the next command. Obviously you'll need to change the particulars for your computer.

continues on next page

3. Type the following and press Return or Enter:

```
gcc -E test.c
```

This command will output the results of *test.c* after running the preprocessor. In other words, the resulting display will be the C code created after replacing every directive with its appropriate value (**Figure 8.4**).

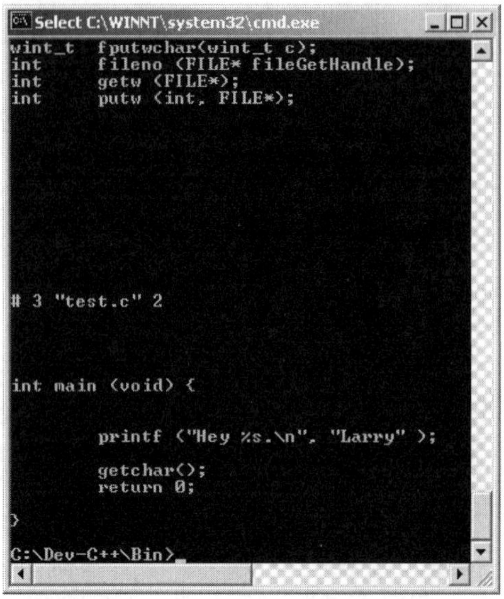

✔ Tips

- If the above sequence gives you problems (particularly on Windows), you can try changing to the gcc directory (*C:\Dev-C++\Bin* perhaps) and using `gcc -E C:\path\to\test.c`. Or, you can just copy *test.c* into gcc's directory and then use the command in Step 3.

- The C preprocessor never replaces tokens with their associated value within double quotation marks in C code. This will not work:

```
#define NUM 10
int main (void) {
     printf ("This does not work:
→ NUM");
     // Rest of main function.
```

- Odd as it may sound, the C preprocessor is essentially a text editor. In layman's terms, you can think of its functionality as a "search and replace" feature for your C code.

- Most of this chapter focuses on the common #include and #define directives, but you will also see the #ifdef, #if, #ifndef, #else, #elif, and #undef directives in the "Creating Conditionals" section at the end of this chapter.

Figure 8.4 The gcc compiler lets you view the results of preprocessing, which is different than the results of executing a C application (see Figure 8.1).

```
1     /* yards.c - Script 8.2 */
2
3     #include <stdio.h> /* Include directive.
      → */
4
5     #define NUM_ELEMENTS 10 /* Number of
      → array elements. */
6
7     int main (void) {
8
9         unsigned int yards[NUM_ELEMENTS]; /*
      → Array to store yard increments. */
10        int i; /* Index variable. */
11
12        /* Populate the array in increments
      → of 5. */
13        for (i = 0; i < NUM_ELEMENTS; i++) {
14            yards[i] = (i + 1) * 5;
15        }
16
17        /* Print a header. */
18        printf ("%10s %10s\n", "Yards",
      → "Meters");
19
20        /* Convert to meters and print. */
21        for (i = 0; i < NUM_ELEMENTS; i++) {
22            printf ("%10d %10.2f\n",
      → yards[i], yards[i] * 0.9144);
23        }
24
25        getchar(); /* Wait for the user to
      → press Enter or Return. */
26
27        return 0;
28
29    }
```

Script 8.2 Using constant macros, like NUM_ELEMENTS here, for array elements is a common and prudent practice.

Using Constants

One of the classic tips for creating readable code is to avoid the use of *magic tokens*: literal values (such as a number) that are generally meaningless without some context. Here is an example of bad programming form:

```
if (num < 90) {
    // Do this.
}
```

Although you probably knew why num had to be less than 90 when you wrote the application, that's exactly the kind of thing you'll forget when revisiting the code some time later. Moreover, there's little chance of another programmer comprehending the meaning of that number.

A constant is a macro that defines a literal value. You can then use the constant whenever you would otherwise use the value. By using constants instead of literal values, you ensure that you or anyone else who reads your code sees a more meaningful description, like A_LEVEL instead of a mysterious *90* literal:

```
#define A_LEVEL 90
int main (void) {
    if (num < A_LEVEL) { ...
    // Rest of main function.
```

Another common use of constants is for setting the dimension of an array. You saw an example of this in Chapter 6, "Working with Arrays," and you'll go through another one here.

To create a constant:

1. Create a new text file in your IDE or text editor.

2. Begin with your standard comments and the #include directive (**Script 8.2**):

   ```
   /* yards.c - Script 8.2 */
   #include <stdio.h>
   ```

continues on next page

3. Add a #define directive to create a constant macro:

```
#define NUM_ELEMENTS 10
```

This directive associates the value *10* with NUM_ELEMENTS. We added a comment (see the corresponding script) so that the purpose of this macro is clear.

4. Define the main function:

```
int main (void) {
```

5. Create the necessary variables:

```
unsigned int yards[NUM_ELEMENTS];
int i;
```

The array **yards** will store a number of integers to be used later in converting yards to meters. It has been defined as an array that is NUM_ELEMENTS long. During the preprocessing stage, NUM_ELEMENTS will be replaced with its value (10).

The second variable, i, is an index variable to be used within two **for** loops.

6. Use a **for** loop to populate the **yards** array:

```
for (i = 0; i < NUM_ELEMENTS; i++) {
    yards[i] = (i + 1) * 5;
}
```

This is a standard **for** loop for accessing every array element. Rather than refer to sizeof(yards) to know when to stop looping, you can more easily refer to the NUM_ELEMENTS value.

The contents of the loop assign increments of 5 to yards, starting at 5. So the first time the loop is run, i is 0, which means that (i + 1) * 5 is 5. On the next iteration, the calculation returns 10, and so on.

Yards	Meters
5	4.57
10	9.14
15	13.72
20	18.29
25	22.86
30	27.43
35	32.00
40	36.58
45	41.15
50	45.72

Figure 8.5 A constant macro is referenced three times in the process of creating this result.

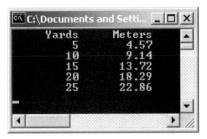

Figure 8.6 Changing the value of one macro constant creates a table of a different length.

✔ Tips

- It is standard practice to name constants with all uppercase letters; this helps differentiate them from variables and other identifiers.

- In a way, using constant macros is another method for working around variable scope. The preprocessor will replace every use of the macro anywhere in the C code—including inside functions—with its respective value. To be clear, this is not the intent of constant macros but only a result of how the preprocessor works.

- When defining constants that will be used in several source files, consider putting all the macros in a single file. This helps ensure that you don't define a macro in multiple ways in separate files or have multiple macros representing the same logical value.

- You may have caught another spot within the *yards.c* application where a constant macro would make sense: having a word like METERS_EQUIV represent the 0.9144 multiplication value.

7. Print a header for the forthcoming data:

```
printf ("%10s %10s\n", "Yards",
→ "Meters");
```

This table header uses spaces to make the data lay out nicely.

8. Create another for loop in which each yard increment and its meters equivalent are printed:

```
for (i = 0; i < NUM_ELEMENTS; i++) {
    printf ("%10d %10.2f\n",
→ yards[i], yards[i] * 0.9144);
}
```

The structure of the loop is the same as the previous loop. In the loop, the value of yards[i] is printed, along with that value times 0.9144, which calculates the meters equivalent. Again, padding is used so that the table has clean columns in the generated display.

9. Complete the main function:

```
    getchar();
    return 0;
}
```

10. Save the file as *yards.c*, compile, and debug.

11. Run the executable (**Figure 8.5**).

12. Change the value of NUM_ELEMENTS, recompile, and rerun the application (**Figure 8.6**).

USING CONSTANTS

171

Function-like Macros

Macros created by the #define directive are named snippets of code. For constants, the name reflects a literal value. On a more complex level, you can also assign actions (executed statements or logical chunks) to a macro, creating a function-like macro:

```
#define ALERT printf("Danger!")
```

With this directive, uses of ALERT in your C code will be replaced with that printf() statement.

As always, there is a catch here: C preprocessor directives must be defined on a single line. Once a new line is encountered, the old directive's definition is over. When the information for a directive won't fit on a single line (which is most likely to happen with function-like macros), you can break up the line by inserting a space followed by a backslash character (\) and continuing the information on the next line. When the preprocessor encounters this, the backslash character and any white space at the beginning of the following line are removed and the lines are joined together before the directive is processed. For example:

```
#define BIG_ALERT printf("*** This \
will get your attention! ***");
```

Function-like macros behave like functions, except that, when they're kept compact, they can execute much more quickly than a function.

To create a function-like macro:

1. Create a new text file in your IDE or text editor.

2. Begin with your standard comments and the #include directive (**Script 8.3**):

```
/* newline.c - Script 8.3 */
#include <stdio.h>
```

```
1   /* newline.c - Script 8.3 */
2
3   #include <stdio.h> /* Include directive.
    → */
4
5   #define NL printf("\n") /* Prints a
    → newline character. */
6
7   int main (void) {
8
9       /* Print text interspersed with
    → newlines. */
10
11      printf ("This is some text.");
12
13      NL;
14
15      printf ("This will show up on the
    → next line.");
16
17      NL;
18      NL;
19
20      printf ("This will show up two lines
    → later.");
21
22      getchar(); /* Wait for the user to
    → press Enter or Return. */
23
24      return 0;
25
26  }
```

Script 8.3 This function-like macro will print the newline character each time the C code refers to NL.

3. Add a #define directive to create a function-like macro:

```
#define NL printf("\n")
```

This line creates a macro that associates the code printf("\n") with the abbreviation NL. The code itself will print a newline character. Note that there's no semicolon after the function call here, because that's the C syntax and this is a C preprocessor realm.

4. Define the main function:

```
int main (void) {
```

5. Print some text and then reference the NL macro:

```
printf ("This is some text.");
NL;
```

Before compilation occurs, the C preprocessor will replace NL with printf("\n"). Thus, the second line here is the equivalent of having

```
printf("\n");
```

in your C code.

6. Print some more text along with calls to the NL macro:

```
printf ("This will show up on the
→ next line.");
NL;
NL;
printf ("This will show up two lines
→ later.");
```

As you can tell, the text itself is rather silly, but the output of this application will show how the C preprocessor inserted the printf("\n") calls as if they were hardcoded into the C.

continues on next page

FUNCTION-LIKE MACROS

7. Complete the main function:

```
getchar();
return 0;
}
```

8. Save the file as *newline.c*, compile, and debug.

9. Run the executable (**Figure 8.7**).

10. If you want, use the compiler to view the post-processed code (**Figure 8.8**).

If you've forgotten the syntax for doing this, review the first part of this chapter.

✔ Tips

■ Because the backslash line continuation will read through any white space on the following line, you can make extended macros more legible by indenting subsequent code:

```
#define BIG_ALERT printf("*** This \
    will get your attention! ***");
```

■ As with all macros, keep in mind that function-like macros are a simple replacement in your C code. No syntax checking is performed on the code until compilation. If you have errors in the syntax of a macro, the compiler may report a syntax error on a line that appears to be perfectly fine.

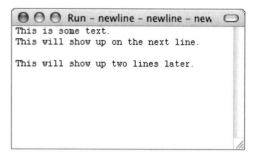

Figure 8.7 This application uses function-like macros to create newlines.

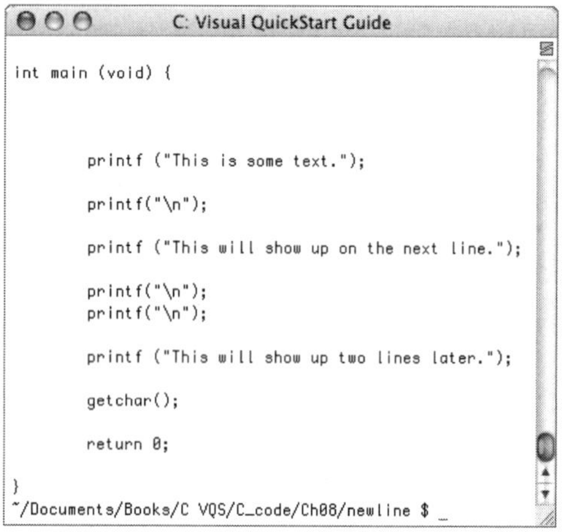

```
int main (void) {

    printf ("This is some text.");

    printf("\n");

    printf ("This will show up on the next line.");

    printf("\n");
    printf("\n");

    printf ("This will show up two lines later.");

    getchar();

    return 0;

}
~/Documents/Books/C VQS/C_code/Ch08/newline $ _
```

Figure 8.8 The post-processed version of the code demonstrates how references to NL are replaced with printf("\n").

Function-like Macros That Take Arguments

Like any user-defined function, user-defined function-like macros can also take arguments:

```
#define OOPS(X) printf("Oh no, %s!", X)
```

With that macro, any C code like this:

```
OOPS("Tim");
```

is turned into

```
printf("Oh no, %s!", "Tim");
```

during preprocessing.

Or, consider the following, more complex example:

```
#define AVE(X,Y)  ((X)+(Y))/2
```

The AVE macro now represents the code for calculating the average of two numbers. So this C code:

```
printf ("The average of %.1f and %.1f is
→ %.2f.\n", 20.0, 118.0,
→ AVE(20.0,118.0));
```

will be turned into this by the C preprocessor:

```
printf ("The average of %.1f and %.1f is
→ %.2f.\n", 20.0, 118.0,
→ ((20.0)+(118.0))/2);
```

Compared with regular function declarations, function-like macros are far simpler. There's no need to indicate the type of value returned (since it won't return any value) or the type or number of arguments it takes. This is because these aren't true functions, but rather sections of code that will be swapped into your C application during preprocessing.

Our next example will use a function-like macro to find the smaller of two numbers.

To use function-like macros with arguments:

1. Create a new text file in your IDE or text editor.

2. Begin with your standard comments and the #include directive (**Script 8.4**):

```
/* smaller.c - Script 8.4 */
#include <stdio.h>
```

Function-like Macro Problems

There are a number of tricky aspects to writing and using function-like macros. Remember that the C preprocessor will go through your C code and replace every macro name with its associated code. Because of this process, your applications can be tripped up due to macro code that doesn't otherwise seem problematic. To avoid such problems, you can take a number of steps when defining macros:

1. You always, always, always want to enclose parameters within parentheses in the macro definition if performing arithmetic. As the preprocessor replaces tokens with their value, precedence can become obscured, and calculations may not be made as intended.

2. Avoid using the macro's name within its own definition.

3. Be careful when referring to other macros within a macro definition.

As an example of just the first rule, if you have this macro:

```
#define SQ(X) (X*X)
```

and then reference it using the C

```
SQ(1+3);
```

the preprocessor will turn that into (1+3*1+3), the result of this calculation being 7 (3 times 1 equals 3 plus one plus 3), not 16 (1 plus 3 equals 4 times 4), as you might have expected. The proper way to define this macro would be

```
#define SQ(X) ((X)*(X))
```

which would turn SQ(1+3) into ((1+3)*(1+3)).

You can find more suggestions, along with detailed examples, by searching the Internet using the keywords *C macro pitfalls*.

```
000                    📄 Script
1     /* smaller.c - Script 8.4 */

2

3     #include <stdio.h> /* Include directive.
      ⇥ */

4

5     #define MIN(X,Y) ( ((X) < (Y)) ? (X) :
      ⇥ (Y) ) /* Return the smaller of two
      ⇥ numbers. */

6

7     int main (void) {

8

9         float num1, num2; /* Two numbers to
      ⇥ compare. */

10

11        /* Assign values to the numbers. */

12        num1 = 20.0;

13        num2 = 103.9;

14

15        /* Print which is smaller. */

16        printf ("The smaller of %.1f and %.1f
      ⇥ is %.1f.\n", num1, num2,
      ⇥ MIN(num1,num2));

17

18        getchar(); /* Wait for the user to
      ⇥ press Enter or Return. */

19

20        return 0;

21

22    }
```

Script 8.4 This more complicated function-like macro can handle arguments. It takes two values and determines the smaller one.

3. Add a #define directive to create a function-like macro that takes arguments:

   #define MIN(X,Y) (((X) < (Y)) ? (X)
   ⇥ : (Y))

   The MIN macro takes two arguments, called X and Y. It is assumed that these will be numbers, but you do not need to define a variable type here because it's a macro, not a real function.

   The code of the macro uses the ternary operator to return either X or Y, depending on whether the condition ((X) < (Y)) is true or false. If X is less than Y, the condition is true and X is returned. If not, Y is returned.

4. Define the main function:

   int main (void) {

5. Create the necessary variables:

   float num1, num2;

   This application uses two numbers, both of type float.

6. Assign values to the numbers:

   num1 = 20.0;
   num2 = 103.9;

   You can assign any decimal values you want to these two numbers.

7. Print both the numbers and then print the smaller one by referencing the macro:

   printf ("The smaller of %.1f and %.1f
   ⇥ is %.1f.\n", num1, num2,
   ⇥ MIN(num1,num2));

continues on next page

FUNCTION-LIKE MACROS THAT TAKE ARGUMENTS

The print statement prints three numbers in context. First it prints the original numbers (num1 and num2), and then it prints the smaller one. This last value is determined by referencing the MIN macro. After preprocessing, the resulting C code is

```
printf ("The smaller of %.1f and %.1f
→ is %.1f.\n", num1, num2, ( ((num1)
→ < (num2)) ? (num1) : (num2) ));
```

8. Complete the main function:

```
    getchar();
    return 0;
}
```

9. Save the file as *smaller.c*, compile, and debug.

10. Run the executable (**Figure 8.9**).

11. Change the value of the two numbers, recompile, and rerun the application (**Figure 8.10**).

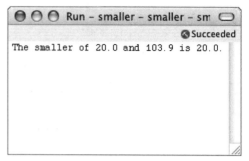

Figure 8.9 A function-like macro called MIN is used to determine the smaller of two numbers.

Figure 8.10 Running the smaller application again, using different numeric values (compare with Figure 8.9).

FUNCTION-LIKE MACROS THAT TAKE ARGUMENTS

✔ Tips

■ When defining a function-like macro, be sure not to insert a space before or after the hash or between the name and the parentheses. Otherwise, the definition creates a constant macro that begins with a pair of parentheses. For example:

```
#define my_malloc () malloc()
```

In this case, `my_malloc` has the literal value of *() malloc()*, and a call to `my_malloc()` in your C code would be expanded to *() malloc()()*.

■ This application may seem like a ridiculous use of a programming language but it's really not. While it's very easy for humans to identify the smaller of two numbers, computers cannot do so without making an actual comparison.

■ If you increment and decrement numbers within function-like macros, it can lead to unexpected consequences due to the way the preprocessor replaces tokens in your C code.

Function or Macro?

Given their similarities, it might seem as if you would always use a function-like macro rather than a function. However, there are some differences.

Function-like macros don't have a function's scope, so you can't declare variables in them. If you're creating anything but the simplest of functions, a macro won't be able to keep up.

On the other hand, if you have a simple function that has few inputs and no local variables, that is no more than a few lines, and that is called a lot, declaring it as a macro rather than as a function may gain you some considerable speed. As a side benefit, the arguments of a macro are *untyped*, so the MIN macro can be used on either integers or floats without alteration.

In the end, as with inline functions (see the previous chapter), modern compilers are great at choosing the most efficient method of performing certain tasks. By writing your applications in different ways and testing their performance, you'll get the best sense of when to use what technique.

Creating and Including Header Files

Although it's feasible to write an entire advanced C program in a single source file, accomplishing that task would be unnecessarily tedious and edits would require more effort than otherwise necessary. By using the C preprocessor, you can break complex applications down into multiple files, while still retaining the same functionality.

The #include directive provides a mechanism for including the contents of another file while compiling a primary file. You've seen this many times with the *stdio.h* include.

Quite often, these included files are in separate source files that exist solely to provide function declarations, macro definitions, and other nonfunction code. These included files are called *header files*.

Two common kinds of header files are system header files and your own header files. System header files define macros (both constants and functions) that allow your C code to work on a particular operating system. When your program needs to use one of those macros, you must include the appropriate header file so the compiler can figure out what you're talking about.

You include system header files by using angle brackets < > around the filename in the directive. This tells the preprocessor to grab that code out of the standard location for your operating system:

```
#include <stdio.h>
#include <ctype.h>
```

Figure 8.11 Maintaining a logical directory structure is even more important as you begin developing your own header files.

You include your own header files by using double quotation marks around the filename:

```
#include "myfile.h"
```

The preprocessor will search the user's source code directories for the file. Or, if a directory is specified, the preprocessor will find the file more quickly. Both of these examples give the file's relative location:

```
#include "./myfile.h"
#include "includes/myfile.h"
```

Over the next few pages, you'll learn how to create and include your own header files, thus making your applications more modular and easier to maintain.

Creating header files

A header file is just a standard text file, given the *.h* extension to signify its header nature. Normally you would place these headers files in the same directory as the rest of the application files or in their own special folder within the application's directory (**Figure 8.11**).

You can use header files to store any pieces of code that the application needs. For example, a header file might define various macros, contain additional #include directives, create function declarations, and so on.

Our next example will place three mathematical macros in their own header file, so that they may be made available to multiple applications with relative ease.

To create and include a header file:

1. Create a new text file in your IDE or text editor.

2. Add detailed comments explaining the purpose of this file (**Script 8.5**):

```
/*
 *  my_math.h - Script 8.5
 *  This header file defines three
→ macros.
 *
 *  Created by Larry Ullman - July
→ 2004.
 *
 */
```

It's a good idea with header files to include even more comments than your standard C files, since the header files may not be apparently related to an application. You can mention such things as creation date, purpose of the file, who created it, the last time it was modified, what contingencies exist, and so forth.

3. Add a #define directive to create the MIN macro:

```
#define MIN(X,Y) ( ((X) < (Y)) ? (X)
→ : (Y) )
```

This is the same code that was used in the previous example, but now it's in its own file.

4. Add another #define directive to create a MAX macro:

```
#define MAX(X,Y) ( ((X) > (Y)) ? (X)
→ : (Y) )
```

This macro's code is exactly like MIN's, except that it checks if X is greater than Y instead of less than.

```
1    /*
2     *  my_math.h - Script 8.5
3     *  This header file defines three
     → macros.
4     *
5     *  Created by Larry Ullman - July 2004.
6     *
7     */
8
9    #define MIN(X,Y) ( ((X) < (Y)) ? (X) :
     → (Y) ) /* Return the smaller of two
     → numbers. */
10
11   #define MAX(X,Y) ( ((X) > (Y)) ? (X) :
     → (Y) ) /* Return the larger of two
     → numbers. */
12
13   #define AVE(X,Y) ((X)+(Y))/2 /* Calculate
     → the average of two numbers. */
```

Script 8.5 Creating your own header files like this one allows you to place several directives in one common location.

5. Add a third #define directive to create an AVE macro:

`#define AVE(X,Y) ((X)+(Y))/2`

You've seen this example earlier in this chapter. It adds two numbers and divides by 2 to find their average.

6. Save the file as *my_math.h*.

✔ Tips

- Although included files can contain any fragments of code, they are typically reserved for declaring functions, defining macros, and declaring variables, structs (user-defined data types), and constants.

- For good examples of how to separate your functions and declarations into header and source files, take a look at the various system header files on your computer or available for viewing online (see Appendix B, "Resources").

- Although this chapter demonstrates how to create and include your own header files, don't forget that the #include directive is most often used to incorporate C header files that are part of the base C library.

Including Header Files

Once you create your own header file, you include it by surrounding the filename with straight double quotation marks in the directive:

```
#include "filename.h"
```

If no pathname is indicated, as in the previous code, the compiler will search the current directory, as well as other logical directories for that environment, to find the file. To eliminate this guesswork, you can use relative pathnames when including your own header files. To state that the file is in the same directory as the including (or parent) file, use an initial period followed by a slash:

```
#include "./filename.h"
```

If the file is in a subdirectory, begin with that subdirectory's name:

```
#include "includes/filename.h"
```

Finally, if the included file is located in a directory above the current directory, use two periods and a slash:

```
#include "../common/filename.h"
```

In our next example, we will include and use the header file we created.

To include a header file:

1. Create a new text file in your IDE or text editor.

2. Begin with your standard comments and the #include directive (**Script 8.6**):

```
/* include.c - Script 8.6 */
#include <stdio.h>
```

```
1    /* include.c - Script 8.6 */
2
3    #include <stdio.h> /* Include directive.
  →  */
4
5    #include "./my_math.h" /* Include
  →  directive. */
6
7    int main (void) {
8
9        float num1, num2; /* Two numbers to
  →  compare. */
10
11       /* Assign values to the numbers. */
12       num1 = 20.0;
13       num2 = 8.4;
14
15       /* Print which is smaller. */
16       printf ("The smaller of %.1f and %.1f
  →  is %.1f.\n", num1, num2,
  →  MIN(num1,num2));
17
18       /* Print which is larger. */
19       printf ("The larger of %.1f and %.1f
  →  is %.1f.\n", num1, num2,
  →  MAX(num1,num2));
20
21       /* Print the average of the two. */
22       printf ("The average of %.1f and %.1f
  →  is %.1f.\n", num1, num2,
  →  AVE(num1,num2));
23
24       getchar(); /* Wait for the user to
  →  press Enter or Return. */
25
26       return 0;
27
28   }
```

Script 8.6 Include your own header file as you would any system file, but use double quotation marks instead of the angle brackets.

3. Include the *my_math.h* header file:

```
#include "./my_math.h"
```

This syntax of this include assumes that the *my_math.h* file is located within the same directory as this one. If you placed the header file in a different location, you'd need to change the pathname so that it accurately points to the header file.

4. Define the `main` function:

```
int main (void) {
```

5. Create the necessary variables and assign values to them:

```
float num1, num2;
num1 = 20.0;
num2 = 8.4;
```

Again, two number variables are declared and initialized with random values.

6. Print the smaller of the two variables:

```
printf ("The smaller of %.1f and %.1f
→ is %.1f.\n", num1, num2,
→ MIN(num1,num2));
```

This code mimics that in the *smaller* application. The C preprocessor will replace `MIN(num1,num2)` with the associated code since `MIN` is defined in *my_math.h*.

7. Print the larger and then the average of the two numbers:

```
printf ("The larger of %.1f and %.1f
→ is %.1f.\n", num1, num2,
→ MAX(num1,num2));
```

```
printf ("The average of %.1f and %.1f
→ is %.1f.\n", num1, num2,
→ AVE(num1,num2));
```

Similar to the code in Step 6, the two number values are printed and then processed by the `MAX` and `AVE` macros.

continues on next page

INCLUDING HEADER FILES

8. Complete the main function:

```
getchar();
return 0;
}
```

9. Save the file as *include.c*, compile, and debug.

10. Run the executable (**Figure 8.12**).

11. Change the value of the two numbers, recompile, and rerun the application (**Figure 8.13**).

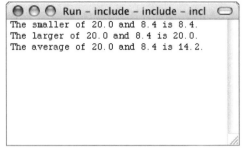

Figure 8.13 The same application run again, working with different number values.

✔ Tips

■ If you want to include files that are located in one of the system include path subdirectories, you can do so with slashes separating the directories. For example, #include <sys/types.h> includes the file *types.h* inside the *sys* directory in one of the standard include file locations.

■ You should avoid absolute pathnames when including files because this makes your code less portable.

■ When you compile a file, you can direct the compiler to search for included files in additional locations as well. The exact syntax for doing so depends upon your compiler and environment, but, for example, you can often use the -I command line argument to gcc.

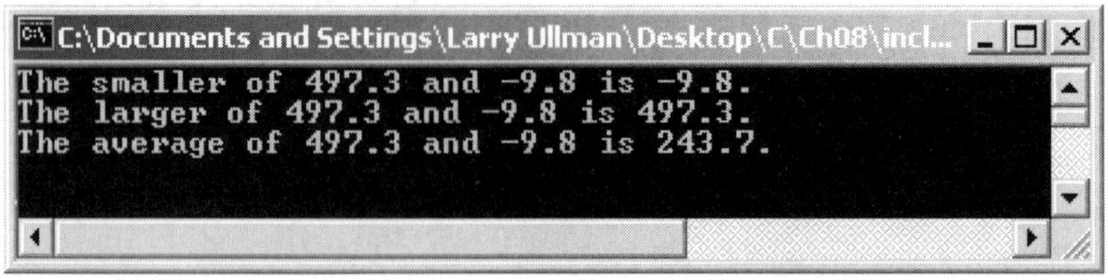

Figure 8.12 By including the *my_math.h* header file (Script 8.5), this application can run two numbers through three different mathematical macros.

Table 8.1 These directives are used to create conditionals for the C preprocessor.

Conditional Directives

DIRECTIVE	EFFECT
#if	Includes code up to the next #else or #endif if the expression is true
#else	Includes code up to the next #endif if the preceding #if expression is false
#elif	Includes code up to the next #else or #endif if the included expression is true; can only follow an #if expression
#endif	Used to indicate the end of a conditional directive
#ifdef	Includes code up to the next #else or #endif if the referenced definition exists
#ifndef	Includes code up to the next #else or #endif if the referenced definition does not exist

Creating Conditionals

Just as you can have conditionals within your C code that may or may not execute code depending on whether a condition is true or false, you can write C preprocessor conditionals. These are directives that instruct the preprocessor to do something (or not do something) based on certain criteria. Unlike your C conditionals, which are checked during execution of an application, C preprocessor conditionals are tested during the preprocessor stage (just before compilation).

There are a number of conditional directives in the C preprocessor (**Table 8.1**), allowing for relatively intricate examples.

One particularly common use of conditional directives is to ensure that a macro is only defined once, no matter how many times an application actually attempts to include the header file that defines it. Our next example demonstrates this concept.

To use a conditional directive:

1. Open *my_math.h* in your text editor or IDE (Script 8.5).

2. Before the first #define directive add this conditional (**Script 8.7** on the next page):

   #ifndef MY_MATH_H

   This begins a C preprocessor conditional whose condition is the equivalent of saying *If the* MY_MATH_H *macro has not been defined...*

   You'll see why and how this conditional works after the next step.

   continues on next page

3. Add a macro defining MY_MATH_H.

#define MY_MATH_H

You don't even need to assign a value to the macro, as long as it is defined. In essence, the MY_MATH_H macro is a marker used for indicating whether the *my_math* header file and its subsequent macro definitions have been included or not. If the file has been included, then MY_MATH_H and the other macros have been defined and do not need to be defined again. If the file has not been included, then all of the macros will be defined here.

4. At the end of the file, close the conditional:

#endif

This terminates the conditional begun in Step 2. Thus, all of the macro definitions are within the conditional.

5. Save the file as *my_math2.h*.

6. Open *include.c* in your text editor or IDE (Script 8.6).

This program will be modified to use this new header file.

```
 ⬤ ⬤ ⬤                    📄 Script
1    /*
2     *  my_math2.h - Script 8.7
3     *  - remake of my_math.h (Script 8.5)
4     *  This header file defines three
     → macros.
5     *
6     *  Created by Larry Ullman on July 2004.
7     *
8     */
9
10   #ifndef MY_MATH_H
11
12   #define MY_MATH_H
13
14   #define MIN(X,Y) ( ((X) < (Y)) ? (X) :
     → (Y) ) /* Return the smaller of two
     → numbers. */
15
16   #define MAX(X,Y) ( ((X) > (Y)) ? (X) :
     → (Y) ) /* Return the larger of two
     → numbers. */
17
18   #define AVE(X,Y) ((X)+(Y))/2 /* Calculate
     → the average of two numbers. */
19
20   #endif
```

Script 8.7 C preprocessor directives can be made more complex by creating conditionals.

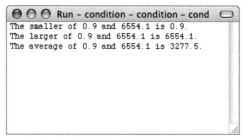

Figure 8.14 A C preprocessor condition has been added to the code ensuring that the header file is included only once. This has no effect on the end result but does add a level of protection.

```
  ● ● ●              📄 Script
1      /* condition.c - Script 8.7 */
2
3      #include <stdio.h> /* Include directive.
   ↪ */
4
5      #include "./my_math2.h"
6
7      int main (void) {
8
9          float num1, num2; /* Two numbers to
   ↪ compare. */
10
11         /* Assign values to the numbers. */
12         num1 = .9;
13         num2 = 6554.1;
14
15         /* Print which is smaller. */
16         printf ("The smaller of %.1f and %.1f
   ↪ is %.1f.\n", num1, num2,
   ↪ MIN(num1,num2));
17
18         /* Print which is larger. */
19         printf ("The larger of %.1f and %.1f
   ↪ is %.1f.\n", num1, num2,
   ↪ MAX(num1,num2));
20
21         /* Print the average of the two. */
22         printf ("The average of %.1f and %.1f
   ↪ is %.1f.\n", num1, num2,
   ↪ AVE(num1,num2));
23
24         getchar(); /* Wait for the user to
   ↪ press Enter or Return. */
25
26         return 0;
27
28     }
```

Script 8.8 This program makes use of the new *my_math2* file, which only defines macros if they have not yet been defined.

7. Change the #include directive so that it includes the *my_math2.h* file (**Script 8.8**):

   #include "./my_math2.h"

8. Make sure that a copy of *my_math.h* is in the same directory as *condition.c* (this file).

9. Save the file as *condition.c*, compile, and debug.

10. Run the executable (**Figure 8.14**).

✔ Tip

■ Conditional directives are most often used to compile code differently depending on the target architecture. This allows you to have a single code base but still allow for OS-dependent optimizations, changes, and so on.

WORKING WITH POINTERS

Every interesting C program that solves a real-world problem uses pointers and dynamic memory. Together, these two tools enable you to create programs that use more complex data structures than the ones you have seen so far (simple scalar values and arrays of scalar values).

This chapter introduces pointers, a prerequisite for working with dynamic memory, the topic covered in the following chapter. The two concepts—and therefore the two chapters—are closely related. Working with pointers also brings you in closer contact with the machine's low-level workings. For example, you will see and work with addresses of the objects in your computer's memory. This is less abstract than working with variables, and you will gain a valuable understanding of the way C programs run.

Pointers can be confusing for beginning readers, so take your time and follow the examples closely. This is definitely one of those chapters you may want to revisit later. Teaching these concepts requires the use of several rather trivial examples at first, but only by going through these exercises can you follow the more advanced, practical applications to follow in the remaining chapters.

Understanding Program Memory

The chapter starts by looking at how the system stores (in the computer's memory) the data used by an application. Having a clear understanding of memory layout makes it easier to get started with pointers.

The point of any computer program is to process data. This data is stored in your computer's main memory. *Every* piece of data in memory has a unique address, defined in bytes. *Some* of the pieces have a name in addition to an address; those pieces are called *variables*, which is what you have been using so far.

Picture your computer's memory as a very long row of cells that store data, each with a unique address, and each 1 byte in size. The system assigns your variables to these memory cells, and every variable gets a unique address.

Different variable types take up a different quantity of cells. Integers take up 4 bytes of space and the chars use only 1 byte each. Floats and doubles will use different amounts of memory too.

To illustrate this, let's look at how C might lay out in memory the variables in the following definitions:

```
int  a = -40;
int  b = 7853;
char c = 74;
char d = 19;
int  e = 449378;
```

Alignment

In Figure 9.1, you can also see that there's a memory gap between variables d and e. This occurs because an integer's starting addresses has to be a multiple of four. So e must be addressed beginning at 16, not 14.

It's said that variable types are aligned on their natural boundaries (like integers start on multiples of four). You don't have to worry about alignment yourself; the C compiler will correctly arrange alignment of all variables automatically.

Like a variable's size, the alignment is system-dependent and it may vary on your system.

Figure 9.1 shows how these five variables might be stored in memory. The actual addresses are system-dependent; this is just one possible example of how the data might be arranged.

So far this book hasn't used data without giving it a name. That concept will be approached in the next chapter. In this chapter you'll see how to access variables (data with names) using their addresses instead of their names, and you'll also find out why this is useful in real programs.

The first thing you need to know, of course, is how to get the address of a variable.

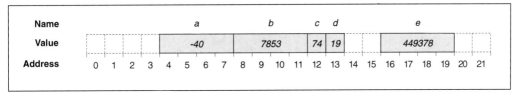

Figure 9.1 One possible memory layout for five different variables.

The Address-of Operator

Finding out a variable's address is very simple: C provides the address-of operator (&) to do just that. This operator takes the name of a variable and returns the variable's starting address in memory. For now, think of an address as a big number.

If you have a variable defined as int counter, the correct syntax to get its address is &counter.

Our first example uses the address-of operator to show how variables are laid out in the memory of your computer. The five variables shown in Figure 9.1 will be used in the example so you can see for yourself how your particular environment stores the data.

To find a variable's address:

1. Create a new file or project in your text editor or IDE.

2. Type the standard beginning lines of code (**Script 9.1**):

   /* pointer1.c - Script 9.1 */
   #include <stdio.h>

   This application, and working with pointers in general, requires no special libraries, but the standard input and output library is included for using the printf() function.

3. Begin the main function:

   int main (void) {

   This function takes no arguments and returns an integer value.

```
1    /* pointer1.c - Script 9.1 */
2
3    #include <stdio.h>
4
5    int main (void) {
6
7        /* Declare five variables of
     → different types. */
8        int  a = -40;
9        int  b = 7853;
10       char c = 74;
11       char d = 19;
12       int  e = 449378;
13
14       /* Print out the addresses of all
     → variables.
15        * This will show their placement in
     → memory */
16       printf("Address of a: %u\n", &a);
17       printf("Address of b: %u\n", &b);
18       printf("Address of c: %u\n", &c);
19       printf("Address of d: %u\n", &d);
20       printf("Address of e: %u\n", &e);
21
22       /* Pause and wait for input before
     → terminating. */
23       getchar();
24
25       return 0;
26
27   }
```

Script 9.1 This program reveals the memory layout of sample variables.

4. Define and initialize the five variables:

```
int  a = -40;
int  b = 7853;
char c = 74;
char d = 19;
int  e = 449378;
```

These are just five sample variables, of different types. Their values are random, helping to indicate how C stores different value types. Notice that we're using the numeric equivalents of characters when assigning values to the different char variables. See the table in Appendix B, "Resources," for their character representation.

5. Use the address-of operator and `printf()` to display the addresses of the variables:

```
printf("Address of a: %u\n", &a);
printf("Address of b: %u\n", &b);
printf("Address of c: %u\n", &c);
printf("Address of d: %u\n", &d);
printf("Address of e: %u\n", &e);
```

We are using the %u sequence so that `printf()` displays the addresses as unsigned integer numbers. See the following tip for more on this idea.

6. Add a `getchar()` call to pause execution on Windows:

```
getchar();
```

7. Complete the `main` function:

```
    return 0;
}
```

8. Save the file as *pointer1.c*, compile, and debug as necessary.

continues on next page

THE ADDRESS-OF OPERATOR

9. Run the application (**Figure 9.2**).

   The actual addresses revealed by this application are more or less irrelevant. The important thing is to look at the differences from one address to the next.

10. If possible, recompile and run the application on another computer (**Figure 9.3**).

    The example might seem a bit trivial, but it is important to understand these basics as they form the foundation of the material that follows.

C:\Documents and Settings\Larry Ullman\Desktop\C\Ch09\pointer...
Address of a: 37814108
Address of b: 37814104
Address of c: 37814103
Address of d: 37814102
Address of e: 37814096

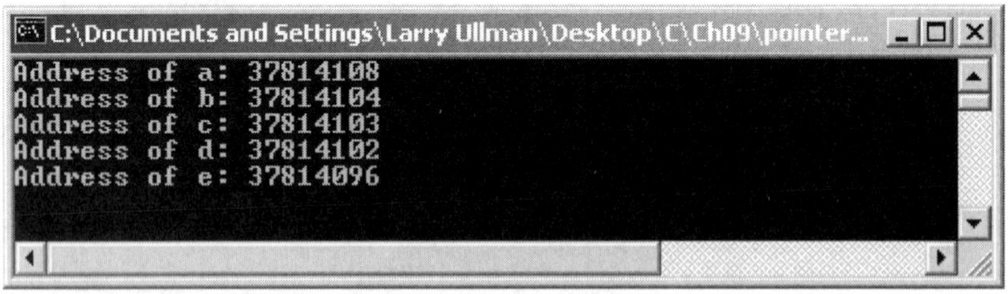

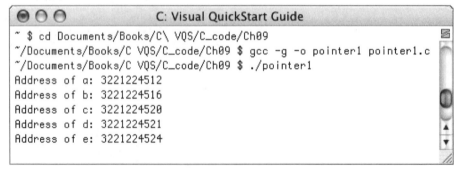

Figure 9.2 The actual memory addresses of five different variables on a Windows computer.

C: Visual QuickStart Guide
~ $ cd Documents/Books/C\ VQS/C_code/Ch09
~/Documents/Books/C VQS/C_code/Ch09 $ gcc -g -o pointer1 pointer1.c
~/Documents/Books/C VQS/C_code/Ch09 $ ./pointer1
Address of a: 3221224512
Address of b: 3221224516
Address of c: 3221224520
Address of d: 3221224521
Address of e: 3221224524

Figure 9.3 The results of running the *pointer1.c* application on another computer, creating different results (because different memory addresses exist).

✔ Tips

- In this example we have used the %u place-holder sequence for unsigned integers when printing the addresses. Technically this is not quite correct since an address might not be the same size as an integer on a particular system (although they are on commonly available systems). There is a special placeholder for addresses: %p. That outputs the value as a hexadecimal number, though, which is not as easy to read as a regular decimal integer. If you wish, you can replace %u with %p in the example and run it again to see the output. The remaining examples in this book will use %p.

- The address-of operator can return the addresses of objects in memory other than variables. For example, it can return addresses of elements in an array, e.g., &(a[9]), and it can even return the addresses of functions, e.g., &my_function (when you define a function, C allocates space in memory for it). You won't need these capabilities nearly as often as you will the ability to point to regular variables.

Storing and Retrieving Addresses in Pointer Variables

The previous example just used the addresses of the variables in the `printf()` function. Now you'll look at how to store these addresses in other variables.

As mentioned earlier, an address is really just a big number. However, you should not treat an address as a regular number and store it in an `int` or `long` variable. If you try to do this, the C compiler will complain and emit a warning message (**Figure 9.4**).

Instead of using the regular numeric variable types to hold addresses, C requires you to store them in a special type of variable called a *pointer* variable. They're called pointer variables because an address *points to* a piece of data.

A pointer variable can only be used to store addresses of a particular type of data. That is, an integer pointer variable can store the address of an integer, a char pointer variable can store the address of a char, and so on. You cannot store the address of an integer in a pointer variable that was defined to hold the address of a char. Again, if you do this, the program will still compile, but the compiler will issue a warning message, and you should fix the mix-up (**Figure 9.5**).

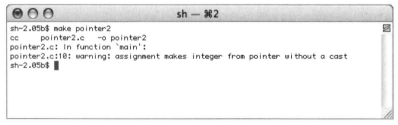

Figure 9.4 Addresses should not be stored in regular integer variables.

Type Safety

You might wonder why C does not allow you to store addresses of different types in the same pointer variable. After all, the addresses of objects in memory are all of the same size, so there is no technical difference between a pointer to an integer and a pointer to a char.

The reason is that explicitly giving a pointer a type allows the compiler to catch programmer mistakes. If the programmer stores the address of a char in a pointer variable that is defined to hold the address of an integer, it is highly likely that later on in the program, that stored address will be *accessed* as an integer, which will produce incorrect results or even crash the program.

If such an address assignment between different types is indeed the right thing to do, there's a special notation called a *type cast* that allows the programmer to indicate to the compiler explicitly that the conversion of pointers is correct and not a mistake. Type casting will be used in a couple of places to ensure that a pointer is of the right type.

To define pointer variables, you combine the variable types like int, char, and float with the asterisk:

```c
int *x;
```

This creates a pointer variable that can hold the address of an integer variable. Defining pointer variables for other types of addresses works in a similar way:

```c
unsigned long *x;
char *y;
float *z;
```

To work with the pointer variable's value, which is the address stored in the variable, you leave off the asterisk. You do that when you want to store a new value (address) into the pointer variable, as well as when you want to read out the currently stored address:

```c
int a; // Integer
int *x; // Integer pointer
x = &a; /* x stores the address where
the a variable data can be found. */
printf("Address of a: %p", x);
```

Our next example will better demonstrate the use of pointer variables.

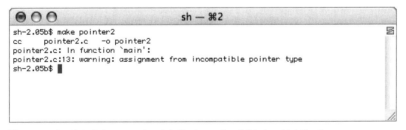

Figure 9.5 A pointer's type must match the type of variable to which it refers.

To store addresses in pointer variables:

1. Create a new file or project in your text editor or IDE.

2. Type the standard beginning lines of code (**Script 9.2**):

```
/* pointer2.c - Script 9.2 */
#include <stdio.h>
```

3. Begin the main function:

```
int main (void) {
```

4. Define and initialize one int and one char variable:

```
int a = 456;
char b = 'J';
```

As with the previous example, these variables are for demonstration purposes, with no specific meaning.

5. Define and initialize one int and one char pointer variable:

```
int *x;
char *y;
```

The x variable will be a pointer used in conjunction with the integer a. The second pointer, y, is for storing b's address. Each pointer matches the type of variable it will point to.

6. Store the addresses of the two variables in the pointer variable of the corresponding type:

```
x = &a;
y = &b;
```

To assign the address to a pointer, refer to the variable while using the address-of operator. The x pointer now stores the address in memory where a's value (*456*) is being stored. Similarly, y contains the address in memory where b's value (*J*) is stored.

```
1    /* pointer2.c - Script 9.2 */
2
3    #include <stdio.h>
4
5    int main (void) {
6
7        /* Define the variables. */
8        int  a = 456;
9        char b = 'J';
10
11       /* Create two pointers, properly
   → typed. */
12       int *x;
13       char *y;
14
15       /* Store the addresses in pointers.
   → */
16       x = &a;
17       y = &b;
18
19       /* Print the results using two
   → different methods. */
20       printf("Address of a: %p\n", &a);
21       printf("Address of a: %p\n", x);
22       printf("Address of b: %p\n", &b);
23       printf("Address of b: %p\n", y);
24
25       /* Pause and wait for input before
   → terminating. */
26       getchar();
27
28       return 0;
29
30   }
```

Script 9.2 This application stores variable addresses in pointers.

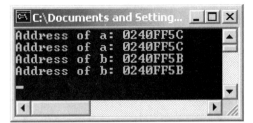

Figure 9.6 The addresses returned by the address-of operator and the ones stored in the pointer variables are identical.

7. Print the addresses of the variables:

```
printf("Address of a: %p\n", &a);
printf("Address of a: %p\n", x);
printf("Address of b: %p\n", &b);
printf("Address of b: %p\n", y);
```

These lines demonstrate the two ways of accessing a variable's address. First, each is printed using the variable name and the address-of operator. Then, each address is printed by using the pointer. The %p signifier is used within printf() to properly print a pointer value.

8. Complete the main function:

```
getchar();
return 0;
}
```

9. Save the file as *pointer2.c*, compile, and debug as necessary.

10. Run the application (**Figure 9.6**).

The application now stores and retrieves the addresses using pointer variables.

✔ Tip

■ A program will probably still compile (depending on the compiler settings) and the program might run if you inadvertently mismatch the type of a pointer to its addressed variable. But compiler warnings are there for a reason and ignoring them is considered sloppy style, possibly leading to incorrect behavior and crashes during program execution.

STORING AND RETRIEVING ADDRESSES

Another Look at Pointer Variables

While pointer variables have a special role, they too are just places in memory used to store a particular kind of data (in their case, the addresses of other pieces of data). Like ordinary variables, they have a size and a location in memory (**Figure 9.7**). And as with ordinary variables, you can use the address-of operator to find a pointer variable's address.

Our next example shows you how these locations and sizes look on your machine. It makes use of the sizeof() function, which returns the number of bytes used by a particular variable.

To list pointer sizes and locations:

1. Open *pointer2.c* (Script 9.2) in your text editor or IDE.

2. Add four more printf() function calls (**Script 9.3**):

   ```
   printf("Size of a: %d\n", sizeof(a));
   printf("Size of b: %d\n", sizeof(b));
   printf("Size of x: %d\n", sizeof(x));
   printf("Size of y: %d\n", sizeof(y));
   ```

   Each of these lines will print the memory size of a variable. It will show the space taken up by both the initial variables as well as their pointers.

```
1    /* pointer3.c - Script 9.3 - rewrite of
   →  Script 9.2 (pointer2.c) */
2
3    #include <stdio.h>
4
5    int main (void) {
6
7        /* Define the variables. */
8        int  a = 456;
9        char b = 'J';
10
11       /* Create two pointers, properly
   → typed. */
12       int  *x;
13       char *y;
14
15       /* Store the addresses in pointers.
   → */
16       x = &a;
17       y = &b;
18
19       /* Print the results using two
   → different methods. */
20       printf("Address of a: %p\n", &a);
21       printf("Address of b: %p\n", &b);
22       printf("Address of x: %p\n", &x);
23       printf("Address of y: %p\n", &y);
```

continues on next page

Script 9.3 Character and integer variables occupy different amounts of memory, which we demonstrate by using the sizeof() function.

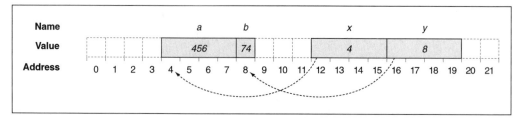

Figure 9.7 The value stored in a pointer variable (x and y) is the memory address of another variable (a and b).

```
24
25        /* Print the sizes of the four
     →  variables. */
26        printf("Size of a: %d\n",
     →  sizeof(a));
27        printf("Size of b: %d\n",
     →  sizeof(b));
28        printf("Size of x: %d\n",
     →  sizeof(x));
29        printf("Size of y: %d\n",
     →  sizeof(y));
30
31        /* Pause and wait for input before
     →  terminating. */
32        getchar();
33
34        return 0;
35
36   }
```

Script 9.3 *continued*

```
"/Documents/Books/C VQS/C_code/Ch09 $ gcc -g -o pointer3 pointer3.c
"/Documents/Books/C VQS/C_code/Ch09 $ ./pointer3
Address of a: 0xbffffc40
Address of b: 0xbffffc44
Address of x: 0xbffffc48
Address of y: 0xbffffc4c
Size of a: 4
Size of b: 1
Size of x: 4
Size of y: 4
```

Figure 9.8 Different data types use different amounts (in bytes) of memory.

3. Save the file as *pointer3.c*.

4. Compile and debug as necessary.

5. Run the application (**Figure 9.8**).

You can see that the char variable takes less memory (1 byte) than either the integer or the pointer variables. You can also see that the pointer variable for a char address requires the same amount of space as the pointer variable that holds an integer address.

✔ Tips

■ The previous example illustrates an important point: when you define a pointer variable to hold some object's address, the system allocates space for that address. It does *not* allocate space for the object itself. So for example if you define a pointer to an integer, you do not get any space to store the integer. You get space (usually 4 bytes) to store an integer's address, but you still need to define (and thereby allocate space for) that integer separately. We will get back to this in the next chapter, where you will learn how to explicitly ask the system for the allocation of a block of memory.

■ The address values in the output of the previous examples were in hexadecimal format. A handy way to convert from hexadecimal to decimal numbers is to use Google. Just search for something like *0xbffff96c in decimal* and Google will return the result *0xbffff96c = 3 221 223 788*.

ANOTHER LOOK AT POINTER VARIABLES

Dereferencing Pointer Variables

So far we've used the address-of operator to find the memory addresses of variables. These values have also been stored in pointer variables. Addresses themselves are not really that interesting, though; in the end we want to work with the actual data stored in memory at those addresses. C provides the dereferencing operator (*****) to do just that.

Given a pointer variable that contains an address, the ***** operator allows you to read and write the value stored at the place in memory whose address is stored in the pointer variable. This process is called *dereferencing* a pointer.

The dereferenced address can be used wherever the original variable could be. So if x is an integer pointer variable, then ***x** can be used wherever an integer is expected.

As always, an example will make this clearer.

To use the * operator:

1. Create a new file or project in your text editor or IDE.

2. Type the standard beginning lines of code (**Script 9.4**):

   ```
   /* pointer4.c - Script 9.4 */
   #include <stdio.h>
   ```

3. Begin the main function:

   ```
   int main (void) {
   ```

4. Define and initialize an integer, a, and an integer pointer variable, x:

   ```
   int a = 456;
   int *x;
   ```

DEREFERENCING POINTER VARIABLES

```
    ● ● ●                Script
1    /* pointer4.c - Script 9.4 */
2
3    #include <stdio.h>
4
5    int main (void) {
6
7        /* Define and initialize an integer
    → variable and
8         * an integer pointer variable. */
9        int a = 456;
10       int *x;
11
12       /* Store the address of the integer
    → variable in
13        * the integer pointer variable. */
14       x = &a;
15
16       /* Print the value of the pointer
    → variable. */
17       printf("Address of a: %p\n", x);
18
19       /* Print the value of the integer
    → variable. */
20       printf("a at start: %d\n", a);
21
22       /* Print the value again, but
    → this time
23        * do so by dereferencing (with the
    → * operator)
24        * the address stored in the pointer
    → variable. */
25       printf("*x at start: %d\n", *x);
26
27       /* Change the value of a
28        * by dereferencing its address
    → stored in the
29        * pointer variable. */
30       *x = 123;
31
```

continues on next page

Script 9.4 The dereferencing operator (*****) is required to access a variable's value through its address.

```
32        /* Print the changed value, both
→ directly using
33         * the variable's name and indirectly
→ using its
34         * address and the dereferencing
→ operator. */
35        printf("a at end:    %d\n", a);
36        printf("*x at end:    %d\n", *x);
37
38        /* Pause and wait for input before
→ terminating. */
39        getchar();
40
41        return 0;
42
43    }
```

Script 9.4 *continued*

Once again, we are using these variables for demonstration purposes, hence their trivial names and values. Make sure, though, that the variable type of the pointer matches the type of the variable to which it points.

5. Store and print the address of the integer *a*:

   ```
   x = &a;
   printf("Address of a: %p\n", x);
   ```

   First, the pointer x is assigned the address of the variable *a*. Then this pointer value is printed.

6. Print the initial value of *a*:

   ```
   printf("a at start: %d\n", a);
   ```

   Through dereferencing, this application will change the value of *a*, so its initial value is printed for comparison.

7. Use the dereferencing operator to access *a*'s value through the address stored in pointer variable x:

   ```
   printf("*x at start: %d\n", *x);
   ```

   Since x is a pointer variable whose value is the address of *a*, printing the value of *x will be the same as printing the value of *a*.

8. Assign a new value to *a* through the address stored in x:

   ```
   *x = 123;
   ```

   This is the equivalent of writing

   ```
   a = 123;
   ```

   Note how *a* and *x are interchangeable after they have been linked by the x = &*a* statement. This application accesses a place in memory directly by its name *a* and indirectly through its address stored in the pointer variable x, with a little help from the dereferencing operator.

continues on next page

9. Print the value of *a* again, using both the variable and its pointer:

```
printf("a at end: %d\n", a);
printf("*x at end: %d\n", *x);
```

These lines will confirm that the change was made to *a*'s value. Again, both *a* and *x refer to that same value.

10. Complete the main function:

```
    getchar();
    return 0;
}
```

11. Save the file as *pointer4.c*, compile, and debug as necessary.

12. Run the application (**Figure 9.9**).

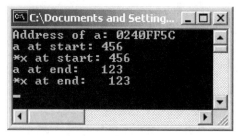

Figure 9.9 A variable can be changed using its address and the dereferencing operator (*).

✔ Tips

■ This example illustrates an important point: Using *x, you are able to read and change a variable without knowing its name. Later in the chapter, this idea will be put to good use when we pass the addresses of variables to a function instead of their values.

■ To clear up the terminology being used, a quick reiteration of this chapter's concepts is in order. First, the *address* is the physical location, in a computer's memory, where the value of a variable is stored. A *pointer variable* is a special type of variable that can be assigned an address. A *pointer*, a term you'll commonly see, is simply another word for *address*.

■ C has two uses for the asterisk. Referring to *var is dereferencing, or accessing the value stored in the variable var points to. You may also see a construct like this, where a pointer variable is defined and initialized in one step:

```
int *x = &a;
```

It is very important to realize that the asterisk in such a line does not act as a dereferencing operator (even though it looks like a dereferencing operation). Rather, this asterisk is part of the pointer variable's type, together with int. Written in two lines it would look like this:

```
int *x;
x = &a;
```

Using Multiple Pointers to the Same Location

The examples so far used only one pointer variable to store the address of some other variable. You can, of course, have multiple pointer variables that store the same address.

If you declare

```
int a = 456;
int *x = &a;
int *y = &a;
int *z = &a;
```

then a, or the dereferenced *x, *y, and *z refer to the same value (**Figure 9.10**). If you change the value stored in a by using any one of them (like *x = 24;), the change will also be visible when you read the value through any of the others.

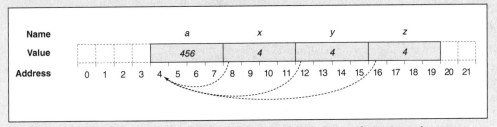

Figure 9.10 Multiple pointer variables can contain the same address of, and therefore point to, the same location in memory.

Passing Addresses to Functions

Now that you have a basic understanding of addresses (albeit thanks to trivial examples), it's time to look at some tasks that cannot be solved without using addresses. The remaining examples will show how useful pointers are.

In this next example, pointers to variables that exist in the main function will be passed to another function. Why is this useful? Consider this example: you want to create a function that swaps the values of two variables. You might be tempted to try a program like **Script 9.5**.

The problem is that such an application will not work because what the main function passes to the swap() function are the *values* of the variables a and b, not the variables themselves. The variables first and second that the swap() function manipulates are local to that function. Changes to such local variables are not visible in the main function, as the program's output would show (**Figure 9.11**).

To get the desired effect, we need to pass the *addresses* of the variables in the main program to the swap function, as the next example demonstrates.

```
1   #include <stdio.h>
2
3   void swap(int first, int second);
4
5   int main(void) {
6
7       int a = 5, b = 10;
8
9       printf("At first, a = %d, b = %d.\n",
    → a, b);
10      swap(a, b);
11      printf("After swapping, a = %d, b =
    → %d.\n", a, b);
12
13      return 0;
14  }
15
16  void swap(int first, int second) {
17      int temp = first;
18      first = second;
19      second = temp;
20  }
```

Script 9.5 Because the swap() function works on copies of the original values, it cannot affect the values of the actual variables defined in the main program.

```
~/Documents/Books/C VQS/C_code/Ch09 $ gcc -g -o pointer5 pointer5.c
~/Documents/Books/C VQS/C_code/Ch09 $ ./pointer5
At first, a = 5, b = 10
After swapping, a = 5, b = 10
~/Documents/Books/C VQS/C_code/Ch09 $ _
```

Figure 9.11 The swap() function could not change the value of main's variables because it only affected the local variable values.

```
  ⊙ ⊙ ⊙          📄 Script
1     /* pointer6.c - Script 9.6 */
2
3     #include <stdio.h>
4
5     void swap(int *first, int *second); /*
      → Function prototype. */
6
7     int main(void) {
8
9         /* Define and initialize two integer
      → variables */
10        int a = 5, b = 10;
11
12        /* Print the initial variable values.
      → */
13        printf("At first, a = %d, b = %d.\n",
      → a, b);
14
15        /* Swap the variable values. */
16        swap(&a, &b);
17
18        /* Print the variables again. */
19        printf("After swapping, a = %d, b =
      → %d.\n", a, b);
20
21        /* Pause and wait for input before
      → terminating. */
22        getchar();
23
24        return 0;
25
26    } /* End of main function. */
27
28    /* Define swap(), taking pointers instead
      → of values. */
29    void swap(int *first, int *second) {
30
                        continues on next page
```

Script 9.6 In this version of the application, the *swap()* function is given the addresses of the variables from the main program and can therefore change their associated values.

To pass addresses to a function:

1. Create a new file or project in your text editor or IDE.

2. Type the standard beginning lines of code (**Script 9.6**):

   ```
   /* pointer6.c - Script 9.6 */
   #include <stdio.h>
   ```

3. Add the function prototype for the swap function:

   ```
   void swap(int *first, int *second);
   ```

   The prototype declares that the function takes two parameters, both of which are addresses of integer variables (pointers to int). Note that these asterisks indicate pointer variables; they are not being used as dereferencing operators.

4. Begin the main function;

   ```
   int main (void) {
   ```

5. Define and initialize two integer variables, then print their values:

   ```
   int a = 5, b = 10;
   printf("At first, a = %d, b = %d.\n",
   → a, b);
   ```

   This application will swap the two variable values. To demonstrate this in action, their original values are first printed.

6. Call the swap function, passing it the addresses of the two variables:

   ```
   swap(&a, &b);
   ```

   Instead of passing the swap() function two values, as in

   ```
   swap (a, b);
   ```

   the swap function will now receive the address of the two variables. This will allow that function to access and alter these variables' values.

   continues on next page

7. Print the variables' values again:

```
printf("After swapping, a = %d,
→ b = %d.\n", a, b);
```

After calling the swap function, the variables' values are printed again to confirm that a swap was made.

8. Complete the main function:

```
    getchar();
    return 0;
}
```

9. Begin the swap function definition:

```
void swap(int *first, int *second) {
```

The function expects to receive two addresses of integer variables as parameters. These addresses will be made available to the function's code in the two pointer variables—first and second—declared here.

10. Define a local integer variable temp and initialize it with the value stored at the first integer address:

```
int temp = *first;
```

As you have already learned, we use the dereferencing operator * to get the value when you have an address.

11. Exchange the two values, again using the dereferencing operators:

```
*first = *second;
*second = temp;
```

The important point here is that the function is actually changing the values of the variables a and b in the main program. This is possible because the two pointer variables first and second contain the addresses of a and b. By dereferencing first and second to work with the values, changing *first is equivalent to changing a and changing *second is equivalent to changing b.

```
    ● ● ●                    Script
31        /* Using a third, temporary integer
→ variable,
32        * swap the values of the two
→ variables whose
33        * addresses were passed as
→ parameters.
34        * We use the dereferencing operator
→ * to get
35        * at the variables' values. */
36        int temp = *first;
37        *first = *second;
38        *second = temp;
39
40    } /* End of swap function. */
```

Script 9.6 *continued*

Figure 9.12 This version of the swap() function was able to change the variables in the main function because it was given their addresses instead of their values.

Revisiting the scanf() Function

Only the use of pointers makes the ability to change a variable's value in another function possible. You have already seen this concept, though, with standard library functions like scanf().

scanf() assigns to variables values parsed from a source, using a formatting pattern to make that association. For example, this code reads in two integers (separated by a space) from the standard input and assigns them to variables:

```
int num1, num2;
scanf("%d %d", &num1, &num2);
```

The scanf() function cannot return more than a single value (a limitation on all functions), so it must find another way to assign values to variables.

What happens instead is that you pass scanf() the addresses of all these variables (like &num1 and &num2). Since scanf() can dereference the addresses using the * operator, it is able to assign the variables values it has parsed out of the input.

Again, without pointers, there would be no way for a function like scanf() to do its job.

12. Complete the swap function:

```
}
```

13. Save the file as *pointer6.c*, compile, and debug as necessary.

14. Run the application (**Figure 9.12**).

This time, the changes performed in the swap() function had the desired effect in the main program.

✔ Tips

- In this chapter, pointers are only used on regular variables. You can also use pointers to pointer variables. This would again allow you to pass the address of a pointer variable to a subroutine and have the subroutine fill your pointer variable with an address. Such techniques are beyond the scope of this book, though.

- To reacquaint yourself with variable scope, turn to the end of Chapter 7, "Creating Your Own Functions."

Arrays, Pointers, and Pointer Arithmetic

You've already learned about arrays (in Chapter 6, "Working with Arrays") and how to use the square brackets to access individual elements (the square brackets are technically referred to as the *subscription operator*). Now that you have an understanding of pointers, you'll learn how to use them to access array elements by performing calculations on the base address of the array. Such address calculations are called *address* or *pointer arithmetic*.

What is an array's base address? The elements of an array are laid out sequentially in memory. An array's base address is simply the address of the array's first element (**Figure 9.13**).

As with any object, you can get the address of this first element by using the address-of operator:

```
char a[] = {3, 23, 14, 7, 12};
&a[0];
```

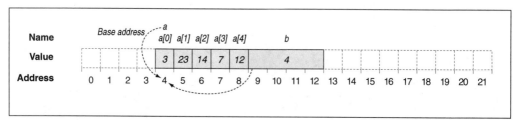

Figure 9.13 An array's base address (stored in the pointer b) is the location of the array's first element. So the base address of the array a is 4.

This is a bit inconvenient to write, so C provides an alternative: you can use the array name, a in this case, as shorthand for the &a[0] expression. So if you use the name of an array anywhere in your code, what you get is actually the array's base address. Thus, these two assignments to b are equivalent:

```
char *b;
b = &a[0];
b = a;
```

Both statements store the array's base address—and therefore the address of the array's first element—in the char pointer variable b.

Building on this concept, you know you can dereference the address stored in a pointer variable to get the value stored at that address. Thus the following two expressions will now give the same value:

```
*b
a[0]
```

Both return the value of the array's first element, the first using a pointer to the base address, the second using the subscription operator. But what do you do if you want to access, using a pointer, an element *other* than the first one? The answer is that you have to change the address value stored in the pointer variable before dereferencing it. This is exactly what pointer arithmetic is about.

For example, to access the next element of the array, you have to increment the address value stored in the pointer variable by 1 so that it points to the next address in memory:

```
b++;
```

*b will now refer to the second array element. Let's try this in a program.

ARRAYS, POINTERS, AND POINTER ARITHMETIC

To use pointer arithmetic to access arrays:

1. Create a new file or project in your text editor or IDE.

2. Type the standard beginning lines of code (**Script 9.7**):

   ```
   /* pointer7.c - Script 9.7 */
   #include <stdio.h>
   ```

3. Define a C preprocessor constant called COUNT with the value 5:

   ```
   #define COUNT 5
   ```

   This value will be used to control the loop for accessing every array element.

4. Begin the main function:

   ```
   int main (void) {
   ```

5. Define the required variables:

   ```
   char a[] = {3, 23, 14, 7, 12};
   char *b;
   int i;
   ```

   Define and initialize an array of chars *a* with five elements. Then define a char pointer variable *b* and an integer variable i. As you can guess from its name, i will be a loop control variable.

6. Assign *a*'s base address to the *b* pointer variable:

   ```
   b = a;
   ```

   a[0] and *b are now equivalent and refer to the first element's value.

```
                   Script

1    /* pointer7.c - Script 9.7 */

2

3    #include <stdio.h>

4

5    #define COUNT 5 /* Number of array
  →  elements. */

6

7    int main(void) {

8

9        /* Define and initialize an array of
  →  chars with 5 elements. */

10       char a[] = {3, 23, 14, 7, 12};

11

12       /* Define a char pointer variable
  →  and an integer */

13       char *b;

14       int i;

15

16       /* Store the base address of the char

17        * array in the char pointer
  →  variable */

18       b = a;

19

20       /* In a for loop, print all array
  →  elements

21        * using the subscript operator. */

22       printf("Using subscript\n");

23       for (i = 0; i < COUNT; i++) {

24           printf("%d\n", (int) a[i]);

25       }

26

27       /* Again in a for loop, print all
  →  array

28        * elements. Use pointer arithmetic
  →  to

29        * increment the value of the
  →  pointer
```

continues on next page

Script 9.7 Incrementing the address stored in the pointer variable b allows the application to access all of the elements in the a array.

```
⊖ ○ ⊖              📄 Script
30        * variable each time through the
    → loop. */
31      printf("Using pointer\n");
32      for (i = 0; i < COUNT; i++) {
33          printf("%d\n", (int) *b);
34          b++;
35      }
36
37      /* Pause and wait for input before
    → terminating. */
38      getchar();
39
40      return 0;
41  }
```

Script 9.7 *continued*

7. Use a for loop to print the values of all elements of the *a* array:

```
printf("Using subscript\n");
for (i = 0; i < COUNT; i++) {
    printf("%d\n", (int) a[i]);
}
```

This first loop uses the array subscript operator and the index of the elements to access every array value. This is very similar to methods you've already seen. i will be incremented from 0 to 4, giving the array the indexes of the five elements.

One new, minor addition is that a[i] is type casted to an integer value to avoid problems on some systems.

8. Add a second for loop to print all elements again using pointer arithmetic:

```
printf("Using pointer\n");
for (i = 0; i < COUNT; i++) {
  printf("%d\n", (int) *b);
  b++;
}
```

In this loop, instead of using the subscription operator (the square brackets), pointers will access each element. Using the dereferencing operator (*), the value *b points to the value stored in a particular memory block. The first time the loop runs, *b points to a[0]. This value is printed and then b is incremented, so that it points to the next array element (a[1]). This process continues through the entire loop.

Again, the dereferenced value (*b) is type casted to avoid problems.

continues on next page

ARRAYS, POINTERS, AND POINTER ARITHMETIC

215

9. Complete the `main` function:

```
getchar();
return 0;
}
```

10. Save the file as *pointer7.c*, compile, and debug as necessary.

11. Run the application (**Figure 9.14**).

✔ Tip

■ You can, of course, do other kinds of calculations rather than using the increment operator ++ on a pointer variable. For example, constructs like `*(b + 3)` are valid. If `b` is again a pointer variable containing the base address of an array `a`, this expression would give you the value of `a`'s fourth element. And in the first `for` loop example above, you could replace `a[i]` with `*(b + i)`.

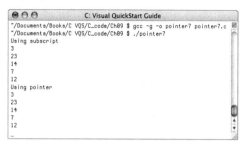

Figure 9.14 Array subscripting and pointer arithmetic—two ways to access all of an array's elements—yield the same results.

Address Arithmetic Using Different Types

There is an interesting point regarding address arithmetic and arrays: Incrementing the pointer by 1 to access the next element does not mean the same thing for different data types.

For example, in an array of chars and an array of ints, the elements typically use 1 byte for the chars and 4 bytes for the ints, as Figure 9.1 illustrates. Thus when the address value (remember: a big number) stored in an integer pointer variable is incremented to point to the next integer value in memory, the address is actually incremented by 4 bytes. When a char pointer variable is incremented, the address changes by 1 byte.

It's useful to know this distinction, but you don't have to worry about it yourself because the C compiler will always take care to use the appropriate increment value.

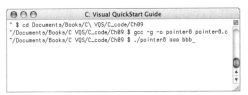

Figure 9.15 C programs can receive a variable number of command-line arguments. The arguments are separated by white space.

Arrays of Pointers

So far you have used only single pointer variables, but you can also use arrays of pointer variables if you need to store a series of addresses. One such need for an array of pointers is when dealing with a series of text strings (character arrays). This will be demonstrated using the command-line arguments that a C program can receive when it is started.

When you run a compiled C program, you can optionally add a number of arguments that are passed to that program. From a command-line interface, arguments are separated by one or more blank spaces, and come after the application name (**Figure 9.15**). In this figure, *pointer9* is the program name and *aaa* and *bbb* are two separate arguments.

How can your C program access these arguments when it may not now how many there are? C always passes two parameters to your main function: the first one is an integer with the number of arguments the application received, and the second one is an array of pointers to where those arguments have been stored in memory. By convention, the first parameter is named argc (for *argument count*) and the second one argv (for *argument vector*, where *vector* means *array*). As usual, each string (which is to say each argument) is a character array, terminated with a null byte. Note that there is always at least one argument because C inserts the program name at the front of the list of arguments (**Figure 9.16**).

Let's write a program that prints the arguments given to the program and displays the memory locations for the different objects shown in Figure 9.16.

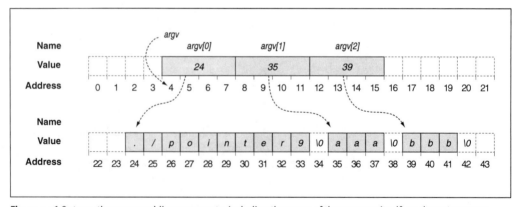

Figure 9.16 C stores the command-line arguments, including the name of the program itself, as character arrays.

ARRAYS OF POINTERS

```
 1   /* pointer8.c - Script 9.8 */
 2
 3   #include <stdio.h>
 4
 5   /* The main function takes two arguments,
 6    * an integer and an array of char
     → pointers. */
 7   int main(int argc, char *argv[]) {
 8
 9       /* Declare an integer variable to
10        * be used as loop index. */
11       int i;
12
13       /* Print the number in the argc
     → parameter. */
14       printf("Number of arguments received:
     → %d\n", argc);
15
16       /* Print the base address of the argv
     → array. */
17       printf("argv base address: %p\n\n",
     → argv);
18
19       /* Print the values of all elements
20        * of the argv array. Each element
     → is a
21        * pointer to a character string,
     → so point that
22        * out too using the %s format
     → sequence. */
23       printf("Address --> Value\n");
24       for (i = 0; i < argc; i++) {
25           printf("%p -> %s\n", argv[i],
     → argv[i]);
26       }
27
28       /* Pause and wait for input before
     → terminating. */
29       getchar();
```

continues on next page

Script 9.8 C programs can access their command-line arguments through an array of pointers to strings.

To use program arguments:

1. Create a new file or project in your text editor or IDE.

2. Type the standard beginning lines of code (**Script 9.8**):

   ```
   /* pointer8.c - Script 9.8 */
   #include <stdio.h>
   ```

3. Begin the main function:

   ```
   int main(int argc, char *argv[]) {
   ```

   This time, the main function is not defined to take no arguments (using void). Instead, it's defined to take the two arguments explained earlier: char *argv[] is the equivalent of saying "argv is an array (of unknown size) of pointers to character variables."

4. Define and initialize an integer i to be used as loop index variable:

   ```
   int i;
   ```

5. Print the argument count:

   ```
   printf("Number of arguments received:
    → %d\n", argc);
   ```

   When the program runs, the argc variable will be assigned the number of arguments the application received. This value is first printed.

6. Print the base address of the argv array:

   ```
   printf("argv base address: %p\n\n",
    → argv);
   ```

   Using the information we presented in the previous section of this chapter, the array's base address—the location where the array's first element is stored—is printed.

continues on next page

7. Add a loop that prints out the addresses and values of each received argument:

```
printf("Address --> Value\n");
for (i = 0; i < argc; i++) {
    printf("%p -> %s\n", argv[i],
 argv[i]);
}
```

The loop goes from 0 (the first item in the argv array) to one less than the number of arguments received (argc). For every element in the argv pointer array, this loop will first print the actual address stored in that element using the %p sequence. Then the character string that starts at that address will be printed as a string. This last value corresponds to the actual command-line argument.

8. Complete the main function:

```
getchar();
return 0;
}
```

9. Save the file as *pointer8.c*, compile, and debug as necessary.

10. Run the application, providing it with some number of arguments (**Figure 9.17**).

```
30
31       return 0;
32
33   }
```

Script 9.8 *continued*

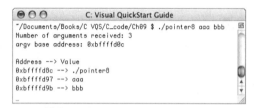

Figure 9.17 The application displays the base address of the argv array and the addresses and pointed values stored in the elements of the array.

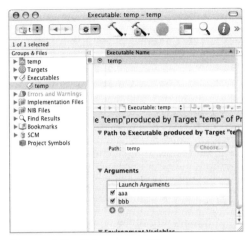

Figure 9.18 Specifying command-line arguments in Xcode.

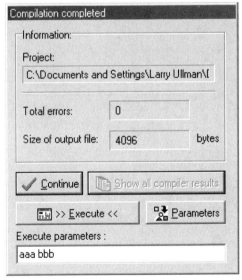

Figure 9.19 Specifying command-line arguments in Dev-C++.

✔ Tips

- You can experiment by running the compiled program with different argument counts and lengths. The dynamic, pointer-based system will work in any situation.

- Most graphical programming environments do not run applications from a command line. In such cases, you have to find out how to pass arguments to your program when running the program. In Apple's Xcode for example, after successful compilation, click on the compiled program's name in the Executables folder. Then, select View > Show Embedded Editor. There, under the Arguments tab, you can add the arguments (**Figure 9.18**).

- In Dev-C++ on Windows, first compile the application. In the resulting window, click on Parameters to display the parameters box. Type any arguments there (**Figure 9.19**), then click on Execute.

10

MANAGING MEMORY

So far, every one of this book's programs has used a fixed amount of memory to accomplish its task. This fixed amount of memory was known and specified (in the form of a variable) when the program was written. These programs could not increase or decrease the amount of memory available for the storage of user data during runtime. Instead, such changes had to be done in the program's source code file, and the program had to be recompiled and re-executed.

But the real world is dynamic, and so is the input that has to be processed by a C program (for example, users need to be able to submit a varying amount of text in most applications). To handle situations where the amount of data to be stored is not known in advance, you have to use dynamic memory in your C programs.

Dynamic memory allows you to create and use data structures that can grow and shrink as needed, limited only by the amount of memory installed in the computer they're running on. In this chapter you'll learn how to work with memory in a flexible manner.

Static and Dynamic Memory

Static memory is what you have seen and used so far: variables (including pointer variables) and arrays of fixed size. You can work with these blocks of memory in your program code using their names as well as their addresses (see Chapter 9, "Working with Pointers").

With static memory you define the maximum amount of space required for a variable when you write your program:

```
char a[1000]; // Fixed at runtime.
```

Whether needed or not, all of that memory will be reserved for that variable and there is no way to change the amount of static memory while the program runs.

Dynamic memory is different. It comes in blocks without names, just addresses. It is allocated when the program runs, in chunks from a large pool that the standard C library manages for you.

You use the standard library's `malloc()` function to request a block of a certain size—in bytes—from the available memory pool. The size is dynamic and can be determined when the program runs (**Figure 10.1**):

```
int memsize;
// memsize gets a value at runtime.
x = malloc(memsize);
```

When you are done with the block, you return it to the pool using the `free()` function:

```
free(x);
```

Every call to `malloc()` must be balanced by a call to `free()`. A missing or double `free()` call is considered a bug (specifically, a missing `free()` statement creates a *memory leak*).

If enough memory is available to satisfy your request, the malloc() function returns the starting address of the newly allocated block. You usually store this address in a pointer variable for later use.

There is a small problem, though. Remember from the previous chapter that a pointer variable can only hold an address of the appropriate type, that is, a char pointer variable can only hold the address of a char, an int pointer variable can only hold the address of an integer, and so on. However, the blocks of memory whose starting addresses malloc() returns are just that: *untyped* blocks of memory of the requested size. The type of the data stored in them is usually determined later on in the program, after the malloc() call.

To accommodate addresses of such untyped blocks of memory, C provides a special type of pointer variable called a *void pointer*. You define such a pointer like so:

```
void *x;
```

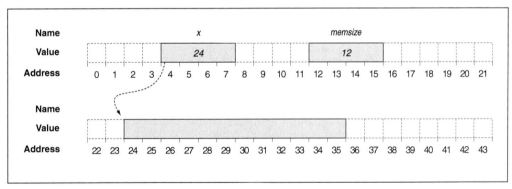

Figure 10.1 A block of dynamic memory (represented in the bottom grid) does not have a name as variables and pointers do (the top grid). Referring to a dynamic memory block's address is the only way to access it.

A void pointer variable can store addresses of any type, including integers, chars, floats, etc. It can also store the addresses of the untyped blocks of memory that malloc() returns:

```
void *x;
x = malloc();
```

Finally, as an extra precaution, the pointer should be set to NULL after you have freed the associated memory:

```
void *x;
x = malloc (size);
free(x);
x = NULL;
```

By taking this final step, the program knows that x no longer refers to a block of memory. This is desired so that any uses of x (unless it is assigned another value beforehand) will fail rather than create hard-to-debug oddities.

Let's write our first dynamic memory example using malloc() and free(). The example is short but introduces the basic syntax that will be used again in all subsequent examples, so it is important for you to understand this process clearly.

To request and return dynamic memory:

1. Create a new file or project in your text editor or IDE.

2. Type the standard beginning lines of code (**Script 10.1**):

   ```
   /* memory.c - Script 10.1 */
   #include <stdio.h>
   #include <stdlib.h>
   ```

   Note the inclusion of the *stdlib.h* header file. It provides the declarations for the malloc() and free() functions required by the compiler when working with dynamic memory.

```
1   /* memory.c - Script 10.1 */
2
3   #include <stdio.h>
4   #include <stdlib.h>
5
6   int main (void) {
7
8       /* Declare a void pointer variable.
         */
9       void *x;
10
11      /* Request a block of memory with
         1000 bytes. */
12      x = malloc(1000);
13
14      /* Print out the starting address
         of the memory block. */
15      printf("Starting block address:
         %p.\n", x);
16
17      /* Return the block to the pool. */
18      free(x);
19      x = NULL;
20
21      /* Pause and wait for input before
         terminating. */
22      getchar();
23
24      return 0;
25
26  }
```

Script 10.1 The malloc() and free() functions are used to allocate and release blocks of dynamic memory.

3. Begin the `main` function:

```
int main (void) {
```

4. Define a void pointer variable:

```
void *x;
```

5. Call the `malloc()` function to request a block of memory 1000 bytes long:

```
x = malloc(1000);
```

The address returned by the `malloc()` function—which indicates the starting address of the requested block of memory—will be assigned to the void pointer x.

6. Print the address:

```
printf("Starting block address:
→ %p.\n", x);
```

To allow you to confirm that the process worked and to view the minimal results, the address stored in the void pointer will be printed. The %p signifier is used, since x is a pointer.

7. Return the block to the pool using the `free()` function:

```
free(x);
x = NULL;
```

The `free()` function takes one argument: the address of the block to be returned to the pool. After this call to `free()`, the specific block of memory pointed to by the address may no longer be used by the program. In other words, referring to x may cause problems since it no longer points to a reserved block of memory. For this reason, the second line sets the value of x to NULL, so that any inadvertent references to x after this will quite clearly be wrong.

continues on next page

STATIC AND DYNAMIC MEMORY

8. Complete the main function:

```
getchar();
return 0;
}
```

9. Save the file as *memory.c*, compile, and debug as necessary.

10. Run the application (**Figure 10.2**).

So far you didn't actually use the memory, but you'll be getting to that in the next sections.

Figure 10.2 The base address of the memory block returned by the malloc() function is printed to confirm that the process worked.

✔ Tips

■ Note that the term *static memory* used in this section has nothing to do with the static C keyword. The static keyword was introduced in Chapter 7, "Creating Your Own Functions," and is pertinent to function variables. The term *static memory* as used in this section means that the amount of memory is set at compile time and cannot be changed during runtime.

■ The block of memory returned by malloc() may be filled with random garbage. Most of the time, this is not a problem because you usually write to memory first before reading from it. In some situations, though, you might need clean memory that has been overwritten with zeros. Instead of writing a for loop to clear the memory yourself, you can use the calloc() function instead of malloc(). It will pre-fill the memory block with zeros, but that process will take some time. Because of the additional time needed to clear the memory, you should not needlessly use calloc() instead of malloc().

■ In case you were curious, the word *malloc* is short for *memory allocation*.

The NULL Pointer

There is a special address value called the NULL pointer (also defined in the *stdlib.h* header file). When a pointer variable is set to this value, it means that the pointer does not point to any object at all:

```
void *x;
x = NULL; /*x doesn't point anywhere.
```

When malloc() fails to allocate a block of the requested size, it returns the NULL pointer value instead of a real address. In your programs, you should *always* check the return value of malloc() to see if it is equal to NULL. Then you can react accordingly:

```
x = malloc(1000);
if (x == NULL) {
    printf("Unable to allocate!\n");
    // Handle the error.
}
```

We have omitted this vital check in the examples for brevity (and because these simple exercises should work regardless), but you should start incorporating it before creating any real-world applications.

Type Casts

You now know enough about dynamic memory to reserve blocks of it, but what you actually want to do is to store and retrieve data in these blocks.

The void pointer variable introduced in the previous section allows you to store and retrieve any kind of *address*, but it specifically does not allow you to read or write any *data* through it using the dereferencing operator (*) as you learned how to do in Chapter 9. The reason for this is that the void pointer variable lacks data type information. Since a void pointer can point to anything, the system cannot know if it should read or write a 1-byte char or a 4-byte integer, or something completely different.

What the system needs in such a situation is a hint from you, the programmer. You have to tell it how you would like that memory address accessed: as a character or as an integer, for example.

The mechanism for giving the system such a hint is called a *cast* or *type cast*. The syntax used for a cast is a pair of parentheses with the desired pointer type between them, followed by the address value:

```
void x*;
(int *)x
```

This tells the system that the address stored in the x pointer variable should be interpreted as the address of an integer value. You can precede this construct with the dereferencing operator to actually read an integer value from that memory address:

```
printf("The value of x is %p.",
→ *(int *)x);
```

Let's try an example so that this idea will make better sense.

To use the type cast operator:

1. Create a new file or project in your text editor or IDE.

2. Type the standard beginning lines of code (**Script 10.2**):

```
/* typecast.c - Script 10.2 */
#include <stdio.h>
#include <stdlib.h>
```

3. Begin the main function:

```
int main (void) {
```

4. Define and initialize a void pointer variable:

```
void *x = NULL;
```

It's good practice to initialize pointer variables with the NULL pointer value. Much like setting such a pointer to NULL after freeing memory, this makes it clear that x points to nothing.

5. Call the malloc() function and ask for a block of memory big enough to hold an integer. Store the address of the block returned by malloc() in the void pointer variable:

```
x = malloc(sizeof(int));
```

Since the amount of memory required to store an integer is machine-dependent, you have to use the sizeof() operator to find out how many bytes will be required. On most contemporary systems, sizeof(int) will return 4.

We have again omitted the check for a NULL return value from malloc(), but you can include it here because you should always check for NULL in a real program.

6. Print the address of the block:

```
printf("Starting address: %p.\n", x);
```

```
 1    /* typecast.c - Script 10.2 */
 2
 3    #include <stdio.h>
 4    #include <stdlib.h>
 5
 6    int main (void) {
 7
 8        /* Define and initialize a void
 →    pointer variable. */
 9        void *x = NULL;
10
11        /* Request a block of memory large
12         * enough to hold an integer. */
13        x = malloc(sizeof(int));
14
15        /* We have omitted the check
 →    for NULL
16         * here. You must always check for
 →    a NULL
17         * return value from malloc(). */
18
19        /* Print out the starting address
 →    of the memory block. */
20        printf("Starting address: %p.\n",
 →    x);
21
22        /* Store an integer in the new
 →    memory block. */
23        *(int *)x = 1234;
24
25        /* Print the value. */
26        printf("Value stored in the memory
 →    block: %d.\n", *(int *)x);
27
28        /* Return the block to the pool. */
29        free(x);
30        x = NULL;
```

continues on next page

Script 10.2 Type casts supply missing type information to the compiler and are critical when working with dynamic memory.

```
  ●  ●  ●                    Script

31
32        /* Pause and wait for input before
    → terminating. */
33        getchar();
34
35        return 0;
36
37    }
```

Script 10.2 *continued*

```
●  ●  ●           C: Visual QuickStart Guide
~ $ cd Documents/Books/C\ VQS/C_code/Ch10
~/Documents/Books/C VQS/C_code/Ch10 $ gcc -g -o typecast typecast.c
~/Documents/Books/C VQS/C_code/Ch10 $ ./typecast
Starting address: 0x300140.
Value stored in the memory block: 1234.
```

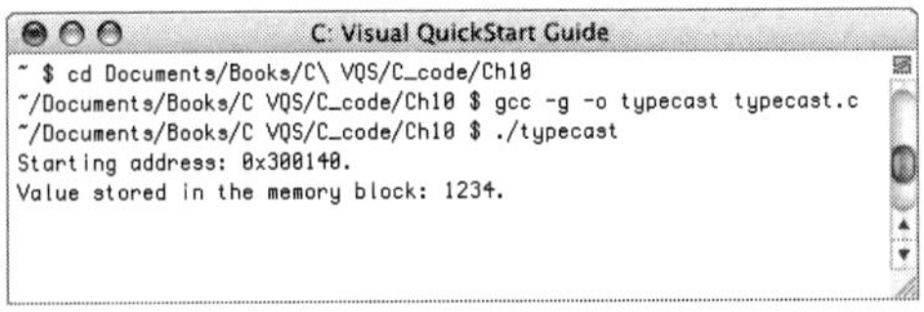

Figure 10.3 Thanks to type casting, a void pointer can be used like an int pointer.

7. Store an integer value into the memory block using the type cast and dereferencing operators:

   `*(int *)x = 1234;`

   The x refers to the address of the dynamically reserved memory block. The (int *) before the x type-casts that as an integer. Finally, the dereferencing operator (the initial *) allows you to read from or write to the memory block. In this case, the value *1234* will be stored there.

8. Print the value stored in the memory block:

   `printf("Value stored in the memory`
   `→ block: %d.\n", *(int *)x);`

   Just as you can use a combination of the type cast and dereferencing operators to assign a value to a memory block, the combination of the two can be used to read in a value stored in a memory block. The %d signifier is used since the value stored is an integer.

9. Return the block to the pool using the free() function:

   `free(x);`
   `x = NULL;`

10. Complete the main function:

    `getchar();`
    `return 0;`
    `}`

11. Save the file as *typecast.c*, compile, and debug as necessary.

12. Run the application (**Figure 10.3**).

continues on next page

TYPE CASTS

✔ Tips

- In more complex expressions involving type casts and the dereferencing operator, you might want to add a pair of parentheses: `*((int *)x)`. This ensures that the expression is evaluated the way you meant it to be.

- If the combination of the dereferencing and type cast operators looks too confusing to you, you can always assign the address stored in the void pointer to a nonvoid pointer variable of the appropriate type:

  ```
  void *x; // void pointer variable
  int *y; // integer pointer variable
  y = x;
  Now you can use *y instead of
  → *(int *)x.
  ```

When You Don't Need Casts

After you've seen type casting in action, here's an important simplification: You do not need the type casts when *assigning* or *comparing* address values if one of the pointers is a void pointer. This means that these statements are all legal without casts:

```
int a, *b;
void *x;
x = &a;
b = x;
if (x == &a) ...
```

It also means that the previous example could be simplified by using an integer pointer variable instead of a void pointer variable:

```
int *x;
x = malloc(sizeof(int));
*x = 1234;
printf("Value stored in the memory
block: %d.\n", *x);
free(x);
x = NULL;
```

It is important to note that the `malloc()` function still returns a void pointer. You are allowed to omit the type cast in the assignment to x because the fact that you are storing the (untyped) address in an integer pointer variable already tells the system how you intend to use the block of memory.

Also note that the `sizeof(int)` expression is *not* what tells the system that you are planning to use the memory block to store an integer; it just specifies how to determine the size (in bytes) of an integer on a particular machine.

Allocating Arrays of Dynamic Size

In the previous section you allocated a block of memory and used it. However, it was a very small block of memory—only the size needed to store an integer. You could have allocated the same amount of memory statically by simply defining a regular integer variable in the program. And, although the amount of memory was determined at runtime, it was still of a fixed size (the size required to store an integer).

Memory management gets a lot more interesting if you determine the amount of memory to request from the pool at runtime, and if the requested amount is larger. In this section you will allocate room for an array of integers. To make it clear that the size of the array is dynamic, this program will ask the user to choose the size at runtime (during the execution of the program).

Before you implement the example, let's review the relationship between arrays and pointers that we introduced in the previous chapter.

The forthcoming example requires an array whose size is not known when the program is written and therefore cannot be inserted between the brackets in the array definition:

```
int a[???]; // How many elements?
```

How can you solve this problem? Recall the discussion in the previous chapter where you learned that the combination of the array's name and the array subscription operator (the square brackets) can be replaced with pointer arithmetic using the array's base address. For example, both a[0] and *x (where x is a pointer containing a's address) refer to the array's first element. Using pointer arithmetic from there, a[1] is equivalent to *(x + 1), a[2] to *(x + 2), and so on.

What helps you here is that this also works in reverse. Given a base address of a chunk of memory stored in a pointer variable (which is exactly what `malloc()` returns), you can use the array subscription operator on the pointer variable's name and treat the chunk of memory exactly like an array. So, if you define x as a block of memory large enough to store 10 integers:

```
int *x = malloc(10 * sizeof(int));
```

then you're allowed to treat x like an array:

```
x[1] = 45;
x[2] = 8;
```

The following example uses this concept.

To allocate a dynamic array:

1. Create a new file or project in your text editor or IDE.

2. Type the standard beginning lines of code (**Script 10.3**):

   ```
   /* array.c - Script 10.3 */
   #include <stdio.h>
   #include <stdlib.h>
   ```

3. Begin the main function:

   ```
   int main (void) {
   ```

4. Define an integer pointer variable and two integers:

   ```
   int *x = NULL;
   int i, count;
   ```

   The x pointer will be used for working with the dynamic memory. The i variable will be used in a loop (as you've seen many times by now), and count will store the number of items in the array, which will be determined by the user.

```
1    /* array.c - Script 10.3 */
2
3    #include <stdio.h>
4    #include <stdlib.h>
5
6    int main (void) {
7
8        /* Define an integer pointer
   →  variable. */
9        int *x = NULL;
10
11       /* Define two integer variables. */
12       int i, count;
13
14       /* Prompt for the number of items.
   →  Store
15        * the user's reply in the count
   →  variable. */
16       printf("Number of items? ");
17       scanf("%d", &count);
18
19       /* Request a block of memory large
20        * enough to hold the requested
   →  number
21        * of integers. */
22       x = malloc(count * sizeof(int));
23
24       /* We have omitted the check for NULL
25        * here. You must always check for
   →  a NULL
26        * return value from malloc(). */
27
28       /* Store a random number in every slot
29        * of the array. */
30       for (i = 0; i < count; i++) {
31           x[i] = rand();
32       }
33
```

continues on next page

Script 10.3 A dynamically allocated block of memory can be used like an array.

```
34        /* Print all values in the array. */
35        for (i = 0; i < count; i++) {
36            printf("The value of array
 ⟶ element %d is %d.\n", i, x[i]);
37        }
38
39        /* Return the block to the pool. */
40        free(x);
41        x = NULL;
42
43        /* Pause and wait for input before
 ⟶ terminating. */
44        getchar();
45        getchar();
46
47        return 0;
48
49  }
```

Script 10.3 *continued*

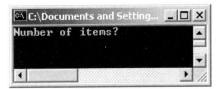

Figure 10.4 The number of elements to be stored in an array will be determined by the input the user enters at this prompt.

5. Prompt the user for the size of the array, storing the user's reply in the count variable:

```
printf("Number of items? ");
scanf("%d", &count);
```

The first line creates a prompt (**Figure 10.4**). The submitted value is then stored in the count variable.

You can also, if you want, add some checks to this process so that a valid integer value is entered. This concept was covered back in Chapter 5, "Standard Input and Output."

6. Request a block of memory large enough to hold this number of integers:

```
x = malloc(count * sizeof(int));
```

To determine how much memory is required, multiply the amount of memory needed for one integer by the number of integers the user wishes to store. This gives the total size of the block to allocate.

7. In a loop, store a random number in every element of the array:

```
for (i = 0; i < count; i++) {
    x[i] = rand();
}
```

This loop runs from 0 to count iterations to access every memory block. Within the loop itself, the rand() function is used to assign a random value to that array's element.

Notice how this code uses the array subscription operator on the pointer variable holding the memory block's base address (x[i]). In essence, you are treating the block of memory like an array, even though you never explicitly defined an array.

continues on next page

8. In another loop, print the array's elements:

```
for (i = 0; i < count; i++) {
  printf("The value of array element
→ %d is %d.\n", i, x[i]);
}
```

9. Return the block to the pool using the `free()` function:

```
free(x);
x = NULL;
```

10. Add two `getchar()` calls to pause execution on Windows:

```
getchar();
getchar();
```

Because this example takes user input, the extra call to `getchar()` may be required.

You can also add one of the techniques for discarding extraneous input, if you desire.

11. Complete the `main` function:

```
    return 0;
}
```

12. Save the file as *array.c*, compile, and debug as necessary.

13. Run the application (**Figure 10.5**).

Enter any number when asked for it by the program.

14. Run the application again, using a different numeric value (**Figure 10.6**).

You can repeat this as many times as you want with different values. A different amount of memory is requested and returned each time.

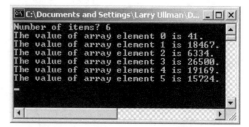

Figure 10.5 An array of varying length—determined by the user-submitted number—is populated with random values, then printed.

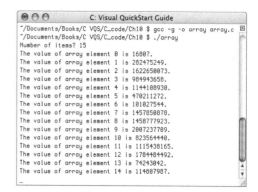

Figure 10.6 Since there is no set array size in this example, the only limitation is the amount of available memory.

✔ Tips

■ You could have used pointer arithmetic on the memory block's base address instead of the array subscription notation. Both pointer arithmetic and array subscription will work.

■ Another example involving the `rand()` function takes place in Chapter 12, "File Input and Output." At that time you'll also see how to generate numbers that are more random.

Resizing a Block of Memory

Sometimes you have to resize a block of dynamic memory after you have already stored data in it. The most common reason for this is the need to grow the block beyond the initial size given to the malloc() call. This often happens if the amount of data to be stored and processed is not known in advance (for example, when you are receiving data over a network connection).

The C library provides the realloc() function for this purpose. It takes two parameters: the address of the memory block to be resized and the desired new size of that block.

```
void *x, *y;
x = malloc(1000); // Initial block
y = realloc(x, 2000); // Doubled
```

Retaining the Original Address

Since realloc() can return a NULL pointer if the operation fails, you have to retain a copy of the old pointer. You should not overwrite the only copy of an address with realloc()'s return value by assigning it to the same pointer variable. In short, this could be bad:

```
x = malloc(1000);
x = realloc(x, 2000);
```

If realloc() fails and returns a NULL pointer, the initial address of the memory block returned by the malloc(1000) call is lost. Since that value can no longer be passed to free(), the originally reserved memory cannot be reclaimed until the program terminates. This is a *memory leak* (see the end of the chapter for more on memory leaks).

The safe usage pattern is to store and examine the return value of realloc() in a second pointer variable before committing it to the original one:

```
void *x, *y;
x = malloc(1000);
y = realloc(x, 2000);
```

This way, the initial value is still available in x if realloc() fails. If you want, you can use a simple conditional on y to reassign the value of x (to the new address) if realloc() worked:

```
if (y) x = y;
```

`realloc()` attempts to grow the original block to accommodate the new requested size. If successful, it returns the block's address unchanged. If it is not possible to grow the old block (because there is not enough adjacent free space in memory), `realloc()` will instead allocate a new block in a different part of the memory pool; copy over all of the old data to the new, bigger block; and return the address of that new block.

This means that upon success, `realloc()` returns the address of the resized memory block. This address might be identical to the one you passed in as parameter, but it doesn't have to be. Upon failure, `realloc()` returns the NULL pointer instead.

This example program asks the user for an arbitrary number of integers. The program stops asking as soon as the number zero or a letter is entered. The application will begin by assuming that a certain amount of memory is required to store these values. Once that amount of memory is used, more memory is requested using `realloc()`. Finally, all the numbers will be sorted (using the C library's `qsort()` function) and printed.

To grow a dynamically allocated array:

1. Create a new file or project in your text editor or IDE.

2. Type the standard beginning lines of code (**Script 10.4**):

```
/* resize.c - Script 10.4 */
#include <stdio.h>
#include <stdlib.h>
```

continues in two pages

```
1    /* resize.c - Script 10.4 */
2
3    #include <stdio.h>
4    #include <stdlib.h>
5
6    /* Function prototype for the sort
     → comparison function. */
7    int sort(const void *x, const void *y);
8
9    int main (void) {
10
11       /* Define an integer pointer
     → variable. */
12       int *numbers;
13
14       /* Define an integer to hold the
     → user's input read
15        * with scanf(). Define another one
     → to hold the
16        * return value of scanf(). */
17       int input, result;
18
19       /* Define an integer to hold the
     → current size of the
20        * dynamically growing array, another
     → one to hold the
21        * index of the next free array
     → element, and a for loop index
22        * counter. */
23       int  size = 4, i, index = 0;
24
25       /* Allocate the integer array to
     → its initial size. */
26       numbers = malloc(size * sizeof(int));
27
28       /* Again note that we have left out
     → the check for NULL. */
29
```

continues on next page

Script 10.4 This more complex example sorts a list of submitted integers. The `realloc()` function can resize a block of memory, where the submitted integers are stored.

```
                                              Script
30      /* Enter an infinite loop that will be left as soon
31       * as the user types the number zero or a non-digit
32       * character. */
33      while (1) {
34
35          /* Prompt the user for input and read a number
36           * using scanf. */
37          printf("Enter a non-zero integer (or 0 to quit): ");
38          result = scanf("%d", &input);
39
40          /* If the number entered was zero, or if it
41           * was not a number at all, leave the infinite
42           * loop using the break statement. */
43          if (result < 1 || input == 0) break;
44
45          /* Before we store the number in our integer array,
46           * check to see if there is any room left. If there
47           * isn't, call realloc() to dynamically grow it. */
48          if (index == size) {
49              size *= 1.5;
50              numbers = realloc(numbers, size * sizeof(int));
51              printf("Reallocation of the memory block. The size is now %d bytes.\n", size);
52          }
53
54          /* Store the new number into the next free slot. */
55          numbers[index] = input;
56
57          /* Increment the index so it indicates the next slot
58           * to be used for the next number. */
59          index++;
60
61      } /* End of while loop body. */
62
63
64      /* At this point we have terminated the infinite
65       * loop. Now use the qsort() function to sort
66       * the numbers in the array into ascending order. */
67      qsort(numbers, index, sizeof(int), sort);
68
```

continues on next page

Script 10.4 *continued*

RESIZING A BLOCK OF MEMORY

3. Add a function prototype for the sort()
function:

```
int sort(const void *x, const void
→ *y);
```

This function assists the qsort() function.

4. Begin the main function:

```
int main (void) {
```

5. Define an integer pointer variable:

```
int *numbers;
```

This pointer variable will hold the base
address of the dynamically allocated
integer array.

6. Define two integers:

```
int input, result;
```

These two integers will hold the user's
input and the return value of the scanf()
function, respectively.

7. Define three more integers:

```
int size = 4, i, index = 0;
```

The size variable will hold the current
size of the dynamically growing array
(the initial size will be 4 elements). The i
variable is a loop counter. The index integer
will track the next free element in the
dynamically growing array.

8. Allocate memory for the integer array:

```
numbers = malloc(size * sizeof(int));
```

Since sizeof(int) is 4 on most machines
and the program starts with 4 elements,
this will allocate a memory block of
16 bytes.

Again, note the missing check for the
NULL return address. You must always
add checks for NULL pointers in your
programs; only authors of C books
may omit them in their examples...

```
69
70      /* Print the numbers in a loop. */
71      for (i = 0; i < index; i++) {
72          printf("The value indexed at %d
→ is %d.\n", i, numbers[i]);
73      }
74
75
76      /* Return the block to the pool. */
77      free(numbers);
78      numbers = NULL;
79
80      /* Pause and wait for input before
→ terminating. */
81      getchar();
82      getchar();
83
84      return 0;
85  } /* End of main() function. */
86
87
88  /* This is a sort comparison function used
89   * by the standard C library function
→ qsort().
90   * See the documentation for your C
→ library for
91   * details. */
92  int sort(const void *x, const void *y) {
93
94      const int *a = x, *b = y;
95
96      if (*a < *b) {
97          return -1;
98      } else if (*a > *b) {
99          return 1;
100     }
101
102     return 0;
103
104 } /* End of sort() function. */
```

Script 10.4 *continued*

Figure 10.7 The user is prompted, indicating what kind of information is requested (a nonzero integer) and how to stop the process (by entering 0).

9. Enter an infinite `while` loop:

   ```
   while (1) {
   ```

   This loop conditional will always be true, making this an infinite loop. This is desired, however, as the loop should be entered at least once (which requires a true condition) and the loop itself includes an escape mechanism (Step 11).

10. During every loop iteration, prompt the user for input and read a number using `scanf()`:

    ```
    printf("Enter a non-zero integer
    → (or 0 to quit): ");
    result = scanf("%d", &input);
    ```

    There is no \n in the prompt string because we want the number entered by the user to line up with the prompt and not on a new line (**Figure 10.7**).

    You have seen `scanf()` before. The format string states to look for an integer number in the user's input. If found, `scanf()` stores it in the integer variable `input`, whose address is passed as an argument. The `scanf()` function returns the number of items successfully read from the user as its result, and that number gets stored into the `result` variable for a check in the next step.

11. Check both the `scanf()` result and the input value, breaking out of the infinite `while` loop if either one is 0:

    ```
    if (result < 1 || input == 0) break;
    ```

    If `result` is 0, it means that the user has entered a non-numeric character that did not satisfy the %d match pattern given to `scanf()` in Step 10. This would apply if the user entered a letter, for example.

    If `input` is 0, it means that the user did input a number, but it was 0.

    continues on next page

RESIZING A BLOCK OF MEMORY

Both cases mean that the user has indicated there are no more numbers to enter so the break statement will exit the while loop. The double pipe (which represents OR) is used to say that if either of those conditions is true, the entire condition is true.

12. Check if there is room left in the dynamically allocated integer array:

```
if (index == size) {
```

index is the array index of the element in which the number that was just read has to be stored. size is the current number of available elements in the array. If index is equal to the current size, the array is already too small because index starts at 0 and the array element with that index does not yet exist.

In this case, the array has to be resized, which is what happens in the if body. If there is still enough room (if index does not equal size), the array stays the way it is and execution proceeds in Step 15.

13. Add the code for resizing the memory block:

```
size *= 1.5;
numbers = realloc(numbers, size *
→ sizeof(int));
printf("Reallocation of the memory
→ block. The size is now %d
→ bytes.\n", size);
```

The first line recalculates the value of size by making it 50 percent bigger. The second line reallocates memory, increasing the reserved block from its current size to size * sizeof(int) bytes. For safety's sake, you should assign the returned realloc() value to another pointer and validate that (see the sidebar) rather than directly assign this to numbers. In the interest of simplicity, this step has been omitted.

RESIZING A BLOCK OF MEMORY

Remember, the `size` variable keeps track of the number of array elements, but `realloc()` operates in bytes, so you have to multiply the new `size` value times `sizeof(int)`.

Finally, a message is printed letting you know that reallocation has taken place.

14. Close the `if` body:

```
}
```

15. Store the number entered by the user in the memory block:

```
numbers[index] = input;
```

This will store the inputted number in the next free array element, whether or not the array was just resized.

Note how you are using the array subscript operator even though `numbers` is not an array name but actually a pointer variable.

16. Increment the array index for the next number:

```
index++;
```

17. Close the `while` loop body:

```
}
```

18. Sort the numbers in the array:

```
qsort(numbers, index, sizeof(int),
→ sort);
```

At this point the `while` loop has terminated and there is a set of numbers stored in memory. Those are sorted using the standard C library's `qsort()` function. See the documentation for your C library for more information about its usage.

continues on next page

RESIZING A BLOCK OF MEMORY

19. Print the sorted numbers:

```
for (i = 0; i < index; i++) {
→ printf("The value indexed at %d
→ is %d.\n", i, numbers[i]);
}
```

This final loop prints the sorted array of numbers. It uses the i counter variable, counting up to index, the number of items stored in the array.

20. Return the memory block to the pool using the free() function:

```
free(numbers);
numbers = NULL;
```

21. Complete the main function:

```
        getchar();
        getchar();
        return 0;
}
```

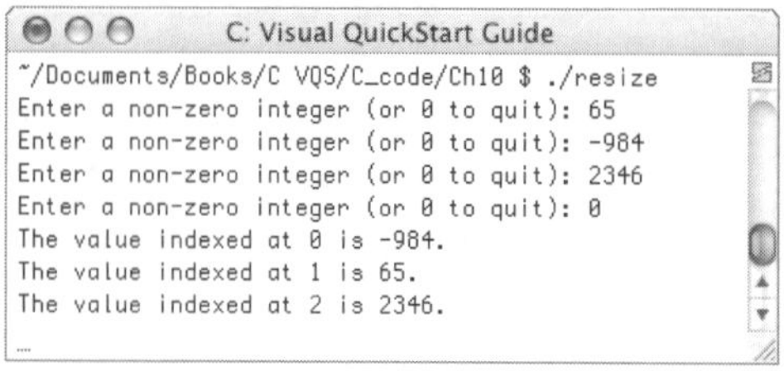

Figure 10.8 The program can sort an arbitrary amount of numbers.

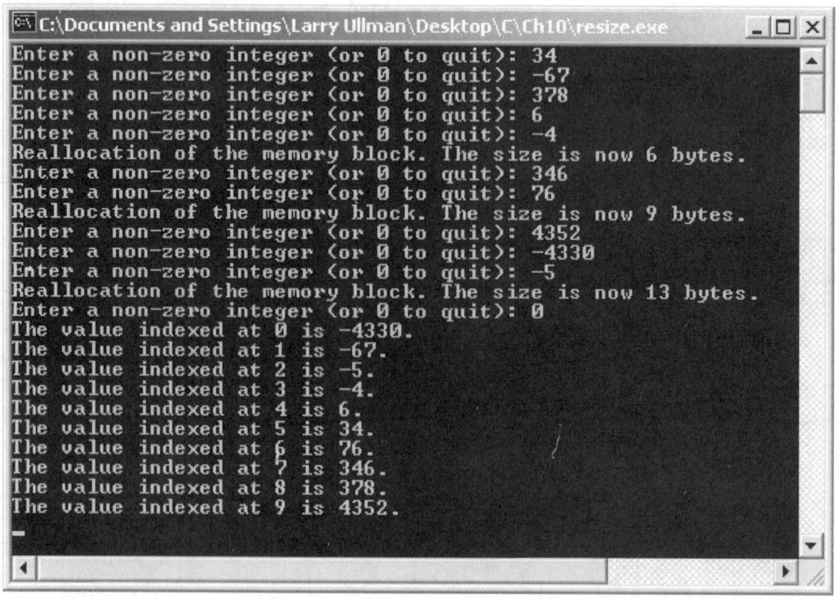

Figure 10.9 If more numbers are entered than there is currently room for, more memory is requested. There is no way to do what this program does without dynamic memory.

22. Add the sort() function:

```
int sort(const void *x, const void
→ *y) {
    const int *a = x, *b = y;
    if (*a < *b) {
            return -1;
    } else if (*a > *b) {
            return 1;
    }
    return 0;
}
```

The sort() function assists the standard C library's qsort() function in sorting the array. It is called repeatedly with two addresses of two values of the array.

Its job is to compare the two values stored at those addresses and then return -1, 0, or 1 depending on whether the first value is smaller than, equal to, or larger than the second value.

Again, see the documentation of your C library for more details.

23. Save the file as *resize.c*, compile, and debug as necessary.

24. Run the application (**Figure 10.8**).

Enter a few numbers, and then enter 0. You should get a sorted list of your numbers, and if you type enough numbers you should get occasional messages reporting that the array was just resized (**Figure 10.9**).

✔ Tips

■ With realloc(), you can not only grow but also shrink a block of memory to a smaller size than the initial value.

■ The realloc() function is a valuable tool that can help you keep fixed limits out of your code. It might take a bit more work to use it than an array whose maximum size you estimate when you write your program, but you will never have to go back to change and recompile the code because your guess about the space requirement for some array was wrong.

■ If you do use realloc(), make sure that you always keep the correct current size of the memory block around in a variable (for which the above example uses the size variable). You need this to check your space requirements during program execution and to trigger the expansion of the block as required. You cannot use sizeof() or any other portable tool to get the current size of a block.

Returning Memory from a Function

Another common use of dynamic memory involves returning pointers to memory blocks from a function. This is especially important when you're working with external libraries written by someone else.

Without this technique, the only things you can return from a function to the calling code are simple scalar values, such as an integer, a floating-point number, or a character. You cannot return more than one value or more complex data structures, like arrays.

This is why you need dynamic memory if you want to return something other than a simple value: you can allocate a block of memory in the function using `malloc()`, fill the block with something useful, and return the pointer to the block to the main part of the application, which can then use the data and free the memory as soon as it is no longer needed. The following example will demonstrate this concept:

To allocate and return memory from a function:

1. Create a new file or project in your text editor or IDE.

2. Type the standard beginning lines of code (**Script 10.5**):

   ```
   /* function.c - Script 10.5 */
   #include <stdio.h>
   #include <stdlib.h>
   #include <assert.h>
   ```

   Note the inclusion of the *assert.h* header file, which defines the `assert()` macro introduced a bit later.

```
1    /* function.c - Script 10.5 */
2
3    #include <stdio.h>
4    #include <stdlib.h>
5    #include <assert.h>
6
7    char *get_name(void); /* Function
     → prototype. */
8
9    int main (void) {
10
11       /* Define a char pointer variable
12        * to hold the base address of an
     → array of
13        * chars, i.e. a string. */
14       char *name = NULL;
15
16       /* Call the subroutine and store
     → the address
17        * value it returns in the pointer
     → variable. */
18       name = get_name();
19
20       /* Check for success and abort upon
     → failure. */
21       assert(name != NULL);
22
23       /* Print the name value. */
24       printf("The entered name was: %s.\n",
     → name);
25
26       /* Return the block to the pool. */
27       free(name);
28       name = NULL;
29
30       /* Pause and wait for input before
     → terminating. */
31       getchar();
```

continues on next page

Script 10.5 This function allocates a block of memory and returns it. The calling code must then free the block.

```
32        getchar();
33
34        return 0;
35    } /* End of main() function. */
36
37
38    /* This function asks for a name
   → and returns
39     * a pointer to the character array with
   → the name. */
40    char *get_name(void) {
41
42        /* Allocate a memory block 100 bytes
   → long. */
43        char *input = malloc(100);
44
45        /* Check if the allocation succeeded.
   → */
46        if (input == NULL) {
47            printf("Unable to allocate
   → memory!\n");
48            return NULL;
49        }
50
51        /* Prompt the user for input. */
52        printf("Enter your name: ");
53
54        /* Store the input in the memory
   → block. */
55        scanf("%99s", input);
56
57        /* Return the address of the memory
   → block. */
58        return input;
59
60    } /* End of get_name() function. */
```

Script 10.5 *continued*

3. Add a function prototype to declare the function you will call from the `main()` routine:

   `char *get_name(void);`

   This definition states that the `get_name()` function takes no arguments (indicated by the void) and that it returns a `char` pointer.

4. Begin the `main` function:

   `int main (void) {`

5. Define a `char` pointer variable and initialize it with the `NULL` pointer value:

   `char *name = NULL;`

   A `char` pointer variable is the usual type to store addresses of text strings, which is what the `get_name()` function returns. Initializing pointer variables to `NULL` is a good practice that can help you catch errors in your program. If you do not initialize a pointer variable to `NULL`, it can initially point to an unpredictable location in memory.

6. Call the `get_name()` function and store the address it returns in the pointer variable:

   `name = get_name();`

   As you'll see, the `get_name()` function returns a character pointer, whose value will be assigned to `name`.

continues on next page

RETURNING MEMORY FROM A FUNCTION

7. Check the return value to make sure that you did get a valid address:

```
assert(name != NULL);
```

`assert()` is a macro that makes it convenient to embed short checks into your program code. If the condition in the parentheses is not true, then the program will abort immediately with an error message (**Figure 10.10**). In English, this line of code says *Confirm that name does not equal NULL*.

This is not the best and most user-friendly way to handle an error condition, but it works well in short programs and doesn't require you to type a lot of code. It is best used to check for failures that are not likely to occur.

8. Print the string returned by the function:

```
printf("The entered name was: %s.
 ⇢ \n", name);
```

9. Return the memory block to the pool using the `free()` function:

```
free(name);
name = NULL;
```

10. Complete the main function:

```
        getchar();
        getchar();
        return 0;
} /* End of main() function. */
```

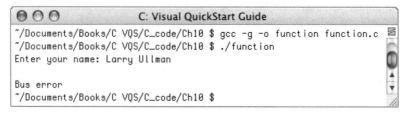

Figure 10.10 The `assert()` macro is an easy way to report upon errors, although it's not very user-friendly.

Figure 10.11 The user is prompted to enter his or her name.

11. Begin the get_name() function:

```
char *get_name(void) {
```

This definition matches the function prototype.

12. Define a character pointer variable and immediately initialize it with the address returned by a call to malloc():

```
char *input = malloc(100);
```

This will allocate space in memory for 100 consecutive char items starting at the address returned by malloc().

13. Check the return value to make sure you did get a valid address:

```
if (input == NULL) {
    printf("Unable to allocate
→ memory!\n");
    return NULL;
}
```

If the allocation fails, then the get_name() function cannot continue. In such a case, the function has to abort and should communicate its failure to the calling code. It does this by returning the NULL pointer value, just as malloc() returned the NULL pointer value to get_name(). This is a very common way to indicate failure for functions that return an address. You will see this pattern a lot in C programs.

14. Prompt the user for input and collect the input using scanf():

```
printf("Enter your name: ");
scanf("%99s", input);
```

As usual with prompt strings, there is no \n and therefore no line break, so the user's input appears on the same line as the prompt (**Figure 10.11**).

continues on next page

scanf()'s pattern (%99s) says that it should store up to 99 characters entered by the user. scanf() stores these characters plus the trailing null byte in the memory block pointed to by the input pointer variable.

15. Return the value of input:

```
return input;
```

The memory block is now filled with the user's input. This should be returned by the calling function. Keep in mind that the function is actually returning the starting address where input is stored, not the actual string value itself.

Note that there is no free() statement in this function. Instead, it is the calling code's responsibility to free the memory when it is finished with the contents of the block, which is the whole point of this example.

16. Save the file as *function.c,* compile, and debug as necessary.

17. Run the application (**Figure 10.12**).

✔ Tip

■ In this scenario where the malloc() and the free() calls are not in the same function, it is especially important to make sure that the block is indeed freed when it is no longer used. If you use a third-party library function you didn't write yourself, read its documentation carefully to make sure all dynamic memory blocks are properly accounted for.

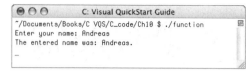

Figure 10.12 The memory for the name was allocated in a subroutine and passed back to the caller.

RETURNING MEMORY FROM A FUNCTION

Why You Shouldn't Return Pointers to Local Variables

At the end of Chapter 7, we discussed the concept of variable scope: functions have their own variables, which are only available within that function. These variables are called *local* variables. In Chapter 9, you saw that you can use pointers to alter a local variable's value in another function, which is one way to circumvent scope.

It should be clarified, however, that a function should never return pointers to a its own local variables. The only kind of pointer you may safely return from a function is the base address of a block of dynamically allocated memory.

For example, the following function is declared as returning a pointer to a character array (a string):

```
char *get_name(void) {
    char name[100];
    // Put some data into name.
    return name; // Wrong!
}
```

When the return statement of this function is reached, the name array has been filled with some useful data. The intention here is to return the array's base address to the calling code (the main part of the application that called this function) so that the main application can use the data.

The problem with this is that the array holding the data is a local variable that ceases to exist at the end of the function, right after the return statement is executed. The space in memory occupied by the array during the execution of the function will be reused for other purposes after the function returns. The address returned does still point to a valid location in memory, but there is no longer an array at that location.

The same is true for any kind of local variable. Pointers to local variables are only valid until a function stops executing.

RETURNING MEMORY FROM A FUNCTION

Avoiding Memory Leaks

You already read that it is an error if a block of memory is allocated but never returned to the pool. Such a block will be freed only when the program terminates. If the program runs for a long time and continuously allocates new blocks while forgetting to give old unused blocks back to the pool, then the program will run out of memory at some point, causing subsequent malloc() requests to fail.

If a program has such a bug, it is said to have a *memory leak*, because the pool of available memory has a leak in it (**Figure 10.13**).

The address returned by malloc() is the only way to access the memory block, and it is also the only way to hand it back to the pool, using the free() function:

```
void *x;
x = malloc (1000);
free(x);
x = NULL;
```

This means that if this address value (stored in x) is lost, a memory leak has occurred.

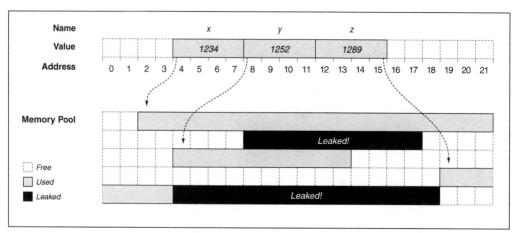

Figure 10.13 Memory leaks occur when reserved blocks are not freed by an application, thereby limiting the amount of available memory.

AVOIDING MEMORY LEAKS

The address value can be lost in many ways, for example by being overwritten in a pointer variable:

```
void *x;
x = malloc(3000); // block 1
x = malloc(4000); // block 2
free(x);
x = NULL;
```

After the second `malloc()` call, the result of the first call—the address of block 1—is lost because the only copy of this address was stored in x, which has been overwritten with the address of the second block. The second block can be returned to the pool using `free(x)`, but the first block cannot be freed because its address is no longer known. This is one cause for a memory leak.

Memory leaks can also occur if a pointer variable holding the block's address does not have the proper scope:

```
void foo(void) {
    void *x;
    x = malloc(1000);
}
```

When this `foo()` function terminates, the pointer variable x goes out of scope, which means it no longer exists and its value is lost. There are two ways to prevent such a leak.

The first option is to call `free()` with x as a parameter, inserted somewhere before the final `return` statement:

```
void foo(void) {
    void *x;
    x = malloc(1000);
    free(x);
    x = NULL;
    return;
}
```

The second possibility is to return the address to the function's caller, as the *function.c* example did.

✔ Tips

- Memory leaks are very common in C programs. You have to be careful about where memory is allocated and freed in your own code, but you also have to study the documentation for any third-party libraries of code you use. The use of external libraries is common in C, so you should understand the memory management philosophy or style of such external libraries. Sometimes they even have memory leak bugs themselves.

- Some programmers recommend writing the malloc() and free() statements at the same time as you program, or at least insert reminder source code comments. You're less likely to forget the free() call this way.

- Because memory management errors are so common, there are many tools to find them in your C programs. Check the documentation of your standard C library for hints. Often, special versions of the malloc() and free() functions are available, or you can use external settings that cause these functions to emit special diagnostic messages.

Memory Scope

Variables and arrays (static memory) have a scope, the part of your program in which they can be used. Usually the scope is the body of the function in which they were defined, main() or any one of your subroutines. If defined outside any function, they have global scope, which means that they can be used across all functions in your program. Still, you should avoid global variables if possible because they can lead to hard-to-debug and incorrect code.

Dynamic memory does not have a scope. Once allocated, it can be used anywhere in your program where the address of the memory block is available. Because there is no scope for dynamic memory, you have to track its usage yourself and give it back to the system as soon as it is no longer used.

Note that the *pointer variables* holding the addresses of blocks of dynamically allocated memory do have a scope that can end, leading to a memory leak unless the block is freed first or there is another copy of the address value.

Working with Strings

In Chapter 6, "Working with Arrays," you learned how to use character arrays as strings. But with C you can also handle strings by using pointers. You saw one example of this at the end of the previous chapter.

In this chapter you'll first learn more about these two ways of creating strings (as arrays and as pointers). Then you'll begin working with the many string functions found in the *string.h* C library file. To understand and use these functions, you'll run through a series of exercises, some of which merely demonstrate a concept, and others that show real-world uses of the ideas.

Basic String Pointer Syntax

A character string is a type of array, each element containing a specific character and terminating with the \0 character. The code

```c
char name[] = "Marc";
```

requires 5 bytes of memory, since a single character in C requires 1 byte.

In Chapter 9, "Working with Pointers," you saw that an array's name can also act as a pointer to that array's address. The following code works fine, demonstrating two different uses of the same name array (**Figure 11.1**):

```c
char name[] = "Marc";
printf ("String: %s \nPointer: %p",
name, name);
```

The name example adds little benefit to your C programs; however, in a multidimensional character array, using pointers can save lots of space. Take, for example, this code:

```c
char name[2][9] = {
"Marc",
"Liyanage"
};
```

Figure 11.1 Character arrays can be printed as strings or as pointers.

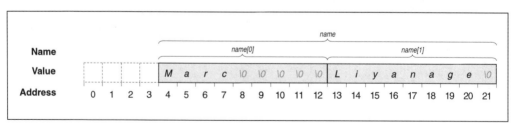

Figure 11.2 A multidimensional character array must have subarrays of equal length, possibly requiring blocks of memory to store extra \0 values.

The name array will require 18 bytes of memory (**Figure 11.2**), as each subarray (*Marc* and *Liyanage*) must be of the same length. By using pointers, you can make *ragged* arrays: an array of character pointers whose values are strings of varying length. The syntax for rewriting name as a character pointer array is

```
char *name[2] = {"Marc", "Liyanage"};
```

In essence, name is now an array consisting of two character pointers. Each pointer contains the address of a string stored in memory (**Figure 11.3**).

In this first example, you'll use C preprocessor directives to help create a multidimensional character array and an array of character pointers. Although this example won't do anything, we will build on in the next example, which will reveal the memory difference between the two.

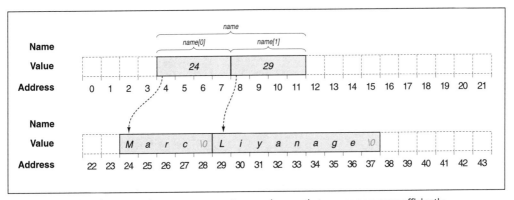

Figure 11.3 By using character pointers, you can create ragged arrays that use memory more efficiently.

To work with string pointers:

1. Create a new file or project in your text editor or IDE.

2. Type the standard beginning lines of code (**Script 11.1**):

```
/* ragged.c - Script 11.1 */
#include <stdio.h>
```

3. Define a constant macro:

```
#define CHAPTER0 "Introduction"
```

The arrays we are building in this example will store the titles of the first five chapters of this book, including the introduction. Rather than having to type each of these twice (once for each array), we will use directives.

4. Define the other chapters:

```
#define CHAPTER1 "Getting Started
→ with C"
#define CHAPTER2 "Introduction to
→ Data Types"
#define CHAPTER3 "Working with
→ Numbers"

#define CHAPTER4 "Control Structures"
```

The double quotation marks are required around each title (they are part of the definition itself), but you should not conclude each directive with semicolons, since they're not C code.

Feel free to type the rest of the chapters in from the table of contents if you aren't satisfied with just the five!

5. Begin the main function:

```
int main (void) {
```

6. Define a multidimensional character array:

```
char chapters[5][27] = {CHAPTER0,
→ CHAPTER1, CHAPTER2, CHAPTER3,
→ CHAPTER4};
```

```
 1    /* ragged.c - Script 11.1 */
 2
 3    #include <stdio.h>
 4
 5    /* Set the different chapter titles as
   → constant macros. */
 6    #define CHAPTER0 "Introduction"
 7    #define CHAPTER1 "Getting Started with C"
 8    #define CHAPTER2 "Introduction to Data
   → Types"
 9    #define CHAPTER3 "Working with Numbers"
10    #define CHAPTER4 "Control Structures"
11
12    int main (void) {
13
14        /* Create a multi-dimensional
   → character array. */
15        char chapters[5][27] = {CHAPTER0,
   → CHAPTER1, CHAPTER2, CHAPTER3,
   → CHAPTER4};
16
17        /* Create an array of character
   → pointers. */
18        char *chapters_ptr[5] = {CHAPTER0,
   → CHAPTER1, CHAPTER2, CHAPTER3,
   → CHAPTER4};
19
20        /* Print the memory requirements of
   → each variable. */
21        printf ("The chapters array uses %zu
   → bytes of memory.\n", sizeof(chapters));
22        printf ("The chapters_ptr array uses
   → %zu bytes of memory.\n",
   → sizeof(chapters_ptr));
23
24        getchar();
25        return 0;
26    }
```

Script 11.1 Using C preprocessor directives to minimize typing, this program defines two arrays that store the same values in different ways. The memory requirements of each variable are then printed.

This is a multidimensional array of five elements, each element containing a string 27 characters long. That number comes from the number of characters in the longest chapter title, plus one for the end-of-string character.

The proper syntax for creating this array will be in place after the C preprocessor does its thing. The C code will then look like this:

```
char chapters[5][27] = {
→ "Introduction", "Getting Started
→ with C", "Introduction to Data
→ Types", "Working with Numbers",
→ "Control Structures" };
```

7. Define an array of character pointers:

```
char *chapters_ptr[5] = {CHAPTER0,
→ CHAPTER1, CHAPTER2, CHAPTER3,
→ CHAPTER4};
```

An array of character pointers is defined using different syntax. The number of elements is still defined (5), but each element's value is more flexibly set.

8. Print the memory usage of both variables:

```
printf ("The chapters array uses %zu
→ bytes of memory.\n",
→ sizeof(chapters));
printf ("The chapters_ptr array uses
→ %zu bytes of memory.\n",
→ sizeof(chapters_ptr));
```

The sizeof() function (or operator) is used to print the memory usage of the two different arrays. Each print statement uses the %zu signifier, corresponding to the type of value returned by sizeof() (you'll learn more about this in the next section).

continues on next page

BASIC STRING POINTER SYNTAX

9. Complete the main function:

```
getchar();
return 0;
}
```

10. Save the file as *ragged.c*, compile, and debug as necessary.

11. Run the application (**Figure 11.4**).

✔ Tips

■ As Figure 11.4 shows, the chapters variable requires 135 bytes of memory. This number is equal to 5 (the number of array elements) times 27 (the number of characters in each array). By definition, a single character requires 1 byte of memory.

■ In addition to having the potential for unnecessary memory usage, regular arrays are limited to a fixed length. On the other hand, pointer character arrays can adapt to longer strings during the running of the application.

■ The memory usage of the chapters_ptr variable indicated in Figure 11.4 is deceptive. That's not the total usage for the values the pointers refer to, but rather the memory usage of the pointers themselves (4 bytes each times 5 elements). Remember that pointers require some space in memory along with the memory required for the values to which the pointers point.

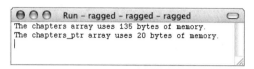

Figure 11.4 Two methods for storing several strings are used and their respective memory requirements are indicated. In the next example, however, you'll see why the second memory listing isn't quite accurate.

BASIC STRING POINTER SYNTAX

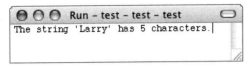

Figure 11.5 The strlen() function does not count a string's terminating \0 character.

Finding the Length of a String

In the previous example, the sizeof() operator was used to determine the memory requirements of a variable. But what if you wanted to just count the number of characters in a string? For that, you can use the appropriately named strlen() function (short for *string length*):

```
num = strlen(my_string);
```

Note that this function does not count the terminating \0 character that concludes every string. For example (**Figure 11.5**):

```
char my_string[] = "Larry";

printf("The string '%s' has %d
→ characters.", my_string,
→ strlen(my_string));
```

Despite the value returned by strlen(), my_string requires 6 bytes of memory since it contains 6 characters: *L, a, r, r, y,* and *\0.*

By using the strlen() function, in conjunction with some loops and arithmetic, you can calculate the actual character count and memory requirements of the arrays in *ragged.c.*

To determine the length of a string:

1. Open *ragged.c* in your text editor or IDE.

2. Add a C preprocessor directive including the *string.h* header file (**Script 11.2**):

   ```
   #include <string.h>
   ```

   To use the `strlen()` function, along with many of the other functions being used in this chapter, you must include the *string.h* header file, where that macro is defined.

3. After the definition of the two arrays, define three integer variables:

   ```
   int i;
   int chapters_count = 0, ptr_count = 0;
   ```

   The first variable, i, will be a for loop counter. The next two variables will be used to total up the number of characters and bytes required by the two arrays.

4. After the original print statements, use a loop to calculate the total length of the strings:

   ```
   for (i = 0; i < 5; ++i) {
       chapters_count +=
   → strlen(chapters[i]);
   }
   ```

   Although the chapters array uses 135 bytes of memory, we'd like to determine how many characters it actually contains. The strlen() function will do this. The loop will go through each subarray of chapters, adding that string's character count to the total.

FINDING THE LENGTH OF A STRING

```
● ● ●                    Script
1    /* length.c - Script 11.2 - rewrite of
     → ragged.c (Script 11.1) */

2

3    #include <stdio.h>

4    #include <string.h>

5

6    /* Set the different chapter titles as
     → constant macros. */

7    #define CHAPTER0 "Introduction"

8    #define CHAPTER1 "Getting Started with C"

9    #define CHAPTER2 "Introduction to
     → Data Types"

10   #define CHAPTER3 "Working with Numbers"

11   #define CHAPTER4 "Control Structures"

12

13   int main (void) {

14

15       /* Create a multi-dimensional
         → character array. */

16       char chapters[5][27] = {CHAPTER0,
         → CHAPTER1, CHAPTER2, CHAPTER3, CHAPTER4};

17

18       /* Create an array of character
         → pointers. */

19       char *chapters_ptr[5] = {CHAPTER0,
         → CHAPTER1, CHAPTER2, CHAPTER3, CHAPTER4};

20

21       /* Declare three integers. */

22       int i; /* Loop counter. */

23       int chapters_count = 0, ptr_count = 0;
         → /* Character counters. */

24

25       /* Print the memory requirements of
         → each variable. */

26       printf ("The chapters array uses %zu
         → bytes of memory.\n", sizeof(chapters));

27       printf ("The chapters_ptr array uses
         → %zu bytes of memory.\n",
         → sizeof(chapters_ptr));

28
```

continues on next page

Script 11.2 The space requirements of the two variables are calculated using the sizeof() and strlen() functions.

```
29        /* Determine the total string length.
  → */
30        for (i = 0; i < 5; ++i) {
31            chapters_count +=
  → strlen(chapters[i]);
32        }
33
34        /* Print the number of characters. */
35        printf ("The chapters array contains
  → %d characters.\n", chapters_count);
36
37        /* Calculate the memory being used
  → by the pointer array. */
38        ptr_count = sizeof(chapters_ptr) +
  → chapters_count + 5; /* Pointer size
  → plus number of characters plus 5 (for
  → the \0). */
39
40        /* Print that result. */
41        printf ("The chapters_ptr array -
  → actually- uses %d bytes of memory.\n",
  → ptr_count);
42
43        getchar();
44        return 0;
45    }
```

Script 11.2 *continued*

5. Print the total string length:

```
printf ("The chapters array contains
  → %d characters.\n", chapters_count);
```

6. Calculate the amount of memory being used by the pointer array and its values:

```
ptr_count = sizeof(chapters_ptr) +
  → chapters_count + 5;
```

Determining the amount of actual memory being used by the pointer array requires a little math and some understanding of how C works. To start with, the `sizeof(chapters_ptr)` chunk will return the memory used for the pointers themselves, which we know is 20 bytes. To this we add the previously determined character count, since each character being stored requires 1 byte. Finally, 5 more bytes are added, representing the terminating \0 character for each string, which were not counted by `strlen()`.

7. Print the amount of actual memory being used:

```
printf ("The chapters_ptr array -
  → actually- uses %d bytes of
  → memory.\n", ptr_count);
```

8. Save the file as *length.c*, compile, and debug as necessary.

continues on next page

FINDING THE LENGTH OF A STRING

9. Run the application (**Figure 11.6**).

✔ Tips

■ The sizeof() function returns a value of type size_t, a special type in C. It's defined as whatever type the sizeof operator returns (which makes sense, in a circular way). Thus, size_t could be an unsigned integer, an unsigned long integer, and so forth. You can print this value using the %z modifier, so %zu represents an unsigned size_t value.

■ Given the fact that all arrays are indexed beginning at 0 and the fact that strings are terminated by a \0 character, it's very easy to improperly refer to a string element. Use the strlen() function and C preprocessor directives to help avoid indexing mistakes.

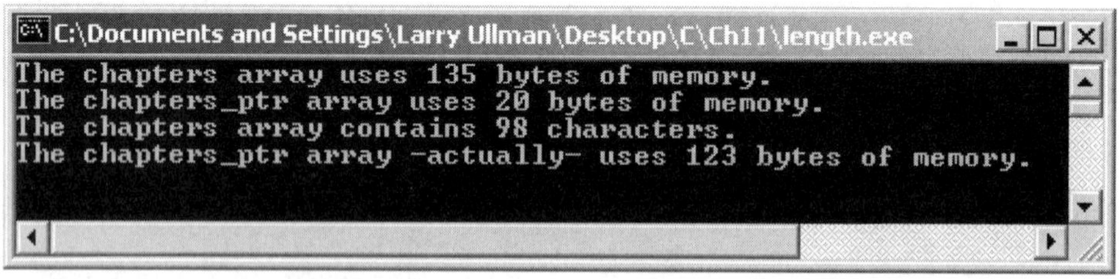

Figure 11.6 This example shows how a specific character array requires 135 bytes of memory to store 98 characters. Using a pointer array, those same 98 characters can be stored using only 123 bytes.

FINDING THE LENGTH OF A STRING

Connecting Strings (Concatenation)

Concatenation is the process of appending one string onto another. It's kind of like addition for words. To perform concatenation, you use the strncat() function:

```
strncat(string1, string2, length);
```

This function will append the value of string2 onto the end of string1. It will append up to *length* number of characters. This *length* value should correspond to the remaining space in string1. For example:

```
char string1[25] = "Mary had a ";
char string2[] = "little lamb.";
strncat(string1, string2, 13);
```

It's very important that you don't try to add more characters to a string than it has room for (see the sidebar), so you'll want to take special precautions before performing concatenation. This next example creates a full name variable from the combination of a person's submitted first and last names.

strn* Functions and Overflow

In earlier C standards, the available string functions were strcat(), strcpy(), and so forth. The problem with these functions is that they allowed for a *buffer overflow*, a serious programming flaw. Overflow occurs when more data is assigned to a memory block than the memory block has room for.

For example, if you define a character array as being 10 characters long and try to assign 12 characters to it, C will write the 2 extra characters to subsequent memory blocks. In other words, the data overflows the original variable's memory allotment.

The new versions of these functions all begin with *strn*: strncat(), strncpy(), etc. Each of these takes a third argument: a number. The number argument dictates how many characters in the second variable should be added or copied or whatever to the first. By ensuring that this number corresponds to the amount of available memory allotted to that variable, you can avoid overflow problems.

While you still might see the *str** functions in some C code, using the *strn** versions is preferable.

To perform concatenation:

1. Create a new file or project in your text editor or IDE.

2. Type the standard beginning lines of code (**Script 11.3**):

   ```
   /* concat.c - Script 11.3 */
   #include <stdio.h>
   ```

3. Include the *string.h* header:

   ```
   #include <string.h>
   ```

   This application makes use of both the strcat() and strncat() functions, defined in this *string.h* file.

4. Define the maximum variable size:

   ```
   #define VARSIZE 50
   ```

   By setting this value—which will be used to define the character arrays—as a constant, we can use it repeatedly in the application to help avoid buffer overflow problems.

5. Begin the main function:

   ```
   int main (void) {
   ```

6. Define two character arrays:

   ```
   char name[VARSIZE];
   char last_name[VARSIZE];
   ```

   The name variable will, in the end, contain the user's entire name. The last_name value will be read in separately and appended to name. Both are of VARSIZE length.

7. Prompt for and read in the user's first name:

   ```
   printf("Enter your first name: ");
   scanf("%48s", name);
   ```

```
1   /* concat.c - Script 11.3 */
2
3   #include <stdio.h>
4   #include <string.h> /* For strcat() and
    → strncat(). */
5
6   #define VARSIZE 50
7
8   int main (void) {
9
10      /* Two name character arrays. */
11      char name[VARSIZE];
12      char last_name[VARSIZE];
13
14      /* Prompt for and read in the
    → first name. */
15      printf("Enter your first name: ");
16      scanf("%48s", name);
17
18      /* Prompt for and read in the last
    → name. */
19      printf("Enter your last name: ");
20      scanf("%49s", last_name);
21
22      /* Add a space. */
23      strcat(name, " ");
24
25      /* Append the last name. */
26      strncat(name, last_name, (VARSIZE - 1)
    → - strlen(name));
27
28      /* Print the result. */
29      printf("You entered your name as
    → %s.\n", name);
30
31      getchar();
32      getchar();
33      return 0;
34  }
```

Script 11.3 Using concatenation, one string (name) is appended with other string values.

The scanf() function will assign input from the keyboard to the name variable. It will read up to 48 characters or until it encounters a space. The 48 limit is imposed as 48 characters, plus the space added in Step 9 and the terminating \0 character, adds up to the 50-character limit for the string.

8. Prompt for and read in the user's last name:

```
printf("Enter your last name: ");
scanf("%49s", last_name);
```

The same process is repeated, this time initializing the last_name variable.

9. Using concatenation, add a space to the name variable.

```
strcat(name, " ");
```

Before appending the last name to the name variable, the script adds a space. If this step were omitted, the name variable would turn out to be something like *LarryUllman*.

In this case you can use the strcat() function instead of strncat(), since you know that exactly one character will be added to name and that the variable has room for it (because a maximum of 48 characters have been assigned already).

10. Append the last name value to the name variable:

```
strncat(name, last_name, (VARSIZE - 1)
→ - strlen(name));
```

Here the strncat() function is used to append a certain number of characters from last_name to name. The number of characters available is calculated by starting with the variable's maximum length and subtracting 1 (for the space), then subtracting the current number of characters already in name. This last number is returned by the strlen() function.

continues on next page

CONNECTING STRINGS (CONCATENATION)

11. Print the final name variable value:

```
printf("You entered your name as
→ %s.\n", name);
```

12. Complete the main function:

```
        getchar();
        getchar();
        return 0;
}
```

13. Save the file as *concat.c*, compile, and debug as necessary.

14. Run the application (**Figure 11.7**).

15. Run the application again, using different values (**Figure 11.8**).

✔ Tips

- Concatenation does not affect the value of the second string. It only alters the value of the first string.

- You can also perform concatenation using sprintf(), which formats a string. Defined in the *stdio.h* header file, the function works much like printf() but assigns the output to a string variable, rather than sending it to the standard output.

- If the sum total of a person's name exceeds the 50-character limit, some characters from the last name will not be appended to the name variable (**Figure 11.9**).

- You might think that this application should use first_name and last_name variables instead of name and last_name. But if you did that, once you appended last_name to first_name, first_name would no longer be an appropriate description of that variable.

- You could also define the name and last_name variables using different lengths, as long as the name size is larger than the size of last_name.

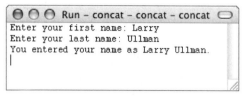

Figure 11.7 Concatenation is used to append the value of a person's last name onto the first name.

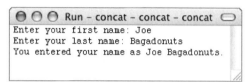

Figure 11.8 The application takes into account the amount of available space so that entering longer or shorter names shouldn't cause problems.

Figure 11.9 By limiting the number of characters involved with concatenation, the end result may seem strange but it won't create buffer overflows.

Comparing Strings

Comparing numbers is a very easy task, involving the standard comparison operators (==, <, >, <=, >=), but you cannot compare strings using them. Instead, there is the strncmp() function:

```
strcmp (string1, string2);
```

This function returns the value *0* if the two strings are the same and returns a nonzero value otherwise. Normally you'll want to use this as a condition in an if-else statement:

```
if (strcmp(string1, string2) == 0) {
    // The same!
} else {
    // Different!
}
```

Our next example creates a tough but functioning guessing game, where the user must guess a three-letter word.

Adjusting for Case

The example is this section—guessing a random three-letter word—is hard enough without trying to adjust for the case of the word. The strcmp() function is case sensitive, meaning that *Cat*, *cat*, and *CAT* do not match each other.

The easiest way to correct for this is to use the strcasecmp() function, which is a case-insensitive version of strcmp().

Another alternative is to convert both strings being compared to either upper or lower case. So *Cat*, *cat*, and *CAT* would all be turned into *cat* or *CAT*, depending upon your preference. You can do that by running every character in a string through either the toupper() or tolower() function, defined in the *ctype.h* file.

To compare two strings:

1. Create a new file or project in your text editor or IDE.

2. Type the standard beginning lines of code (**Script 11.4**):

```
/* guess.c - Script 11.4 */
#include <stdio.h>
```

3. Include the *string.h* header:

```
#include <string.h>
```

Since this application makes use of the `strcasecmp()` function, you must include the *string.h* file where it is defined.

4. Add a function prototype:

```
void discard_input (void);
```

Because this application relies so heavily on precise user input, it will utilize the `discard_input()` function, first defined in Chapter 7, "Creating Your Own Functions." This prototype indicates that the function takes no arguments and returns no values.

5. Begin the `main` function:

```
int main (void) {
```

6. Define two character arrays:

```
char guess[10];
const char answer[] = "coy";
```

The first array will store the user's guess. The second array is a constant that stores the right answer, which is initialized here as well.

If you wanted, you could make the game less exact by limiting the size of `guess[]` to four characters. That way, only the first three characters entered (plus the \0) would be assigned to `guess`. The end result would be that the user-submitted word *doggerel* would still match the answer *dog*.

```
1    /* guess.c - Script 11.4 */
2
3    #include <stdio.h>
4    #include <string.h> /* For strcasecmp().
     → */
5
6    void discard_input (void); /* Function
     → prototype. */
7
8    int main (void) {
9
10       /* Two character arrays. */
11       char guess[10];
12       const char answer[] = "coy"; /*
     → Word to guess. */
13
14       /* Prompt for and read in an answer.
     → */
15       printf("Guess what three-letter word
     → I'm thinking of: ");
16       scanf("%9s", guess);
17       discard_input();
18
19       /* Check for a match, re-prompt if
     → wrong. */
20       while (strcasecmp(answer, guess)) {
21           printf("Incorrect! Guess again: ");
22           scanf("%9s", guess);
23           discard_input();
24       }
25
26       /* Must be correct to get here. */
27       printf("You are correct!");
28
29       getchar();
30       return 0;
31   }
32
```

continues on next page

Script 11.4 This guessing game reads in a word and compares it to the right answer. The process continues until the user guesses the correct word.

COMPARING STRINGS

```
                    Script
33   /* This function discards all of the
  → input until a newline. */
34   void discard_input (void) {

36       char junk; // To get rid of extra
  → input.

37

38       // Loop through the input and ignore
it.

39       do {
40           junk = getchar();
41       } while (junk != '\n');

42

43   } /* End of discard_input() function. */
```

Script 11.4 *continued*

7. Prompt for and read in the user's first guess:

```
printf("Guess what three-letter word
 → I'm thinking of: ");
scanf("%9s", guess);
```

All of this is familiar territory, where the user is prompted and that entered text is assigned to the **guess** variable.

8. Discard any extraneous input:

```
discard_input();
```

Calling this function here will discard any other characters typed after the application has read in the nine (or up to nine) characters assigned to **guess**. By using this, we ensure that any extraneous characters will be discarded instead of being read in as part of the next guess.

9. Begin a **while** loop to compare the user's answer against the right word:

```
while (strcasecmp(answer, guess)) {
```

The **while** loop evaluates a condition and, if true, executes the code therein. With this specific loop, the condition is a call to the **strcasecmp()** function, comparing the value of **answer** to the value of **guess**. If the two strings do not have the same value, the function will return a nonzero value, which is true in C. In such cases, the contents of the loop (Step 10), which says the guess was wrong and that the user should try again, are executed.

If the submitted guess matches the right answer, the **strcasecmp()** function will return *0*, which is false in C, and the loop will not be entered.

continues on next page

COMPARING STRINGS

10. Complete the `while` loop, re-prompting the user, reading in the answer, and discarding any extraneous input:

```
    printf("Incorrect! Guess again:
→ ");
    scanf("%9s", guess);
    discard_input();
}
```

The contents of the `while` loop will only be executed if the `strcasecmp()` function determines that `guess` and `answer` are different. If so, the user is re-prompted, the next guess is read in, and the remaining input is discarded. After these three lines of code have been executed, the loop's condition will be reevaluated—testing the new guess against the right answer. The process will continue until the user guesses the correct answer.

11. Tell the user they got it right:

```
    printf("You are correct!");
```

The application will only reach this point in the code—after the `while` loop—if the user enters the correct answer.

12. Complete the `main` function:

```
        getchar();
        return 0;
}
```

13. Define the `discard_input()` function:

```
void discard_input (void) {
    char junk;
    do {
            junk = getchar();
    } while (junk!= '\n');
}
```

This function must be defined in order to use it. Revisit Chapter 7 for the description of this particular syntax.

14. Save the file as *guess.c*, compile, and debug as necessary.

15. Play the game (**Figures 11.10** and **11.11**).

✔ Tips

■ If you're curious, strcmp() returns a negative number if string1 comes before string2 alphabetically and returns a positive number if string2 comes before string1.

■ The strncmp() function compares two strings character by character until a difference is found or until n number of characters have been compared:

```
char s1[] = "catastrophic";
char s2[] = "catalog";
strcmp(s1, s2); // positive number
strncmp(s1, s2, 4); // 0
```

■ If you're only comparing single characters, use the standard equality operator:

```
if ('A' == 'B') { …
```

Figure 11.10 The application continues to run until the user enters the right answer.

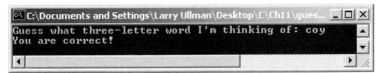

Figure 11.11 If the answer is guessed on the first try, the while loop is never entered (see Script 11.4).

Searching Through Strings

If what you'd like to do is find a particular character within a string, rather than compare one string to another, there are a few C functions you can use.

The strchr() function searches a string for a character, returning the address of that character in the string, or NULL if it was not found:

```
char string[] = "That was quick.";
char *address = NULL;
address = strchr(string, 'q');
printf ("At %p you'll find %c.", address, *address);
```

Conversely, strrchr() finds the last occurrence of a character in a string, returning that address if it was found.

```
char string[] = "That was quick.";
char *address = NULL;
address = strrchr(string, 'a');
printf ("At %p you'll find %c.", address, *address);
```

The strpbrk() function takes this concept one step further by searching a string for the first occurrence of any of a list of characters:

```
char string[] = "That was quick.";
char *address = NULL;
address = strpbrk(string, "aeiou");
printf ("At %p you'll find %c.",
→ address, *address);
```

Finally, strstr() finds the first location of *string2* within *string1*:

```
char haystack[] = "Is there a needle in here?";
char *address = NULL;
address = strstr(haystack, "needle");
printf ("%s was found beginning at %p. ", "needle", *address);
```

Obviously, in each of these examples, you'd want to check that address contained a non-null value (meaning that the search succeeded) before reporting on the results.

Copying Strings

Sometimes you'll need to create a copy of a string in an application so that you can manipulate the value without affecting the original. When you work with strings and pointers, you have two ways of copying strings. The first method makes use of the `strncpy()` function:

```
strncpy(string1, string2, length);
```

Once again, the *length* value should correspond to the available room in `string1`. This function makes a literal copy of the value of `string2` and assigns this to `string1`.

The `strncpy()` is fine when you want a second copy of a string, but it does require twice the memory, as that second string must also be stored. If you want to work with a second reference to a string value instead, you can copy a string pointer:

```
char *string1 = "Sophia";
char *string2;
string2 = string1;
```

The `string1` variable is a pointer to the location in memory where the literal string `Sophia` is stored. The `string2` variable is also a pointer to this same location. The end result is two pointers—each of which requires very little memory—that can point to the same string value. This also means that a change to the string value through either pointer will be visible when the string is read through the other pointer, because only one string is really being stored.

In our next example, several words will be read in from the keyboard and stored in memory. The `strncpy()` function will help make this process possible.

To copy a string:

1. Create a new file or project in your text editor or IDE.

2. Type the standard beginning lines of code (**Script 11.5**):

   ```
   /* copy.c - Script 11.5 */
   #include <stdio.h>
   ```

3. Include the *string.h* header:

   ```
   #include <string.h>
   ```

   For this application, *string.h* is required since it defines the strncpy() function.

4. Add a function prototype:

   ```
   void discard_input (void);
   ```

   This application will also make use of the discard_input() function, as did the guessing game.

5. Set two constant macros:

   ```
   #define NUM_STRINGS 10
   #define STR_LEN 10
   ```

   The words entered by the user will be stored in a multidimensional character array whose parameters are set by these constants. The application will take up to NUM_STRINGS words, each of which can be up to STR_LEN characters long.

6. Begin the main function:

   ```
   int main (void) {
   ```

7. Define two character arrays:

   ```
   char words[NUM_STRINGS][STR_LEN];
   char input[STR_LEN];
   ```

   The first array will store all of the submitted words. The second character array will be used to retrieve the keyed input.

```
1    /* copy.c - Script 11.5 */
2
3    #include <stdio.h>
4    #include <string.h> /* For strncmp()
     → and strcmp(). */
5
6    void discard_input (void); /* Function
     → prototype. */
7
8    #define NUM_STRINGS 10
9    #define STR_LEN 10
10
11   int main (void) {
12
13       /* Define character array. */
14       char words[NUM_STRINGS][STR_LEN];
15
16       char input[STR_LEN]; /* For user
     → input. */
17
18       int i; /* Loop counter. */
19       int count = 0; /* To count number of
     → words entered. */
20
21       /* Get up to NUM_STRINGS words. */
22       for (i = 0; i < NUM_STRINGS; ++i) {
23
24           /* Prompt and read in word. */
25           printf("Enter a word (or 0 to
     → quit): ");
26           scanf("%9s", input);
27           discard_input();
28
29           /* Check for a 0. */
30           if (input[0] == '0') break;
31
32           /* Copy the input to the array.
     → */
```

continues on next page

Script 11.5 This application reads in up to 10 (NUM_STRINGS) words of 10 (STR_LEN) characters in length, copying them each into an array.

```
33        strncpy(words[i], input,
→ STR_LEN);

34

35            /* Count another word entered. */

36            ++count;

37

38        } /* End of while loop. */

39

40        printf("A total of %d words was
→ entered.\n", count);

41

42        getchar();

43        return 0;

44

45  }

46

47  /* This function discards all of the
→ input until a newline. */

48  void discard_input (void) {

49

50        char junk; // To get rid of
→ extra input.

51

52        // Loop through the input and
→ ignore it.

53        do {

54            junk = getchar();

55        } while (junk != '\n');

56

57  } /* End of discard_input() function. */
```

Script 11.5 *continued*

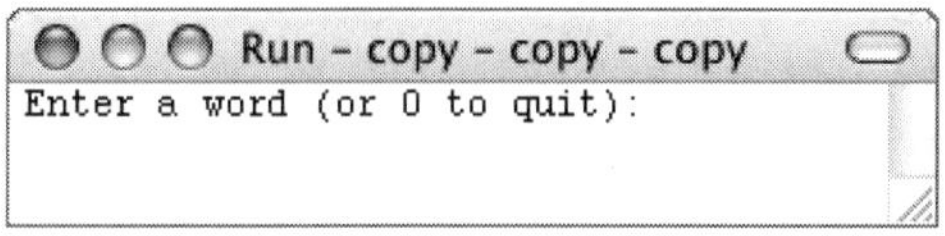

Figure 11.12 The application's prompt indicates how the user can terminate the application.

8. Define two integers:

   ```
   int i;
   int count = 0;
   ```

   The i variable is a loop counter. To track the total number of words the user entered—which can be up to 10, the count variable will be incremented.

9. Define a for loop:

   ```
   for (i = 0; i < NUM_STRINGS; ++i) {
   ```

   To read in all 10 words, a loop will be used. This iterates from *0* to 1 less than NUM_STRINGS.

10. Prompt for and read in a word:

    ```
    printf("Enter a word (or 0 to quit):
    → ");
    scanf("%9s", input);
    discard_input();
    ```

    A word will be read in of up to 9 characters in length (allowing for the tenth available spot to be filled with \0). The read-in value is assigned to the input character array and then any extraneous input is discarded.

11. Check that the user didn't type a *0*:

    ```
    if (input[0] == '0') break;
    ```

    If the user wants to exit the application and enter no more words, they can indicate this by entering *0* (see the prompt, **Figure 11.12**). This conditional then checks if the first character in the input array is equal to *0*. If so, the break will exit the for loop (it has no effect on the if conditional). Since the break is the only if statement, curly braces can be omitted for brevity.

    Another way to write this condition would be to use

    ```
    if (strncmp(input, "0", 1) == 0)
    → break;
    ```

    continues on next page

In that code, 0 is within double quotation marks, as you must compare two strings. In the application's code, 0 is within single quotation marks, as it is comparing the first character in input to the character 0.

12. Copy the inputted word into the array:

```
strncpy(words[i], input, STR_LEN);
```

With each iteration of the loop, the input variable will be replaced with a new word. Therefore, the original value will be copied over to the words array. By using i—the loop counter—as its index, we ensure that each entered word will populate the next available spot in the array.

Even though we know that input is at most 9 characters long, the third argument in strncpy() is set to STR_LEN so that buffer overflow cannot occur.

13. Complete the while loop:

```
    ++count;
}
```

The count variable will be used to count the number of submitted words, so its value is incremented by 1.

14. Print the number of submitted words.

```
printf("A total of %d words was
→ entered.\n", count);
```

15. Complete the main function:

```
        getchar();
        return 0;
}
```

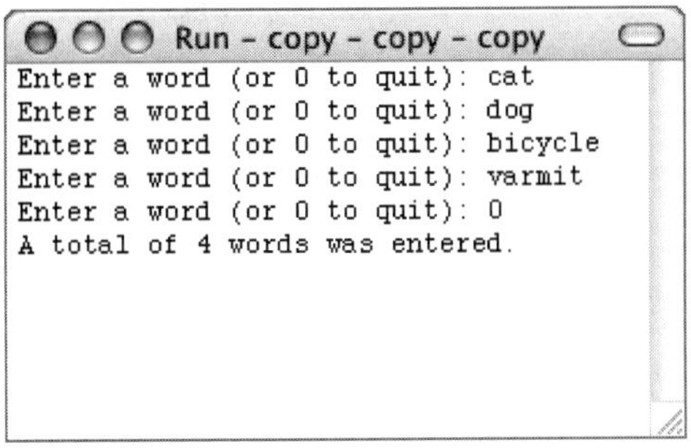

Figure 11.13 The application reads up to 10 words, or until the user enters a *o*. The number of read words is then displayed.

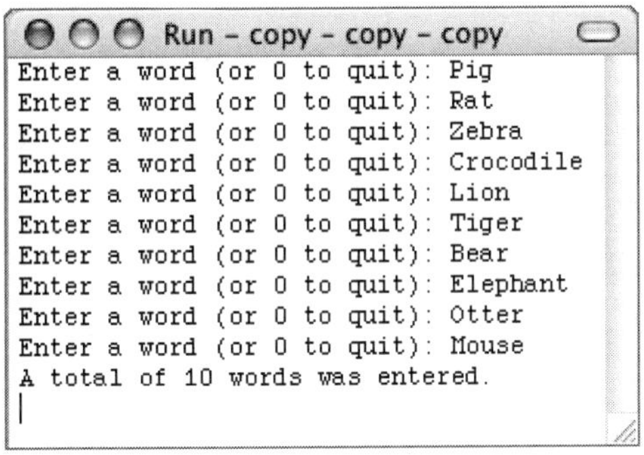

Figure 11.14 The application automatically stops reading in words once 10 have been entered.

16. Define the `discard_input()` function:

```
void discard_input (void) {
    char junk;
    do {
            junk = getchar();
    } while (junk!= '\n');
}
```

17. Save the file as *copy.c*, compile, and debug as necessary.

18. Run the application (**Figures 11.13** and **11.14**).

✔ Tips

■ The `strncpy()`function will not copy the terminating \0 character if `string2` has *length* or more characters in it. For this reason, after making a copy, you should make the last character of the new `string1` equal to \0. Thus, the proper code for using `strncpy()` can look something like this (where `LENGTH` is a C preprocessor macro):

```
strncpy(string1, string2, LENGTH-1);
→ string1[LENGTH-1] = '\0';
```

In the previous example, this was not an issue as we knew that `string2` would have a terminating \0 on it already (because it was limited from the keyboard input).

■ The `strncpy()` function can be used to assign a value to a string, without using a second string variable:

```
char string1[10];
strncpy(string1, "Sophia",
→ strlen(string1));
```

Sorting Strings

For our last example in this chapter, you'll learn how to sort strings alphabetically. The type of sort being demonstrated is a called a *bubble sort*. A bubble sort is easy to comprehend but relatively slow.

It works by repeatedly looping through the list of items, comparing two at a time. If item b should come before item a, their places are switched. As you might guess, to make the comparison on strings, we will use the strcmp() function.

We say this is a slow sort because it requires a pair of nested for loops that bubbles every item through the entire list of items. If you had a list of, say, 10 words, a total of 90 (9 * 10) comparisons would need to be made.

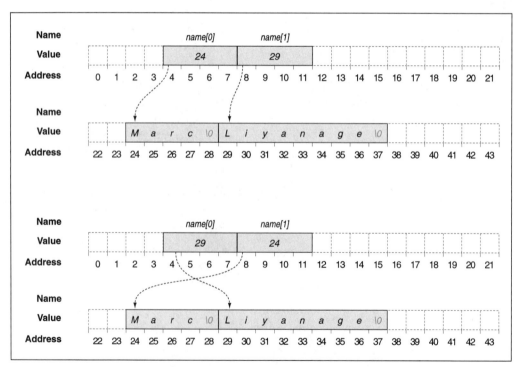

Figure 11.15 Instead of rearranging the actual string values in memory, it's more efficient to reorder the values of the pointers to those strings.

```
                    Script
1   /* sort.c - Script 11.6 - rewrite of
  → copy.c (Script 11.5) */

2

3   #include <stdio.h>
4   #include <string.h> /* For strncmp()
  → and strcmp(). */

5

6   void discard_input (void); /* Function
  → prototype. */

7

8   #define NUM_STRINGS 10
9   #define STR_LEN 10

10

11  int main (void) {

12

13      /* Define character array. */
14      char words[NUM_STRINGS][STR_LEN];

15

16      char input[STR_LEN]; /* For user
  → input. */

17

18      /* Pointers. */
19      char *words_ptr[NUM_STRINGS];
20      char *temp;

21

22      int i, j; /* Loop counters. */
23      int count = 0; /* To count number
  → of words entered. */

24

25      /* Get up to NUM_STRINGS words. */
26      for (i = 0; i < NUM_STRINGS; ++i) {

27

28          /* Prompt and read in word. */
29          printf("Enter a word (or 0 to
  → quit): ");
30          scanf("%9s", input);
31          discard_input();

32
```

continues on next page

Script 11.6 By adding a bubble sort to the *copy* application, the submitted words can be sorted alphabetically and then reprinted.

Aside from the type of sort being used, a more important consideration is how the strings are moved around. Continually swapping around long strings in order to place them in the right order is a processor-intensive process. Instead, you can more quickly rearrange pointers. In other words, instead of moving the actual stored strings around, change the pointers so that the pointers are ordered according to the alphabetical order of the strings (**Figure 11.15**).

To demonstrate this concept, let's modify the *copy* application so that it sorts the submitted list of words. To do so, we need to create an array of pointers and add a bubble sort.

To sort a list of strings:

1. Open *copy.c* (Script 11.5) in your text editor or IDE.

2. Define an array of character pointers (**Script 11.6**):

   `char *words_ptr[NUM_STRINGS];`

   To move around the order of the strings, you'll need a set of pointers to those string addresses. Thus, `words_ptr` is an array of character pointers of the same length as the `words` array.

3. Define a temporary character pointer:

   `char *temp;`

   To swap the order of the pointer addresses, a temporary pointer of the same type is required.

4. Add another loop counter:

   `int i, j;`

   The bubble sort uses two `for` loops, so another counter is necessary.

continues on next page

5. Within the for loop, copy each string's address to the pointer array:

```
words_ptr[i] = &words[i];
```

The &words[i] construct returns the address of the first character in the newly added string. This address is assigned to the pointer, in the corresponding index position. It will be these addresses that will be moved around in the bubble sort.

6. After the print statement, begin defining the bubble sort:

```
for (i = 0; i < (count - 1); ++i) {
    for (j = (i + 1); j < count;
→ ++j) {
```

A bubble sort uses a pair of nested loops. The first should go from 0 to 1 less than the number of items in the list (the last item will already be in its proper place after sorting every other item). The count variable—which was incremented while the words were read in—stores the number of items in the list.

The second, inner loop starts at i + 1. The first time both loops run, i will be 0 and j will be 1. Then i will be 0 and j will be 2; i will be 0 and j will be 3; and so forth.

This construct, complicated as it may seem, merely allows the code to compare each item in the list against every other item in the list.

7. Make the comparison on the two strings:

```
if (strcmp(words_ptr[i],words_ptr[j])
→ > 0) {
```

Using i and j (which always point to two different items), we make a simple comparison. If the result is greater than 0, it means that words_ptr[j] should come before words_ptr[i] and the two values should be swapped.

```
33
34          if (input[0] == '0') break;
35
36          /* Copy the input to the array. */
37          strncpy(words[i], input, STR_LEN);
38
39          /* Copy the address to the
→ pointer. */
40          words_ptr[i] = &words[i];
41
42          /* Count another word entered. */
43          ++count;
44
45      } /* End of while loop. */
46
47      printf("A total of %d words was
→ entered.\n", count);
48
49      /* This is the bubble sort. */
50      for (i = 0; i < (count - 1); ++i) { /*
→ Loop through each word. */
51
52          for (j = (i + 1); j < count; ++j)
→ { /* Loop through each word again. */
53
54              if
→ (strcmp(words_ptr[i],words_ptr[j]) > 0)
→ { /* Compare words. */
55
56                  temp = words_ptr[i]; /*
→ Swap word 1 to the temp location. */
57                  words_ptr[i] =
→ words_ptr[j]; /* Assign word 2 to
→ word 1. */
58                  words_ptr[j] = temp; /*
→ Assign temp (original word 1) to
→ word 2. */
59
60              } /* End of IF. */
61
62          } /* End of inner FOR. */
```

continues on next page

Script 11.6 *continued*

```
63
64        } /* End of outer FOR. */
65
66        printf("In alphabetical order,
    → the words are:\n");
67
68        /* Print the numbers in a loop. */
69        for (i = 0; i < count; i++) {
70            printf("%s\n", words_ptr[i]);
71        }
72
73        getchar();
74        return 0;
75
76    } /* End of main() function. */
77
78    /* This function discards all of the input
    → until a newline. */
79    void discard_input (void) {
80
81        char junk; // To get rid of extra
    → input.
82
83        // Loop through the input and ignore
    it.
84        do {
85            junk = getchar();
86        } while (junk != '\n');
87
88    } /* End of discard_input() function. */
```

Script 11.6 *continued*

If the result is 0, the two strings are the same and no swapping needs to occur. If the result is a negative number, then the two strings are already in the proper order.

8. Swap the string addresses, if applicable:

```
temp = words_ptr[i];
words_ptr[i] = words_ptr[j];
words_ptr[j] = temp;
```

The two addresses are swapped using an intermediary value. First, the value of `words_ptr[i]` (which is the address to a specific string) is assigned to `temp`. Then the value of `words_ptr[j]` is assigned to `words_ptr[i]` since the string referenced by `words_ptr[j]` should come first. Finally, the value of `temp`, which is the original value of `words_ptr[i]`, is assigned to `words_ptr[j]`. This is similar to the `swap()` function defined in the previous chapter.

9. Complete the `if` conditional and the two `for` loops:

```
        } /* End of IF. */
    } /* End of inner FOR. */
} /* End of outer FOR. */
```

Using comments and indentation to mark what each curly brace is doing will help keep things clear.

10. Print the list of words in alphabetical order:

```
printf("In alphabetical order, the
    → words are:\n");
for (i = 0; i < count; i++) {
    printf("%s\n", words_ptr[i]);
}
```

continues on next page

To reprint the words, use another `for` loop, and refer to the pointers in the print statement. To clarify what has occurred, the order of the strings in the `words` array has remained unchanged. Instead, the `words_ptr` array has been sorted so that it lists the addresses of the strings in their respective alphabetical order.

11. Save the application as *sort.c*, compile, and debug as necessary.

12. Run the application (**Figures 11.16** and **11.17**).

```
○ ○ ○   Run – sort – sort – sort
Enter a word (or 0 to quit): John
Enter a word (or 0 to quit): Lorraine
Enter a word (or 0 to quit): Brian
Enter a word (or 0 to quit): Sommar
Enter a word (or 0 to quit): Eric
Enter a word (or 0 to quit): Mark
Enter a word (or 0 to quit): Shauna
Enter a word (or 0 to quit): Ali
Enter a word (or 0 to quit): Mike
Enter a word (or 0 to quit): 0
A total of 9 words was entered.
In alphabetical order, the words are:
Ali
Brian
Eric
John
Lorraine
Mark
Mike
Shauna
Sommar
```

Figure 11.16 The submitted words are now displayed in alphabetical order.

```
○ ○ ○   Run – sort – sort – sort
Enter a word (or 0 to quit): cat
Enter a word (or 0 to quit): Dog
Enter a word (or 0 to quit): mouse
Enter a word (or 0 to quit): Moose
Enter a word (or 0 to quit): deer
Enter a word (or 0 to quit): Elk
Enter a word (or 0 to quit): Rat
Enter a word (or 0 to quit): rabbit
Enter a word (or 0 to quit): Owl
Enter a word (or 0 to quit): Octopus
A total of 10 words was entered.
In alphabetical order, the words are:
Dog
Elk
Moose
Octopus
Owl
Rat
cat
deer
mouse
rabbit
```

Figure 11.17 Since the bubble sort uses the `strcmp()` function, which performs a case-sensitive comparison, capitalized letters will come before lowercase.

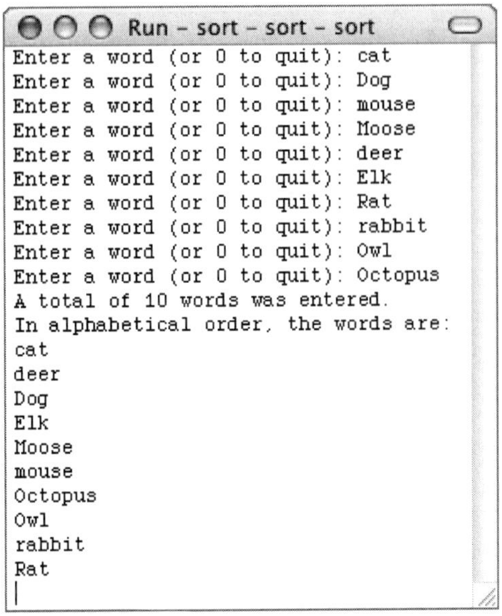

```
●○○  Run – sort – sort – sort          ⊂⊃
Enter a word (or 0 to quit): cat
Enter a word (or 0 to quit): Dog
Enter a word (or 0 to quit): mouse
Enter a word (or 0 to quit): Moose
Enter a word (or 0 to quit): deer
Enter a word (or 0 to quit): Elk
Enter a word (or 0 to quit): Rat
Enter a word (or 0 to quit): rabbit
Enter a word (or 0 to quit): Owl
Enter a word (or 0 to quit): Octopus
A total of 10 words was entered.
In alphabetical order, the words are:
cat
deer
Dog
Elk
Moose
mouse
Octopus
Owl
rabbit
Rat
|
```

Figure 11.18 By using the strcasecmp() function instead, the sort is case-sensitive (compare with Figure 11.17).

✔ Tips

- If you wanted to do a case-insensitive sort (**Figure 11.18**), replace the use of strcmp() with strcasecmp().

- A faster but slightly more complex sorting method is C's qsort(). Chapter 10, "Managing Memory," used an example of this to sort numbers.

FILE INPUT
AND OUTPUT

Most of the examples in this book read from the standard input—which is the keyboard—and write to the standard output—the console or terminal screen. C can also read from and write to files, giving your applications the ability to store and retrieve data.

Working with files is similar to working with standard input and output, although the process does make use of pointers. For the most part, though, your main considerations are what type of file is being referenced and what, exactly, you want to do with that file.

In this chapter you'll learn how to open, write to, read from, and close files. You'll also go through an example for parsing the stored data and, finally, learn how to work with binary files, which have different properties than standard plain-text files.

Opening and Closing Files

Working with a file starts by opening it and ends by closing that file. But before doing anything with a file, you must create a variable as a file pointer. The syntax is

```
FILE *file_pointer_name;
```

For the sake of simplicity, you'll often see fp used to represent a file pointer:

```
FILE *fp;
```

This variable is assigned a value during the process of opening the file for reading or writing. The file pointer will then point to all the information C needs to work with that file.

The functions used to read from and write to files reside in the *stdio.h* header file, which you're already including in your applications. The first function, fopen(), is used to initialize the file pointer:

```
fp = fopen (file_name, mode);
```

The file_name can be as simple as *data.txt* or be a relative path to the file, like *data.txt*, *./files/data.txt*, or *C:\\storage\\data.txt* (see the sidebar). Which mode you use depends on what you want to do with that file: write to it, read from it, append new data to it, or a combination of those tasks (**Table 12.1**). When choosing a mode, keep in mind that the w mode will always erase any existing contents in an existing file. You should use this mode only when you want to begin with a clean slate.

Table 12.1 These modes are used for setting the actions that can be done with a file. Note that the b flag can be used with w, r, or a.

fopen() Modes	
MODE	**OPEN FILE FOR…**
w	Writing, creating the file if it doesn't exist
r	Reading
a	Appending new data to the end of the file, creating the file if it doesn't exist
w+	Reading and writing, creating the file if it doesn't exist
r+	Reading and writing
a+	Reading and writing, appending new data to the end of the file, creating the file if it doesn't exist
b	Binary mode, in conjunction with the other modes (e.g., wb, rb+, etc.)

So, to open a file for reading, you code

```
fp = fopen("data.txt", "r");
```

If C cannot open the file in the designated mode, `fp` will be assigned a value of NULL. Before doing anything else—such as trying to write to this file—you should check the value of your pointer:

```
if (fp != NULL) {
    // Do whatever.
}
```

Once you've finished using the file, you should close it, using the appropriately named `fclose()` function. This function takes one argument: the name of the pointer initialized when opening the file:

```
fclose (fp);
```

To make certain that this process works, let's write a simple application that opens and closes a file.

OPENING AND CLOSING FILES

One Slash Forward, Two Slashes Back

On non-Windows operating systems (Unix, Linux, Mac OS X, and others), forward slashes are used to reference directories (or folders). To refer to a file in the directory above the current location, you would use *../filename*, where the *../* construct points to the parent folder of the current directory. To refer to a file located in a subdirectory of the current one, you would use *subdirectory/filename* or, more precisely, *./subdirectory/filename*, where *./* points to the current directory.

The Windows operating system uses the backslash (\) to reference folders. But since the backslash has a special meaning already—it's used to create escape sequences like newline (\n)—you must use two backslashes to properly refer to directories. So *subdirectory\\filename* and *C:\\somefolder\\filename* are proper Windows references. This construct is actually a type of escape, in which the backslash character is escaped with the escape character (which happens to be a backslash) in order to produce a single backslash.

To open and close a file:

1. Create a new file or project in your text editor or IDE.

2. Type the standard beginning lines of code (**Script 12.1**):

   ```
   /* test.c - Script 12.1 */
   #include <stdio.h>
   ```

3. Set the file path and name as a C preprocessor macro:

   ```
   #define THEFILE "path/to/filename"
   ```

   The actual syntax will depend on your operating system and where you want the file to be created. Here are possible examples for Mac OS X and Windows:

   ```
   #define THEFILE
   → "/Users/larry/Desktop/data.txt"
   #define THEFILE "C:\\Documents and
   → Settings\\Larry
   → Ullman\\Desktop\\data.txt"
   ```

   By setting this value as a C preprocessor directive, you won't need to go hunting through your code to find the filename if you want to change it later.

   You have to use the double quotation marks as part of the definition, since the fopen() function, which uses this macro later, expects a string.

4. Begin the main function:

   ```
   int main (void) {
   ```

5. Create a file pointer:

   ```
   FILE *fp;
   ```

   This is the file pointer that will be used to reference the file.

```
1    /* test.c - Script 12.1 */
2
3    #include <stdio.h>
4
5    /* Set the file path and name. */
6    #define THEFILE
     → "/Users/larry/Desktop/data.txt"
7
8    int main (void) {
9
10       /* Need a pointer of type FILE. */
11       FILE *fp;
12
13       /* Attempt to open the file for
     → writing. */
14       fp = fopen(THEFILE, "w");
15
16       /* Report on the success of file
     → opening. */
17       if (fp != NULL) {
18          printf ("The file is now
     → open.\n");
19       } else {
20          printf ("The file could not
     → be opened.\n");
21          /* Abort the application, if you
     → want. */
22       }
23
24       /* Close the file and report if
     → a problem occurred. */
25       if (fclose(fp) != 0) {
26          printf ("The file could not
     → be closed.\n");
27       } else {
28          printf ("The file is now
     → closed.\n");
29       }
30
31       getchar(); /* Pause. */
32       return 0;
33    }
```

Script 12.1 This application opens and then closes a text file to ensure that the process works.

6. Open the file for writing:

```
fp = fopen(THEFILE, "w");
```

This line uses the C preprocessing macro defined earlier (see Step 3). Before compilation of the C code, the compiler will replace THEFILE here with the value established earlier. The w mode is used, indicating that we want to write to the file, that it should be created if it doesn't exist, and that any existing contents will be overwritten.

7. Create a conditional to report on the file opening:

```
if (fp != NULL) {
    printf ("The file is now
→ open.\n");
} else {
    printf ("The file could not be
→ opened.\n");
}
```

This conditional compares the value of the file pointer against NULL. As long as fp does not equal NULL, the file was successfully opened for writing.

In this example, if the file could not be opened, a simple message is printed. An alternative to this is to abort the execution of the application (by using a return statement), which you'll see in later examples.

8. Close the file:

```
if (fclose(fp) != 0) {
    printf ("The file could not be
→ closed.\n");
} else {
    printf ("The file is now
→ closed.\n");
}
```

The fclose() function returns the number *0* if it worked properly, so this conditional reports on its success. This may be overkill, but it's worthwhile knowing how you would validate that a file was closed.

continues on next page

OPENING AND CLOSING FILES

9. Complete the main function:

```
    getchar();
    return 0;
}
```

Figure 12.1 Successfully running the *test* application on Windows.

10. Save the file as *test.c*, compile, and debug as necessary.

11. Run the application (**Figures 12.1** and **12.2**).

✔ Tips

- On the one hand, absolute pathnames (*/Users/larry/Desktop/filename* or *C:\\Documents and Settings\\Larry Ullman\\Desktop\\filename*) are obviously less portable (because that path may not exist on another computer). On the other hand, they have an advantage over relative pathnames (*../filename* or *subdirectory /filename*) in their precision.

Figure 12.2 Successfully running the *test* application on Mac OS X using Xcode.

- When using Dev-C++ on Windows, the starting point for relative pathnames is the location of the Dev-C++ application itself, not the location of the compiled *test* application.

- A single file pointer can be used to reference multiple file openings in the same application but only one open file at a time. For example:

```
fp = fopen("data1.txt", "r");
// Do whatever.
fclose(fp);
fp = fopen("data2.txt", "r");
// Do whatever.
fclose(fp);
```

- There is a limit as to how many files your C application can open at once. Fortunately, for most applications this limit (as high as several hundred) shouldn't be an issue.

- Because there are many reasons a call to `fopen()` could fail, you'll always want to ensure that the open call worked—by using a conditional that compares the returned value to `NULL`—before doing anything with the file.

- For that matter, if `fp` is `NULL` (because the file could not be opened), the `fclose()` line in this application will fail (because it will be fed a `NULL` pointer). Subsequent examples demonstrate how you can avoid this potential problem.

Binary and Plain-Text Files

When you're working with files, it's important to understand the two basic file types: plain text (or ASCII) and binary. A plain-text file is human readable and contains no formatting, like your C source code files. A binary file is in a format that a computer can use more quickly but is unreadable to humans (if you've ever opened a file and seen a bunch of gibberish, that's binary data).

Another distinction between the two types is that plain-text files can contain multiple lines of data, whereas a binary file is one long stream of information without any breaks. On the other hand, because it's a more native format, computers can often deal with binary files faster than plain-text files. Another benefit of binary files is that a computer does not have to access them linearly as it normally does plain-text files (which are often read one line or character at a time).

When programming in C, the distinction between binary and ASCII files is most important for Windows users, because that operating system distinguishes between the two formats. People using Unix (including Linux and Mac OS X) don't need to worry about this since those operating systems see no difference between the two file types. Because the Unix variants (including Mac OS X) do not distinguish between binary and plain text files, the use of **b** to indicate binary mode when opening a file has no effect on those operating systems.

In these first few examples, you'll be using plain-text files. At the end of the chapter, you'll also see several examples of working with binary files.

Writing to Files

Once you've opened a file for writing (meaning that you used either the w or a mode, or a variant thereof), you can write data to it. To do so, you can use the fprintf() function, which works like printf() except that it takes a file pointer as its first argument:

fprintf (*file_pointer, formatting, extra_arguments*);

The formatting signifiers are exactly the same as those used with printf() and scanf() (**Table 12.2**). So, to write an unsigned integer to a file, you would code

fprintf (fp, "%u", 30);

As with the printf() function, you can include literal values (like punctuation and words) or newlines in the formatting area:

fprintf (fp, "%s\n", name);

Here, the newline character will ensure that each time the fprintf() statement is executed, the data is written on its own line in the text file.

Our next example will take input from the keyboard in the form of a date and that day's high and low temperatures (**Figure 12.3**). This data will be stored in a text file to be read by the next example in the chapter.

Table 12.2 The different signifiers used with printf(), sprintf(), and fprintf().

fprintf() Signifiers	
SIGNIFIER	MEANING
d	integer
f	floating point number
hd	short integer
ld	long integer
hu	unsigned short integer
u	unsigned integer
lu	unsigned long integer
lf	double
Lf	long double (not always available)
c	character
s	string

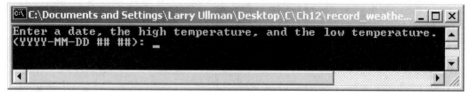

Figure 12.3 The application's prompt indicates what information is to be keyed and in what format.

```
          Script
1    /* record_weather.c - Script 12.2 */
2
3    #include <stdio.h>
4
5    /* Set the file path and name. */
6    #define THEFILE
   → "/Users/larry/Desktop/weather.txt"
7
8    int main (void) {
9
10       /* Need a pointer of type FILE. */
11       FILE *fp;
12
13       int high, low; /* Temperatures. */
14       char date[11]; /* In the form of
   → YYYY-MM-DD, plus \0 character. */
15
16       /* Attempt to open the file for
   → appended writing. */
17       fp = fopen(THEFILE, "a");
18
19       if (fp != NULL) { /* The file
   → is open. */
20
21          /* Prompt the user. */
22          printf ("Enter a date, the high
   → temperature, and the low
   → temperature.\n(YYYY-MM-DD ## ##): ");
23
24          /* Handle the input. */
25          if (scanf ("%10s %d %d", date,
   → &high, &low) == 3) {
26
27             /* Write the data. */
28             fprintf(fp, "%s %d %d\n",
   → date, high, low);
29             printf ("The data has been
   → written.\n");
```

continues on next page

Script 12.2 The *record_weather* application takes three user input values (a date, the day's high temperature, and the day's low temperature) and writes them to a text file.

To write to files:

1. Create a new file or project in your text editor or IDE.

2. Type the standard beginning lines of code (**Script 12.2**):

   ```
   /* record_weather.c - Script 12.2 */
   #include <stdio.h>
   ```

3. Set the file path and name as a C pre-processor macro.

   Again the actual syntax will depend on your operating system and where you want the file to be created. Here are possible examples for Mac OS X and Windows:

   ```
   #define THEFILE
   → "/Users/larry/Desktop/weather.txt"
   #define THEFILE "C:\\Documents and
   → Settings\\Larry Ullman\\Desktop\\
   → weather.txt"
   ```

4. Begin the main function and create a file pointer:

   ```
   int main (void) {
   FILE *fp;
   ```

5. Define the required variables:

   ```
   int high, low;
   char date[11];
   ```

   The first two variables are integers that will store the entered high and low temperatures. The date variable is a character array to store dates in the format *YYYY-MM-DD*, like *2005-01-01*.

   continues on next page

6. Open the file for appended writing:

```
fp = fopen(THEFILE, "a");
```

This code is similar to that in the *test* application except that the *a* mode is used instead of *w*. By using *a*, each new record will be appended to the end of the file, rather than wiping out any existing data.

7. Start a conditional based on the file pointer and prompt the user:

```
if (fp != NULL) {
    printf ("Enter a date, the high
→ temperature, and the low
→ temperature.\n(YYYY-MM-DD ## ##):
→ ");
```

The conditional is the same as it was before. If the file could be opened, then the user will be prompted for the required information (Figure 12.3).

8. Handle the keyed input:

```
if (scanf ("%10s %d %d", date, &high,
→ &low) == 3) {
```

Using the `scanf()` function, the application attempts to read one string (of up to 10 characters long) and two integers from the standard input. The string will be stored in `date`, which, as a character array, can be listed directly. The two integer values go into `high` and `low`, which, as numbers, must be referenced in their address form (&).

If `scanf()` successfully read in three items, the user entered the information properly, so the conditional checks if the returned value is equal to *3*.

See Chapter 5, "Standard Input and Output," for more on the syntax of `scanf()`.

```
30
31        } else {
32            printf ("The data was not in
→ the proper format.\n");
33        }
34
35    } else {
36        printf ("The file could not be
→ opened.\n");
37        return 1; /* Exit the
→ function/application. */
38    }
39
40    /* Close the file. */
41    if (fclose(fp) != 0) {
42        printf ("The file could not
→ be closed.\n");
43    }
44
45    getchar(); /* Pause. */
46    getchar(); /* Pause. */
47    return 0;
48
49 }
```

Script 12.2 *continued*

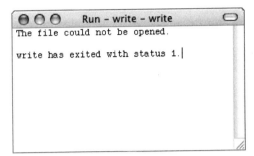

Figure 12.4 If the file could not be opened for appended writing, this is the result.

9. Write the data to the text file:

```
fprintf(fp, "%s %d %d\n", date, high,
→ low);
```

The `fprintf()` function will write the values to the text file. The formatting is simple: separating each value by a space and ending with a newline.

10. Complete the `scanf()` conditional:

```
    printf ("The data has been
→ written.\n");
} else {
    printf ("The data was not in
→ the proper format.\n");
}
```

The first message completes the conditional if `scanf()` worked, indicating that the data was written to the file. If `scanf()` did not return a value of 3, the input was not of the proper format and the second message is printed to the screen.

11. Complete the `fp` conditional:

```
} else {
    printf ("The file could not
→ be opened.\n");
    return 1;
}
```

If the application could not open the file for writing, there's no reason to continue. So, unlike the previous example, in this case an error message will be printed and the function will return the number *1* to indicate that a problem occurred (**Figure 12.4**). Because functions always stop running after a `return` statement, this effectively stops the application.

continues on next page

WRITING TO FILES

12. Close the file:

```
if (fclose(fp) != 0) {
    printf ("The file could not
→ be closed.\n");
}
```

Rather than indicating if the file was closed successfully, this code now indicates if it *wasn't* closed successfully. You can also use a `return 1;` line here, if you want.

13. Complete the `main` function:

```
    getchar();
    getchar();
    return 0;
}
```

The extra use of `getchar()` is to make the application stick around a while longer on Windows, after reading the user input. You could also use the `discard_input` function (see Chapter 7, "Creating Your Own Functions") to get rid of extraneous input.

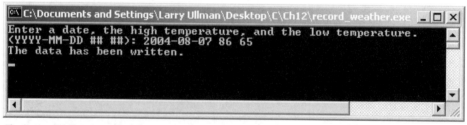

Figure 12.5 Adding a record to the weather file.

Figure 12.6 Entering another set of data for a particular date.

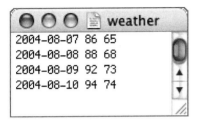

Figure 12.7 The text file contains all of the submitted records in the order they were entered.

14. Save the file as *record_weather.c*, compile, and debug as necessary.

15. Run the application multiple times to populate the text file (**Figures 12.5** and **12.6**).

16. Open the *weather.txt* file in any text editor to confirm that the data was written (**Figure 12.7**).

The next example in this chapter will formally read the *weather.txt* file but you can quickly confirm that the process is working by using a text editor.

✔ Tips

- The fprintf() function returns the number of characters written to a file or the number *-1* if no writing occurred.

- The fputc() function is an easy way to write a single character to a file:

    ```
    fputc ('B', fp);
    ```

- You can also use the fputs() function to write a string to a file:

    ```
    fputs ("I like it.\n", fp);
    ```

- As far as C is concerned, the standard output, text files, printers, and many other things are all considered "files" that C writes to.

Documenting Your Files

Even though the text files in this chapter are written to and read from using a C application, there's something to be said for documenting their format. By doing so, if a user ever opens the data file, it will still have meaning. Or, future developers using your code will be better able to understand why data was written or read in a certain way.

One way to add documentation is to place comments in the C program itself. This will help out the programmer:

```
/* The text file stores data in the format:
YYYY-MM-DD ## ##
```

where the first number is the high temperature and the second is the low. */

A companion option is to add a line indicating the format at the top of the data file, like

```
Date            High    Low
2004-08-29      94      72
2004-08-30      90      70
```

Then, when the C program reads the text file, you would have the application ignore the first line.

Finally, you could add comments to your text file, like this:

```
# This is weather.txt.
# It records the high and low
# temperatures for a particular date.
```

Again, you would then have your C application ignore lines beginning with #.

Reading from Files

To read from a file in C, you can use the `fgets()` function. It was first introduced in Chapter 5 as a reliable way to read numeric input from the keyboard. The syntax for using `fgets()` is

```
fgets (var, length, pointer);
```

The function reads up to *length* amount of data from the file and assigns this to *var*. You should take precautions to ensure that the function does not attempt to read in more data than can be stored in the variable. A reliable way to do this is to use the `sizeof()` operator:

```
fgets (var, sizeof(var), pointer);
```

Finally, there is the pointer value. Previously the pointer being used was `stdin` (standard input), but now the pointer should refer to the file opened for reading:

```
fgets (var, sizeof(var), fp);
```

As a clarification, we stated that `fgets()` reads *up to length* amount of data. Technically the `fgets()` function will read from a file until any of the following conditions are met:

- A newline (\n) is encountered.

- The end of the file is reached (see the sidebar).

- It has read one character less than the maximum number of characters to read.

Since `fgets()` reads in a string, it will read up to `length - 1` characters. These will be assigned to the string, along with a final \0, which terminates every string. Also note that `fgets()` will retain any newline characters it reads in. So if `fgets()` encounters a newline character, that will terminate the read, but that newline will be part of the value of `var`.

Line and File Endings

One of the nice things about C with respect to working with files is that it will automatically convert line endings. Different operating systems use different characters to mark the end of a line. On Windows, a combination of a carriage-return (\r) and the newline or linefeed (\n) characters is used, resulting in \r\n. Pre–Mac OS X Macs used \r, while Unix uses \n. In C, you can just use \n, and that will be interpreted appropriately for the operating system in use.

These line-ending characters only apply to text files, since binary files contain one long stretch of data.

Another concept to consider is the end of file, referred to as EOF. Each operating system also uses its own way of marking the end of a file. When a C application reads in EOF, it knows there's no more data to be read. This EOF constant is also defined within the *stdio.h* header file so that it's environment specific.

Our next example will open the *weather.txt* file and print out its contents line by line, exactly as they were stored. Much of this example's code will be similar to the previous two applications.

To read from files:

1. Create a new file or project in your text editor or IDE.

2. Type the standard beginning lines of code (**Script 12.3**):

   ```
   /* read_weather.c - Script 12.3 */
   #include <stdio.h>
   ```

3. Set the file path and name as a C preprocessor macro:

   ```
   #define THEFILE
   → "/Users/larry/Desktop/weather.txt"
   ```

   or

   ```
   #define THEFILE "C:\\Documents and
   → Settings\\Larry Ullman\\Desktop\\
   → weather.txt"
   ```

   Adjust this line accordingly, making sure only that it points to the same *weather.txt* file used by the *record_weather* application (Script 12.2).

4. Begin the main function and create a file pointer:

   ```
   int main (void) {
   FILE *fp;
   ```

5. Define the required variable:

   ```
   char line[30];
   ```

   Only one variable is necessary for this application (aside from the pointer). The line character array will store the data retrieved from the text file. Its length (30) allows for a reasonable amount of data, based on what we expect the text file to contain.

```
1    /* read_weather.c - Script 12.3 */
2
3    #include <stdio.h>
4
5    /* Set the file path and name. */
6    #define THEFILE
     → "/Users/larry/Desktop/weather.txt"
7
8    int main (void) {
9
10       /* Need a pointer of type FILE. */
11       FILE *fp;
12
13       /* Character array for reading
     → the file. */
14       char line[30];
15
16       /* Attempt to open the file for
     → reading. */
17       fp = fopen(THEFILE, "r");
18
19       if (fp != NULL) { /* The file
     → is open. */
20
21          /* Caption. */
22          printf("The contents of the
     → 'weather.txt' file:\n");
23
24          /* Loop through the file,
     → printing each line. */
25          while (fgets(line, sizeof(line),
     → fp)) {
26             printf("%s", line);
27          }
28
29       } else {
30          printf ("The file could not be
     → opened.\n");
```

continues on next page

Script 12.3 The *record_weather* application retrieves and prints the contents of the *weather.txt* file.

```
                    ● ● ●              📄 Script
31              return 1; /* Exit the
      → function/application. */
32          }
33
34          /* Close the file. */
35          if (fclose(fp) != 0) {
36              printf ("The file could not
      → be closed.\n");
37          }
38
39          getchar(); /* Pause. */
40          return 0;
41      }
```

Script 12.3 *continued*

6. Open the file for reading:

   ```
   fp = fopen(THEFILE, "r");
   ```
   The r mode is used to only read from
   a file.

7. Start a conditional based on the file
   pointer and print a caption:

   ```
   if (fp != NULL) {
       printf("The contents of the
   → 'weather.txt' file:\n");
   ```

8. Read and print the file's contents in
   a loop:

   ```
   while (fgets(line, sizeof(line), fp))
   → {
       printf("%s", line);
   }
   ```
   This loop will continue to use the fgets()
   function to read in from the file as long
   as it can (which is until it reaches the
   file's end). With each iteration of the loop,
   the data read with fgets() is assigned to
   the line variable, which is then printed
   as a simple string.

9. Complete the fp conditional:

   ```
   } else {
       printf ("The file could not
   → be opened.\n");
       return 1;
   }
   ```

10. Close the file:

    ```
    if (fclose(fp) != 0) {
        printf ("The file could not
    → be closed.\n");
    }
    ```

11. Complete the main function:

    ```
        getchar();
        return 0;
    }
    ```

continues on next page

READING FROM FILES

12. Save the file as *read_weather.c*, compile, and debug as necessary.

13. Run the application (**Figure 12.8**).

✔ Tips

■ The feof() function takes a file pointer as an argument and returns *1* if you've reached the end of a file; it returns *0* otherwise.

■ C also has a fgetc() function, which will read in a single character at a time from a file:

```
character = fgetc (fp);
```

■ The fscanf() function can be used to read from files as well, but can easily choke on formatting problems in the text file. Its syntax is like scanf():

```
fscanf(fp, format, &var…);
```

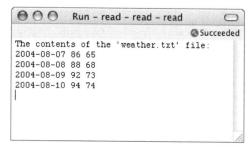

Figure 12.8 The application prints the contents of the *weather.txt* file, along with a caption.

```
  ● ● ●              📄 Script
1     /* parse_weather.c - Script 12.4 - rework
    → of read_weather.c (Script 12.3) */

2

3     #include <stdio.h>

4

5     /* Set the file path and name. */
6     #define THEFILE
    → "/Users/larry/Desktop/weather.txt"

7

8     int main (void) {

9

10        /* Need a pointer of type FILE. */
11        FILE *fp;

12

13        /* Character array for reading
    → the file. */
14        char line[30];

15

16        int high, low; /* Temperatures. */
17        char date[11]; /* In the form of
    → YYYY-MM-DD, plus \0 character. */

18

19        /* Attempt to open the file for
    → reading. */
20        fp = fopen(THEFILE, "r");

21

22        if (fp != NULL) { /* The file is
    → open. */

23

24            /* Caption. */
25            printf("%10s %5s %5s\n", "Date",
    → "High", "Low");

26

27            /* Loop through the file, parsing
    → each line. */
28            while (fgets(line, sizeof(line),
    → fp)) {
```

continues on next page

Script 12.4 This variation on the *read_weather* application uses the sscanf() function to break the stored data into its individual parts.

Parsing File Input

The *read_weather* application is fine if all you want to do is print the contents of a file verbatim. However, if you'd like to do more with your stored data, you'll need a method of parsing the read lines into their respective parts.

This can be accomplished using the sscanf() function. This function, first introduced in Chapter 5, can break one string down into different pieces, using formatting parameters like those used with printf() and fprintf(). The basic syntax is

sscanf(*string_to_parse, formatting,*
→ *arguments…*);

Obviously the number of arguments depends on how many elements are expected to be extracted from *string_to_parse*. Our next example will rework *read_weather*, breaking each line into its date, high temperature, and low temperature, just as they were first entered.

To parse file input:

1. Open *read_weather.c* (Script 12.3) in your text editor or IDE.

2. After defining the line variable, define three more variables (**Script 12.4**):

   int high, low;
   char date[11];

   These lines should look familiar: they're taken straight out of the *record_weather* application (Script 12.2).

3. Change the caption (inside the fp conditional) to read

   printf("%10s %5s %5s\n", "Date",
   → "High", "Low");

   Using a little printf() formatting, this application will print out the retrieved data in columns.

continues on next page

4. Change the contents of the `while` loop to read

```
sscanf (line, "%10s %d %d", date,
→ &high, &low);
printf("%10s %5d %5d\n", date, high,
→ low);
```

The condition of the `while` loop will continue to use `fgets()` to read through the entire file. Within the `while` loop, the process changes. First, the `sscanf()` function is used to break the read line into its three distinct parts. This structure parallels that used to key in the data in *record_weather*.

Then the three variables are printed, using the same formatting as the caption in Step 3.

5. Save the file as *parse_weather.c*.

6. Compile and debug as necessary.

7. Run the compiled application (**Figure 12.9**).

✔ Tips

- For more review of `sscanf()`, see Chapter 5.

- The `sscanf()` function returns the number of elements it excised. You could use this information to check that each line contained three distinct elements. If you wanted, you could make the `sscanf()` line a condition, checking that it returns *3*. That way, you could weed out nondata lines in the file, such as comments.

- Now that you know how to parse file input, you can use your existing knowledge to determine the highest high temperature or the lowest low temperature, or to calculate median temperatures. You could start by building a dynamically sized array (see Chapter 10, "Managing Memory"), populated from the file data, and then perform calculations or sorts on this array.

```
29          sscanf (line, "%10s %d %d",
→ date, &high, &low);
30          printf("%10s %5d %5d\n",
→ date, high, low);
31      }
32
33    } else {
34      printf ("The file could not be
→ opened.\n");
35      return 1; /* Exit the
→ function/application. */
36    }
37
38    /* Close the file. */
39    if (fclose(fp) != 0) {
40      printf ("The file could not be
→ closed.\n");
41    }
42
43    getchar(); /* Pause. */
44    return 0;
45 }
```

Script 12.4 *continued*

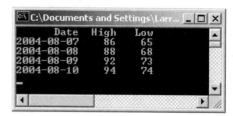

Figure 12.9 The application now breaks the file's contents into its individual parts and prints them in a table-like structure.

Writing to Binary Files

At the very beginning of this chapter, the two file types were mentioned: plain text (formally called ASCII) and binary. All of the previous examples have used plain-text files, which are human readable, but you can also write to and read from binary files using C. The basic ideas for working with binary files are the same, but the specific functions are different.

Binary files are opened and closed like ASCII files, except that you should use the **b** modifier on the mode:

```
FILE *fp;
fp = fopen ("thefile", "wb");
// Write to the file.
fclose(fp);
```

Once you've successfully opened the file, you can write data to it using `fwrite()`. Its syntax is more complex than you've seen so far:

```
fwrite (write_data_pointer,
→ bytes_to_write, blocks, fp);
```

The first argument to `fwrite()` is a pointer to the address of the data being written. This can be an actual pointer (like to a string or a number) or an array (which, as you've seen, has pointer-like qualities). The second argument indicates the size, in bytes, of each block of data. The third argument represents the number of blocks being written. For example, you might write one block, which is a number, or one hundred blocks, which are the elements of an array. The final argument is the file pointer.

In this next example, an array of 50 random numbers will be generated (see the sidebar) and then written to a binary file. Subsequent examples will read the entire file and grab random values from it.

WRITING TO BINARY FILES

Generating Random Numbers

This application requires the generation of 50 random numbers. However, computers aren't very good at doing things randomly—given the same set of instructions, they should produce the same results—so to reliably create random numbers requires a few lines of code that will be new to you.

The C *stdlib.h* file contains the definition for the rand() function, which returns a random number between 0 and 32,767. While multiple calls to this function within an application will return different numbers, each time you run the application, it will most likely return the *same set of random numbers*. To compensate for this, the srand() function is first called to *seed* the process. The standard code for using srand() is

```
srand((unsigned)time(NULL));
```

Basically this line feeds srand() one argument, using the time() function to generate that argument. The time() function, found in the *time.h* library file, returns the number of seconds since midnight on January 1, 1970. Thus, every time the application is run, srand() is fed a different value, as time() returns an increasingly larger number of seconds.

Lastly, this application wants to limit the range of random numbers to be less than 100. The easiest way to accomplish this is to use the remainder of dividing a random number by 100. So if a random number is 32,767, the remainder of dividing that by 100 would be 67. If the number is 22,584, its modulus would be 84.

In the end, the key to this exercise is to learn how to write binary data to a file. The actual generation of random numbers within a particular range is just a secondary requirement. Do not be too confused or concerned with the particulars of that syntax.

```
●●●                     Script
1    /* binary_write.c - Script 12.5 */
2
3    #include <stdio.h>
4    #include <stdlib.h> /* For rand() and
     → srand(). */
5    #include <time.h> /* For time(), used
     → with srand(). */
6
7    /* Set the file path and name. */
8    #define THEFILE
     → "/Users/larry/Desktop/numbers.dat"
9
10   /* Number of items being written. */
11   #define ITEMS 50
12
13   int main (void) {
14
15       /* Need a pointer of type FILE. */
16       FILE *fp;
17
18       int i; /* Loop counter. */
19       int numbers[ITEMS]; /* Array of
     → numbers. */
20
21       /* Attempt to open the file for
     → binary writing. */
22       fp = fopen(THEFILE, "wb");
23
24       if (fp != NULL) { /* The file is
     → open. */
25
26           /* Seed the rand() function. */
27           srand((unsigned)time(NULL));
28
29           /* Populate the array with random
     → numbers less than 100. */
30           for (i = 0; i < ITEMS; i++) {
31               numbers[i] = rand() % 100;
32           }
                  continues on next page
```

Script 12.5 This program writes fifty random numbers (between 0 and 99) to a binary file.

To write to a binary file:

1. Create a new file or project in your text editor or IDE.

2. Type the standard beginning lines of code (**Script 12.5**):

   ```
   /* binary_write.c - Script 12.5 */
   #include <stdio.h>
   ```

3. Require two more standard libraries:

   ```
   #include <stdlib.h>
   #include <time.h>
   ```

   The first library makes the rand() and srand() functions available to this application. The second makes the time() function available, which will be needed with srand(). See the sidebar for more.

4. Set the file path and name as a C preprocessor macro:

   ```
   #define THEFILE
   → "/Users/larry/Desktop/numbers.dat"
   ```

   or

   ```
   #define THEFILE "C:\\Documents and
   → Settings\\Larry Ullman\\Desktop\\
   → numbers.dat"
   ```

   Because the file will store binary data, not plain text, you don't want to use the *.txt* extension. You can either omit the extension entirely or use *.dat* (a three-letter extension representing *data*).

5. Create a constant macro representing the number of items in the array:

   ```
   #define ITEMS 50
   ```

   How many items are stored in the array will be a relevant number many times over in this application, so it makes sense to set it as a preprocessor macro.

   continues on next page

6. Begin the main function and create a file pointer:

```
int main (void) {
FILE *fp;
```

7. Define the required variables:

```
int i;
int numbers[ITEMS];
```

The i variable will be a loop counter; numbers is the array in which random numbers will be stored.

8. Open the file for binary writing:

```
fp = fopen(THEFILE, "wb");
```

This call opens the file for writing, creating the file if it doesn't exist, and wiping out any existing data. The binary mode is indicated by adding the b. This is only required on Windows but is still a good idea on all operating systems.

9. Start a conditional based on the file pointer:

```
if (fp != NULL) {
```

10. Seed the rand() function:

```
srand((unsigned)time(NULL));
```

This line is required to generate truly random numbers. See the sidebar for a more detailed explanation of the purpose and syntax.

11. Populate the array with random numbers:

```
for (i = 0; i < ITEMS; i++) {
    numbers[i] = rand() % 100;
}
```

The for loop counts from i to ITEMS, the number of elements in the array. Within the loop, each element is assigned a random value between 0 and 99. This limit is accomplished by assigning the remainder of dividing the random number by 100, rather than assigning the random number itself (which could be as high as 32,767).

Script

```
33
34          /* Write the array elements to
   → the file. */
35          fwrite (numbers, sizeof(int),
   → ITEMS, fp);
36          printf ("The data has been
   → written.\n");
37
38      } else {
39          printf ("The file could not be
   → opened.\n");
40          return 1; /* Exit the
   → function/application. */
41      }
42
43      /* Close the file. */
44      if (fclose(fp) != 0) {
45          printf ("The file could not be
   → closed.\n");
46      }
47
48      getchar(); /* Pause. */
49      return 0;
50  }
```

Script 12.5 continued

12. Write the array elements to the binary file and print a message to the user:

```
fwrite (numbers, sizeof(int), ITEMS,
→ fp);
printf ("The data has been
→ written.\n");
```

The `fwrite()` line starts by using the `numbers` variable as its pointer. This works because an array name is equivalent to its address in C (see Chapter 9, "Working with Pointers"). The function is then told to write `ITEMS` number of blocks, each of which is `sizeof(int)` bytes in size. We use `sizeof(int)` because `numbers` is an array of integers.

In layman's terms, the `fwrite()` line could be described as: go to the memory block, which starts where the `numbers` array starts, then take the next 50 blocks of data (each block being 4 bytes—the common size of an integer—in length) and write these to the file referenced by `fp`.

The `printf()` line just gives you something to see when the application runs. You could also print out all of the randomly generated numbers, if you want.

13. Complete the `fp` conditional:

```
} else {
    printf ("The file could not
→ be opened.\n");
    return 1;
}
```

14. Close the file:

```
if (fclose(fp) != 0) {
    printf ("The file could not
→ be closed.\n");
}
```

continues on next page

WRITING TO BINARY FILES

15. Complete the main function:

```
    getchar();
    return 0;
}
```

16. Save the file as *binary_write.c*, compile, and debug as necessary.

17. Run the application (**Figure 12.10**).

18. Open *numbers.dat* in a text editor (**Figure 12.11**).

✔ Tips

■ Whereas the fprintf() function writes text to a text file, the fwrite() function copies data stored in memory—which is always binary—to a file. This is why the first argument is a pointer (the address of a memory block), not a simple variable.

■ If you inadvertently open an ASCII file as binary on Windows, C will not handle the line endings properly, meaning you'll need to cope with them in your C code.

■ In case you were curious, ASCII stands for *American Standard Code for Information Interchange*.

■ Instead of using a loop to populate the array and then writing the entire array to the file, this application could write the random number directly to the binary file inside of the loop. In such a case you would change your fwrite() line so that it writes a single block of sizeof(int) size to the file at a time, rather than ITEMS number of blocks of sizeof(int) data. In other words, instead of creating an array of, say, 50 elements and then writing 50 blocks of data in one fwrite() call, you would just write a single block of data 50 times.

Figure 12.10 The results of successfully writing 50 random numbers to a binary data file.

Figure 12.11 The illegible binary contents of the *numbers.dat* file.

Reading from Binary Files

As you might expect, reading from binary files is just the opposite of writing to them. To do so, you'll make use of the `fread()` function:

```
fread (var_pointer, size, blocks, fp);
```

The first argument is a pointer to, or the address of, the variable to which the read data should be assigned. The second value is the size (in terms of bytes) of one block of data to be read in. This value should correspond to the size of the receiving variable. The *blocks* argument works like its counterpart in `fwrite()`: dictating how many chunks of data to read in. Finally, the file pointer is referenced.

In our next example, we use `fread()` to read the entire contents of the data file back into an array. In the subsequent example, `fread()` will be used differently, reading in just one number.

To read from a binary file:

1. Create a new file or project in your text editor or IDE.

2. Type the standard beginning lines of code (**Script 12.6**):

```
/* binary_read.c - Script 12.6 */
#include <stdio.h>
```

3. Set the file path and name as a C pre-processor macro:

```
#define THEFILE
→ "/Users/larry/Desktop/numbers.dat"
```
or
```
#define THEFILE "C:\\Documents and
→ Settings\\Larry Ullman\\Desktop\\
→ numbers.dat"
```

continues on next page

```
1    /* binary_read.c - Script 12.6 */
2
3    #include <stdio.h>
4
5    /* Set the file path and name. */
6    #define THEFILE
     → "/Users/larry/Desktop/numbers.dat"
7
8    /* Number of items being written. */
9    #define ITEMS 50
10
11   int main (void) {
12
13       /* Need a pointer of type FILE. */
14       FILE *fp;
15
16       int i; /* Loop counter. */
17       int numbers[ITEMS]; /* Array of
     → numbers. */
18
19       /* Attempt to open the file for
     → reading. */
20       fp = fopen(THEFILE, "rb");
21
22       if (fp != NULL) { /* The file
     → is open. */
23
24           printf("The contents of the
     → numbers file:\n");
25
26           /* Read the entire contents into
     → the numbers array. */
27           fread (numbers, sizeof(int),
     → ITEMS, fp);
28
29           /* Print each element. */
30           for (i = 0; i < ITEMS; i++) {
31               printf("%d\n", numbers[i]);
32           }
```

continues on next page

Script 12.6 You can read a binary file in a linear fashion using a program like this one.

Again, your directive should point to the same *numbers.dat* or just *numbers* file used by the *binary_write* application (Script 12.5).

4. Create a constant macro representing the number of items in the array:

```
#define ITEMS 50
```

This value will again be used repeatedly in this application, so we define it as a preprocessor directive.

5. Begin the `main` function and create a file pointer:

```
int main (void) {
FILE *fp;
```

6. Define the required variables:

```
int i;
int numbers[ITEMS];
```

These variables correspond to those in the previous example.

7. Open the file for binary reading:

```
fp = fopen(THEFILE, "rb");
```

The r mode is used to only read from a file; the b indicates it's a binary file.

8. Start a conditional based on the file pointer and print a caption:

```
if (fp != NULL) {
printf("The contents of the numbers
→ file:\n");
```

9. Read the entire contents of the file into the `numbers` array:

```
fread (numbers, sizeof(int), ITEMS,
→ fp);
```

This call to `fread()` says that it should read `ITEMS` number of blocks of `sizeof(int)` length, and store this data in the `numbers` array. This is essentially the inverse of the `fwrite()` call in *binary_write.c*.

```
 000                    📄 Script
33
34        } else {
35            printf ("The file could not be
→ opened.\n");
36            return 1; /* Exit the
→ function/application. */
37        }
38
39        /* Close the file. */
40        if (fclose(fp) != 0) {
41            printf ("The file could not be
→ closed.\n");
42        }
43
44        getchar(); /* Pause. */
45        return 0;
46  }
```

Script 12.6 *continued*

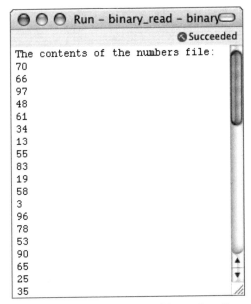

Figure 12.12 The binary contents of the numbers file are retrieved and then printed in text format. (Only part of the results are shown here.)

✔ Tips

- If you wanted, you could store the definitions of ITEMS and THEFILE in their own header file, which is then included by all three binary examples in this chapter. That way, a simple edit to the one file would keep each application working properly.

- The portability of a binary file may be limited due to how different processors store multibyte data. A *big endian* machine orders the most important bytes of the data first. A *little endian* machine orders the most important bytes last. Consequently, a binary file written on one type of computer may not be properly read on the other type.

10. Print each element of the array:

```
for (i = 0; i < ITEMS; i++) {
    printf("%d\n", numbers[i]);
}
```

Since the numbers array has now been populated with the data from the numbers file, it can be printed in a for loop, like any array.

11. Complete the fp conditional:

```
} else {
    printf ("The file could not
→ be opened.\n");
    return 1;
}
```

12. Close the file:

```
if (fclose(fp) != 0) {

    printf ("The file could not
→ be closed.\n");

}
```

13. Complete the main function:

```
    getchar();
    return 0;
}
```

14. Save the file as *binary_read.c*, compile, and debug as necessary.

15. Run the application (**Figure 12.12**).

Moving Around Within Binary Files

One of the benefits of working with binary files is that it's very easy to move around within the binary data. When you open a file, C creates a marker pinpointing a location within this file. (This marker is commonly called a *pointer* but we don't want to confuse you since it's not the same kind of pointer you've been working with.) When you read from a file, the data is read and the marker is moved forward. When you write, the data is added at that location and, again, the marker is moved forward.

You can also move the marker directly to a specific point using `fseek()`:

`fseek(fp, offset, starting_point);`

The first argument is our file pointer, which refers to an opened binary file. The second argument dictates how many bytes the virtual marker should move from the starting point. If the offset is positive, the marker is moved forward from the starting point. If the offset is negative, the marker is moved backwards from the starting point. The starting points themselves are specified using the constants or numeric equivalents listed in **Table 12.3**, and refer to the beginning of, the end of, or an arbitrary point in the file.

In this chapter's final example, the marker will be moved to a random point within the *numbers* file. From there, a number will be read and printed.

Table 12.3 These constants or their numeric equivalent are used with `fseek()` to move the marker around.

fseek() Starting Point Constants		
CONSTANT	NUMERIC	MEANING
SEEK_SET	0L	The beginning of the file
SEEK_CUR	1L	The current marker position within the file
SEEK_END	2L	The end of the file

```
1   /* random_read.c - Script 12.7 */
2
3   #include <stdio.h>
4   #include <stdlib.h> /* For rand() and
    → srand(). */
5   #include <time.h> /* For time(), used
    → with srand(). */
6
7   /* Set the file path and name. */
8   #define THEFILE
    → "/Users/larry/Desktop/numbers.dat"
9
10  /* Number of items being written. */
11  #define ITEMS 50
12
13  int main (void) {
14
15      /* Need a pointer of type FILE. */
16      FILE *fp;
17
18      /* Two integers are required. */
19      int offset, number;
20
21      /* Attempt to open the file for
    → binary reading. */
22      fp = fopen(THEFILE, "rb");
23
24      if (fp != NULL) { /* The file is open.
    → */
25
26          /* Find a random offset in bytes.
    → */
27          srand((unsigned)time(NULL));
28          offset = rand() % ITEMS;
29          offset *= sizeof(int);
30
31          /* Read in the number found at
    → the random location. */
32          fseek (fp, offset, SEEK_SET);
```

continues on next page

Script 12.7 A random point in the data file is used to return a "lucky number."

To navigate a binary file:

1. Create a new file or project in your text editor or IDE.

2. Type the standard beginning lines of code (**Script 12.7**):

   ```
   /* random_read.c - Script 12.7 */
   #include <stdio.h>
   ```

3. Require two more standard libraries:

   ```
   #include <stdlib.h>
   #include <time.h>
   ```

   Because this application will use the rand() function (as *binary_write* did), these extra libraries are necessary.

4. Set the file path and name as a C pre-processor macro:

   ```
   #define THEFILE
   → "/Users/larry/Desktop/numbers.dat"
   ```

   or

   ```
   #define THEFILE "C:\\Documents and
   → Settings\\Larry Ullman\\Desktop\\
   → numbers.dat"
   ```

5. Create a constant macro representing the number of items in the array:

   ```
   #define ITEMS 50
   ```

6. Begin the main function and create a file pointer:

   ```
   int main (void) {
   FILE *fp;
   ```

7. Define the required variables:

   ```
   int offset, number;
   ```

   The first integer will be used as the off-set: the location within the *numbers* file to move to. The second will store the read-in number value.

continues on next page

8. Open the file for binary reading:

```
fp = fopen(THEFILE, "rb");
```

9. Start a conditional based on the file pointer:

```
if (fp != NULL) {
```

10. Determine a random offset value:

```
srand((unsigned)time(NULL));
offset = rand() % ITEMS;
offset *= sizeof(int);
```

The first line seeds the `rand()` function, using the timestamp returned by `time()`. The second line picks an arbitrary offset, as a random number up to the number of items stored. After this second line of code, `offset` will be equal to a number between 0 and 49, corresponding to the 50 items originally stored in the file (like an array, though, we begin counting at 0).

The third line multiplies the value of `offset` by the size of an integer. This is necessary because we need to specify the offset in bytes. For example, if the randomly generated value is 10, then the offset needs to be 40 bytes: 10 times `sizeof(int)`, normally 4 bytes.

11. Move to the random location and read in a number:

```
fseek (fp, offset, SEEK_SET);
fread (&number, sizeof(number),
→ 1, fp);
```

The first line moves the virtual marker `offset` bytes into the file, starting from the beginning of the file. The second line reads one block of data of `sizeof(number)` bytes and stores this in the `number` variable. Remember that the `fread()` function takes an address of a variable as its first argument, so `&number` is used (the memory address for the `number` variable).

```
                                    Script
33          fread (&number, sizeof(number),
     → 1, fp);

34

35          /* Print the number. */
36          printf("Your lucky number is:
     → %d.\n", number);

37

38     } else {
39          printf ("The file could not be
     → opened.\n");
40          return 1; /* Exit the
     → function/application. */
41     }

42

43     /* Close the file. */
44     if (fclose(fp) != 0) {
45          printf ("The file could not
     → be closed.\n");
46     }

47

48     getchar(); /* Pause. */
49     return 0;
50 }
```

Script 12.7 *continued*

Figure 12.13 A random number is retrieved from the binary file and printed.

Figure 12.14 Another execution of the same application retrieves a different random value.

12. Print the number:

```
printf("Your lucky number is: %d.\n",
→ number);
```

Once the number has been retrieved, its value can be printed.

13. Complete the `fp` conditional:

```
} else {
    printf ("The file could not
→ be opened.\n");
    return 1;
}
```

14. Close the file:

```
if (fclose(fp) != 0) {
    printf ("The file could not
→ be closed.\n");
}
```

15. Complete the `main` function:

```
    getchar();
    return 0;
}
```

16. Save the file as *random_read.c*, compile, and debug as necessary.

17. Run the application (**Figure 12.13**).

18. Run the application again to see a different value (**Figure 12.14**).

✔ Tips

- The `fseek()` function, like many functions, returns the value 0 if it worked and -1 otherwise.

- The `ftell()` function returns the current location of the marker in the text file as a number of bytes.

- The `rewind()` function moves the marker back to the beginning of the file.

- The `fseek()` and `ftell()` functions will work on plain ASCII files as well, although doing so is trickier.

MOVING AROUND WITHIN BINARY FILES

319

ADVANCED DATA TYPES

All of the data types covered in this book so far—numbers, characters, and arrays—have been relatively basic, storing simple values. None of these data types can adequately mimic the kind of real-world information you'll often have to work with. To better handle complex records, you need the more advanced data types discussed in this chapter.

The bulk of the material covers structures, an important tool for the C programmer. We will build on the many ways you can use structures, culminating with linked lists. We'll also briefly introduce enumerated types and unions, two other special formats C has, although neither is as necessary as structures.

ADVANCED DATA TYPES

Introduction to Structures

Structures are not a data type in themselves but rather a way for you to define your own data type. Moreover, with structures you can better model real-world objects. For example, if you wanted to create a list of books, storing the author, publication date, and title of each, you could do that with arrays: one array for the authors, one for the publication years, and a third for the titles (**Figure 13.1**). But such a construct would be less than ideal, at the very least because the three arrays would be seemingly unrelated. A better solution is to create one type of variable that can store the author's name, the title, and the publication date, all under one umbrella. This is where structures come in.

To use structures, you first define the structure, using the data types with which you are already familiar. The syntax requires the struct keyword:

```
struct structure_name {
    var_type member_var1;
    var_type member_var2;
};
```

For the books example, you can create a structure like this:

```
struct books {
    char author[40];
    char title[60];
    int pub_year;
};
```

The author, title, and pub_year variables are now all *members* of the books structure.

Once you've defined the structure model, you can create variables of that type:

```
struct structure_name variable_name;
struct books my_book;
```

authors

index	value
0	Nick Hornby
1	Melissa Bank
2	David Sedaris

pub_year

index	value
0	1992
1	1999
2	1997

titles

index	value
0	Fever Pitch
1	Girls' Guide to...
2	Naked

Figure 13.1 Using arrays, all of the required information is stored but the association between the records isn't clear.

```
 ● ● ●          📄 Script
 1     /* weather_structure.c - Script 13.1 */

 2

 3     #include <stdio.h>

 4

 5     /* Set the file path and name. */
 6     #define THEFILE
      → "/Users/Larry/Desktop/weather.dat"

 7

 8     int main (void) {

 9

10         /* Define a structure and create
      → a variable of that type. */
11         struct weather_record {
12             char date[11]; /* YYYY-MM-DD */
13             int high;
14             int low;
15         };

16

17         struct weather_record today; /* One
      → structure variable of type
      → weather_record. */

18

19         /* Need a pointer of type FILE. */
20         FILE *fp;

21

22         /* Attempt to open the file for
      → appended binary writing. */
23         fp = fopen(THEFILE, "ab");

24

25         if (fp != NULL) { /* The file
      → is open. */

26

27             /* Prompt the user. */
28             printf ("Enter a date, the high
      → temperature, and the low
      → temperature.\n(YYYY-MM-DD ## ##): ");

29
```

continues on next page

Script 13.1 This new version of the *record_weather* application uses structures to create records. One structure at a time is then written to the binary file.

To refer to a specific structure member, use the *variable_name.member* syntax:

```
my_book.pub_year = 2005;
```

In this next example, the *record_weather* application from Chapter 12, "File Input and Output," will be rewritten to use structures. Each structure will then be written to a binary file.

To use structures:

1. Create a new file or project in your text editor or IDE.

2. Type the standard beginning lines of code (**Script 13.1**):

   ```
   /* weather_structure.c - Script 13.1
   → */

   #include <stdio.h>
   ```

3. Set the file path and name as a C pre-processor macro:

   ```
   #define THEFILE
   → "/Users/larry/Desktop/weather.dat"
   ```
   or
   ```
   #define THEFILE "C:\\Documents and
   → Settings\\Larry Ullman\\Desktop\\
   → weather.dat"
   ```

   The exact syntax will depend on your operating system, but you should use an absolute path to the file here. Also, a *.dat* file extension is being used—since it will be a binary data file—instead of *.txt*.

4. Begin the main function:

   ```
   int main (void) {
   ```

   continues on next page

5. Define the structure and create a variable of that type:

```
struct weather_record {
    char date[11];
    int high;
    int low;
};
struct weather_record today;
```

This structure will be called `weather_record`. It contains three members: a character array called `date`, an integer called `high`, and another integer called `low`. Each of these correspond to the variables that were used in the previous version of this application.

One variable of the `weather_record` type is created, called `today`. Note that you have to use both the keyword `struct` as well as the structure name in defining this variable.

6. Create a file pointer and open the file for appended binary writing:

```
FILE *fp;
fp = fopen(THEFILE, "ab");
```

The `fp` file pointer is being used exactly as in the previous chapter. The second line opens the file in binary mode for appended writing. Each record written to the file will be added after any existing data.

7. Start a conditional based on the file pointer and prompt the user:

```
if (fp != NULL) {
    printf ("Enter a date, the high
→ temperature, and the low
→ temperature.\n(YYYY-MM-DD ## ##):
→ ");
```

The prompt (**Figure 13.2**) is exactly like the prompt used before, indicating what information is expected, in what order, and in what format.

```
 ● ● ●                    Script

30          /* Handle the input, assigning it
→ to the structure fields. */
31          if (scanf ("%10s %d %d",
→ today.date, &today.high, &today.low)
→ == 3) {
32
33              /* Write the data. */
34              fwrite (&today, sizeof(struct
→ weather_record), 1, fp);
35              printf ("The data has been
→ written.\n");
36
37          } else {
38              printf ("The data was not
→ in the proper format.\n");
39          }
40
41      } else {
42          printf ("The file could not
→ be opened.\n");
43          return 1; /* Exit the
→ function/application. */
44      }
45
46      /* Close the file. */
47      if (fclose(fp) != 0) {
48          printf ("The file could not
→ be closed.\n");
49      }
50
51      getchar(); /* Pause. */
52      getchar(); /* Pause. */
53      return 0;
54
55  }
```

Script 13.1 *continued*

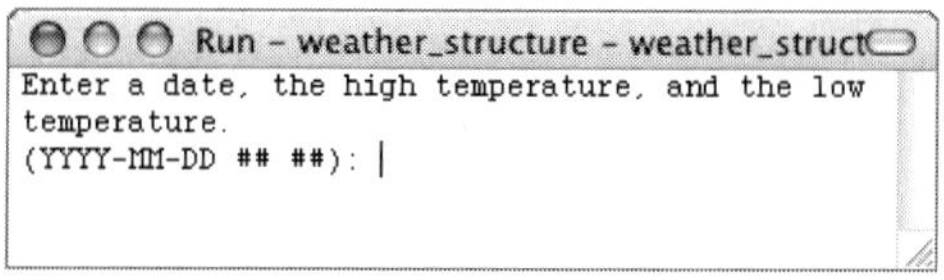

Figure 13.2 Prompting the user to enter a day's date, and high and low temperatures.

8. Read in the keyed input as part of a conditional, assigning each value to the appropriate structure field:

```
if (scanf ("%10s %d %d", today.date,
→ &today.high, &today.low) == 3) {
```

Here the `scanf()` function is working as you've seen it before: reading in a string and two integers, and assigning them to variables. To refer to the structure's members, the `var.members` syntax is used, so `today.date` refers to `today`'s `date` field. The number fields are preceded by the address of operator (`&`), in keeping with the proper `scanf()` syntax.

This conditional checks the value returned by `scanf()` to see if it's equal to 3, meaning that the data was properly entered.

9. Write the structure to the binary file and print a message to the user:

```
fwrite (&today, sizeof(struct
→ weather_record), 1, fp);
printf ("The data has been
→ written.\n");
```

The `fwrite()` line starts by using the `&today` variable as its pointer. This is necessary since `fwrite()` expects an address in memory (where it will find the data to be written) as its first argument. The function is then told to write **1** block of data, which is `sizeof(struct weather_record)` bytes in size. In other words, take 1 `weather_record` structure's worth of data from the memory and write it to the file.

continues on next page

INTRODUCTION TO STRUCTURES

The printf() line just gives you something to see when the application runs. You could also print out the entered values, if you want (**Figure 13.3**), by using

```
printf("You entered the date as %s,
→ the high temperature as %d, and
→ the low temperature as %d.\n",
→ today.date, today.high, today.low);
```

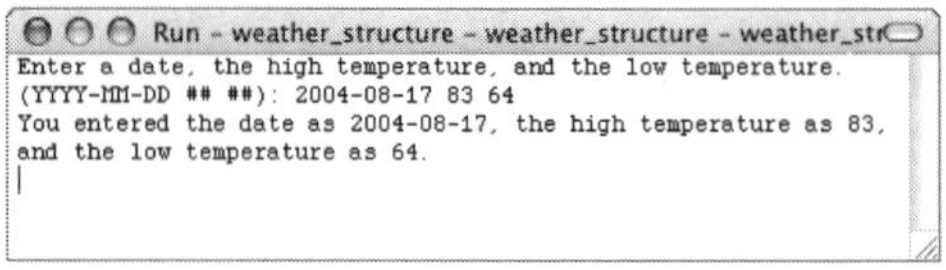

Figure 13.3 You can change the responsive print statement (line 35 of Script 13.1) to be more informative, if you desire.

10. Complete the scanf() conditional:

```
} else {
    printf ("The data was not in
→ the proper format.\n");
}
```

11. Complete the fp conditional:

```
} else {
    printf ("The file could not
→ be opened.\n");
    return 1;
}
```

12. Close the file:

```
if (fclose(fp) != 0) {
    printf ("The file could not
→ be closed.\n");
}
```

13. Complete the main function:

```
    getchar();
    getchar();
    return 0;
}
```

14. Save the file as *weather_structure.c*, compile, and debug as necessary.

15. Run the application, populating the data file (**Figures 13.4** and **13.5**).

✔ Tips

■ You can define a specific structure variable during the declaration of the structure:

```
struct student {
    char name[30];
    float gpa;
} timmy;
```

■ As with other variables, the value of a structure can be initialized during the declaration:

```
struct student {
    char name[30];
    float gpa;
} timmy = { "Timmy Noonan", 3.65};
```

■ You cannot use an existing keyword as your structure or variable name.

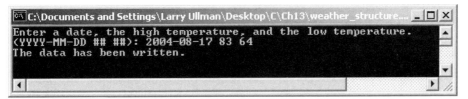

Figure 13.4 The end user cannot tell what goes on behind the scenes (assuming everything works) but this version of the application now uses structures.

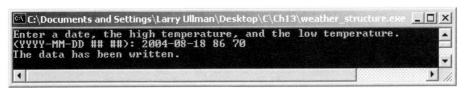

Figure 13.5 Entering another record.

A Look at Unions

A union is somewhat like a structure in its flexible design but can contain only a single value at a time. It can be defined to hold many *types* of values, but only one of those values will ever be stored.

For example, if you wanted to define a variable that would store one type of identification—mother's maiden name, user's date of birth, or the last four digits of the user's social security number—you can use a union:

```
union id {
    char maiden[20];
    char dob[11];
    int ssn;
};
```

Once you've defined the union, you can create variables of that type:

```
union id person;
```

The union variable can now be assigned values like a structure, using the `variable.member` syntax:

```
strncpy(person.maiden, "Malawey", 7);
```

The `person` union now stores the value `Malawey` in the `maiden` field.

```
person.ssn = 1234;
```

The `person` union now stores the value `1234` in the `ssn` field and the `maiden` field no longer has a value.

As you can tell from this example, unions have limited use but they can definitely come in handy under the right circumstances.

Using typedef

The `typedef` operator lets you rename a data type, like creating an alias. One of its main uses is to increase the portability of C applications: a common header file can include aliases to specific data types for different computers. By changing the particulars of the header file, the application should work on another system.

As an example, before the C99 standard supported the boolean type, you could have used `typedef` to create it yourself (which would store *0* or *1*):

```
typedef int boolean;
boolean correct;
```

The `typedef` operator can be used nicely with structures to simplify your declarations:

```
structure students {
   char name[30];
   gpa float;
};
```

The formal way to create a variable of this structure's type is

```
struct students timmy;
```

By using `typedef`, you can create an alias:

```
typedef struct students student_type;
```

Now, to declare a variable of this structure's type, just use

```
student_type timmy;
```

The `typedef` line of code makes the word `student_type` act as shorthand for `struct students`.

Using `typedef` like this can make your code easier to type and easier to read. It will be used in our next example, *read_weather*, which will retrieve all the data from the binary *weather.dat* file and display it.

To use typedef:

1. Create a new file or project in your text editor or IDE.

2. Type the standard beginning lines of code (**Script 13.2**).

```
/* read_weather.c - Script 13.2 */
#include <stdio.h>
```

3. Set the file path and name as a C preprocessor macro:

```
#define THEFILE
→ "/Users/larry/Desktop/weather.dat"
```

or

```
#define THEFILE "C:\\Documents and
→ Settings\\Larry Ullman\\Desktop\\
→ weather.dat"
```

This should point to the exact same file we used in *weather_structure.c* (Script 13.1).

4. Begin the main function:

```
int main (void) {
```

5. Define the structure:

```
struct weather_record {
    char date[11];
    int high;
    int low;
};
```

The structure also matches the same structure defined in the previous example.

6. Use typedef to redefine the structure type, then create a structure variables:

```
typedef struct weather_record wr;
wr day;
```

The first line makes an alias so that wr (short for weather_record) stands for struct weather_record. Then wr is used to create a day variable of type struct weather_record.

```
 1    /* read_weather.c - Script 11.2 */
 2
 3    #include <stdio.h>
 4
 5    /* Set the file path and name. */
 6    #define THEFILE
    →  "/Users/Larry/Desktop/weather.dat"
 7
 8    int main (void) {
 9
10        /* Define the structure. */
11        struct weather_record {
12            char date[11];
13            int high;
14            int low;
15        };
16
17        /* Use typedef to create an alias.
    →  */
18        typedef struct weather_record wr;
19
20        /* Create a structure variable. */
21        wr day;
22
23        /* Need a pointer of type FILE. */
24        FILE *fp;
25
26        /* Attempt to open the file for
    →  binary reading. */
27        fp = fopen(THEFILE, "rb");
28
29        if (fp != NULL) { /* The file is
    →  open. */
30
31            /* Loop through the entire file,
    →  assigning each structure to day. */
32            while (fread (&day, sizeof(wr),
    →  1, fp)) {
```

continues on next page

Script 13.2 The typedef operator can help shorten how you refer to structures. This application uses those structures to read data from a binary file.

USING TYPEDEF

```
○ ○ ○              Script
33
34                /* Print the information,
   → using the structure's fields. */
35                printf ("Date: %s\nHigh:
   → %d\nLow: %d\n\n", day.date, day.high,
   → day.low);
36
37           }
38
39      } else {
40           printf ("The file could not
   → be opened.\n");
41           return 1; /* Exit the
   → function/application. */
42      }
43
44      /* Close the file. */
45      if (fclose(fp) != 0) {
46           printf ("The file could not
   → be closed.\n");
47      }
48
49
50      getchar(); /* Pause. */
51      return 0;
52
53  }
```

Script 13.2 *continued*

7. Create a file pointer and open the file for binary reading:

   ```
   FILE *fp;
   fp = fopen(THEFILE, "rb");
   if (fp != NULL) {
   ```

8. Read in the contents of the data file in a loop:

   ```
   while (fread (&day, sizeof(wr), 1,
    → fp)) {
   ```

   This line says that 1 block of `sizeof(wr)` bytes should be read from the file and assigned to **day**. Without using the **typedef** operator, the second parameter would have to be formally written out as `sizeof(struct weather_record)`.

   As long as this condition is true—that a block could be read from the binary file—the contents of the loop will be executed.

9. Print each record:

   ```
   printf ("Date: %s\nHigh: %d\nLow:
    → %d\n\n", day.date, day.high,
    → day.low);
   ```

   A simple print statement is used to send each record to the standard output. To access the individual members (which are stored in the **day** structure), use the **day**.*membername* syntax.

10. Complete the **while** loop:

    ```
    }
    ```

11. Complete the **fp** conditional:

    ```
    } else {
        printf ("The file could not
     → be opened.\n");
        return 1;
    }
    ```

continues on next page

USING TYPEDEF

12. Close the file:

```
if (fclose(fp) != 0) {
    printf ("The file could not
→ be closed.\n");
}
```

13. Complete the main function:

```
    getchar();
    return 0;
}
```

14. Save the file as *read_weather.c*, compile, and debug as necessary.

15. Run the application (**Figure 13.6**).

✔ Tips

■ Although you should place your typedef statements toward the top of your code, the only requirement is that they are defined before they are used.

■ When you have a series of applications all of which use the same data file and structure definition (like *weather_structure* and *read_weather*), you could benefit from using an external library file. Place the #define macro and the structure definition is a plain-text file called *defs.h* and then include this in your other C files.

■ Overusing typedef or using it in ways that's not clear can lead to confusing code. Each alias you make should be fairly obvious and useful.

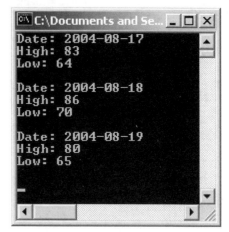

Figure 13.6 This application uses structures to parse individual elements out of a binary file.

Enumerated Types

Although the enumerated type is not the most popular or useful data type in C, it does have its place and being familiar with it is worth your while. An enumerated type is a special variable type you define that limits the possible values a variable can have. For example, a weekday variable can have only one of seven possible values (Sunday, Monday, Tuesday, etc.) or a month variable can be only one of 12 possible values.

To define an enumerated type, use the enum keyword:

```
enum type_name {possible values};
enum weekdays {Sunday, Monday, Tuesday, Wednesday, Thursday, Friday, Saturday};
```

Once you've defined the type itself, you can create a variable of that type:

```
enum weekdays appt_day;
```

Now the appt_day can only be assigned one of those seven values:

```
appt_day = Tuesday;
```

Notice that quotation marks are not being used in either the enumerated type definition or in assigning the specific variable a value. This is because the different values become named constants in C. Enumerated types are actually of type int. C will, behind the scenes, assign the numbers 0, 1, etc. to the possible values.

Because the enumerated values are actually integers, you can specify their values:

```
enum months {January = 1, February = 2, …};
```

or just

```
enum months {January = 1, February, March, …};
```

Another nice feature of enumerated types is that they can be used in switch statements, unlike strings.

Essentially the enumerated type does two things for you:

◆ It allows you to use words instead of numbers to represent values.

◆ It forces a variable to have an appropriate value.

Whether or not you use enumerated types is mostly a matter of preference. It won't hurt to never use them, but you may appreciate what they offer. Some programmers use enumerated types more like comments, as a way of documenting how a variable is supposed to behave.

Using Arrays of Structures

Structures, just like integers, floats, and characters, can be used in arrays. The syntax for creating one is just like you'd expect:

```
struct students {
    char name[30];
    float gpa;
};
struct students class[20];
```

To refer to an individual array element, you would of course refer to the array's index, like `class[19]`. To refer to an individual structural member of an individual array element, the syntax is

```
array_name[index].field_name
class[10].gpa = 2.78;
```

In our next example, we create a list of student names and grades by taking input from the user and storing it in an array of structures.

To use arrays of structures:

1. Create a new file or project in your text editor or IDE.

2. Type the standard beginning lines of code (**Script 13.3**).

   ```
   /* grades.c - Script 13.3 */
   #include <stdio.h>
   ```

3. Include the *string.h* library file:

   ```
   #include <string.h>
   ```

   In order to use the `strncpy()` function, the *string.h* file must be included.

4. Define two macro constants:

   ```
   #define STR_LEN 20
   #define NUM_STUDENTS 10
   ```

```
1    /* grades.c - Script 13.3 */
2
3    #include <stdio.h>
4    #include <string.h> /* For string
        → functions. */
5
6    #define STR_LEN 20
7
8    #define NUM_STUDENTS 10
9
10   int main (void) {
11
12       /* Define the structure. */
13       struct student_grade {
14           char first_name[STR_LEN];
15           char last_name[STR_LEN];
16           float grade;
17       };
18
19       /* Rename the structure syntax. */
20       typedef struct student_grade sg;
21
22       /* Create an array of structures. */
23       sg class[NUM_STUDENTS];
24
25       /* Need some counters. */
26       int i, num;
27       int count = 0;
28
29       /* Need some strings to handle
        → the input. */
30       char classname[12], fn[STR_LEN],
        → ln[STR_LEN];
31
32       /* Need a temporary float. */
33       float g; /* grade */
34
```

continues on next page

Script 13.3 An array of structures is used to represent an entire class of students. Each array element stores the student's first name, last name, and grade.

```
  ● ● ●              📄 Script
35        /* Prompt the user. */
36        printf ("Enter the classname (without
   → spaces): ");
37        scanf ("%11s", classname);
38
39        /* Insert a check on the classname,
   → if you want. */
40
41        /* Loop to read in all the student
   → data. */
42        for (i = 0; i < NUM_STUDENTS; ++i) {
43
44            /* Prompt the user. */
45            printf ("Enter the student's name
   → and their grade. Enter 0 0 0 to
   → quit.\n(First Last ##.#): ");
46
47            /* Read in the input. */
48            num = scanf ("%11s %11s %f", fn,
   → ln, &g);
49
50            /* Check if the user is done. */
51            if (fn[0] == '0') {
52                break;
53            }
54
55            /* Handle the input. */
56            if (num == 3) {
57
58                strncpy(class[i].first_name,
   → fn, STR_LEN-1);
59                class[i].first_name[STR_LEN-
   → 1] = '\0';
60                strncpy(class[i].last_name,
   → ln, STR_LEN-1);
61                class[i].last_name[STR_LEN-1]
   → = '\0';
62                class[i].grade = g;
63                ++count;
64
                        continues on next page
```

Script 13.3 *continued*

The first value represents the maximum string length (for a person's first and last names). The second will be the number of elements in the array.

5. Begin the main function:

```
int main (void) {
```

6. Define the structure:

```
struct student_grade {
    char first_name[STR_LEN];
    char last_name[STR_LEN];
    float grade;
};
```

The structure has two character arrays and one float.

7. Use typedef to rename the structure syntax, then create an array of structures:

```
typedef struct student_grade sg;
sg class[NUM_STUDENTS];
```

Again, the typedef simplifies the process of referring to a structure. Then an array of structures called class is created.

8. Create the other variables:

```
int i, num;
int count = 0;
float g;
char classname[12], fn[STR_LEN],
    → ln[STR_LEN];
```

Several standard variables are required to handle the user input. Three integers are declared: i, a loop counter; num, which will be used to validate the input; and, count, which will count the number of entered records. One float is required to store the grade point average (which will then be stored in the array of structures). Finally there are three character arrays. Two match up with the first_name and last_name structure members and the third is for storing a class name.

continues on next page

USING ARRAYS OF STRUCTURES

9. Prompt the user and read in the class name:

```
printf ("Enter the classname (without
→ spaces): ");
scanf ("%11s", classname);
```

The application begins by taking the name of the class for which student records will be entered (**Figure 13.7**). The assumption is that this will be something like *Algebra*, *English*, or *EN302*.

10. Begin a loop:

```
for (i = 0; i < NUM_STUDENTS; ++i) {
```

The user will be prompted to enter several student records. This process takes place within a loop, which goes from 0 to 1 less than NUM_STUDENTS (the size of the array).

11. Prompt the user and read in the input:

```
printf ("Enter the student's name
→ and their grade. Enter 0 0 0 to
→ quit.\n(First Last ##.#): ");
num = scanf ("%11s %11s %f", fn, ln,
→ &g);
```

First the user is prompted so that they know what information is requested and in what format (**Figure 13.8**). Then the scanf() function is called, assigning the input to the fn, ln, and g variables.

12. Check if the user has finished entering records:

```
if (fn[0] == '0') {
    break;
}
```

As you can tell from the prompt (see Figure 13.8), if the first character entered is a *0*, the user has no more records to enter. This conditional checks for that contingency and exits the for loop (via the break statement) if it is true.

```
   ○ ○ ○                    Script
65           } else { /* Improper input
   → format. */
66               printf ("The data was not
   → in the proper format.\n");
67               break;
68           }
69       }
70
71       /* Print the data. */
72       printf ("Students and grades for the
   → class '%s':\n", classname);
73       for (i = 0; i < count; ++i) {
74           printf("%s %s %0.1f\n",
   → class[i].first_name,
   → class[i].last_name, class[i].grade);
75       }
76
77       getchar(); /* Pause. */
78       getchar(); /* Pause. */
79       return 0;
80
81  }
```

Script 13.3 *continued*

13. Check if the proper input was entered:

```
if (num == 3) {
```

The num variable is assigned a value from the scanf() function. If that function read in three items and assigned them to the three variables, we can assume that the data was entered correctly.

14. Assign the input to the structure:

```
strncpy(class[i].first_name, fn,
→ STR_LEN-1);
class[i].first_name[STR_LEN-1]
→ = '\0';
strncpy(class[i].last_name, ln,
→ STR_LEN-1);
class[i].last_name[STR_LEN-1] =
→ '\0';
class[i].grade = g;
++count;
```

Assigning values to an array of structures is easier than you might think. Begin by identifying the specific array element: class[i]. Then refer to each member number using the .member syntax.

continues on next page

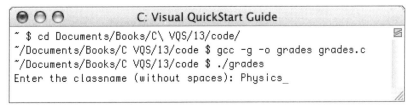

```
● ● ●          C: Visual QuickStart Guide
~ $ cd Documents/Books/C\ VQS/13/code/
~/Documents/Books/C VQS/13/code $ gcc -g -o grades grades.c
~/Documents/Books/C VQS/13/code $ ./grades
Enter the classname (without spaces): Physics_
```

Figure 13.7 The user is first prompted to enter the name of a class.

```
● ● ●          C: Visual QuickStart Guide
~/Documents/Books/C VQS/13/code $ gcc -g -o grades grades.c
~/Documents/Books/C VQS/13/code $ ./grades
Enter the classname (without spaces): Physics
Enter the student's name and their grade. Enter 0 0 0 to quit.
(First Last ##.#): Larry Ullman 85.6_
```

Figure 13.8 Reading in one student record at a time.

The `strncpy()` function is used to assign values to the two character arrays and the `grade` value is assigned using the assignment operator. After each name value is assigned, their final character (`STR_LEN - 1`) is assigned a terminating `\0` character. This is a safety precaution, as each string may not have been properly terminated during the copy.

15. Complete the `num` conditional and the loop:

```
    } else {
            printf ("The data was
→ not in the proper format.\n");
            break;
    }
}
```

If the value returned by `scanf()`—`num`—is not equal to 3, the data wasn't entered properly and the loop should be exited.

16. Print all of the records:

```
printf ("Students and grades for the
→ class '%s':\n", classname);
for (i = 0; i < count; ++i) {
    printf("%s %s %0.1f\n",
→ class[i].first_name,
→ class[i].last_name,
→ class[i].grade);
}
```

Printing the records requires another for loop. Instead of counting up to `NUM_STUDENTS`, it goes to `count`, which is the actual number of records entered.

Within the loop itself, each array element and structure member is fed to the print statement.

17. Complete the `main` function:

```
    getchar();
    getchar();
    return 0;
}
```

Structures and Pointers

You can, naturally, create a pointer to a structure. As with any pointer, the type of pointer must match the type of variable it points to. So

```
struct student {
    char name[30];
    float gpa;
};
struct student timmy, * struct_ptr;
struct_ptr = &timmy;
```

Once you've done this, you can do all the wonderful things with the pointer that you've now (possibly) grown accustomed to. For example, you can pass the structure's pointer to a function.

To refer to a structure's member by using a pointer, there are two options:

```
(*struct_ptr).member
```

or

```
struct_ptr->member
```

The first, more complex example requires the parentheses, since the dot has a higher precedence than the dereferencing operator (*). The second option is syntactically easier and means the same thing.

Finally it should be said that when working with pointers to structures, the programmer must clearly understand how memory is being allocated. If it's dynamically allocated using `malloc()`, as in the next example, you must be certain to free any used memory. If the memory is statically allocated, you do not need to worry about freeing it.

18. Save the file as *grades.c*, compile, and debug as necessary.

19. Run the application, varying the number of entries (**Figure 13.9**).

✔ Tips

■ Arrays of structures can be initialized during declaration, but the syntax can be very complicated.

■ Structures can also be nested, where the definition of one structure includes a field of a structure type.

■ In a way, understanding structures is a good first step toward understanding object-oriented programming (OOP). OOP involves the definition of classes, composed of both variables and functions.

■ You could improve upon this application in many ways—such as storing the records in a binary file, putting more thorough validation routines in place, or using the discard_input() function—but, as it stands, it's a good representation of how to use an array of structures.

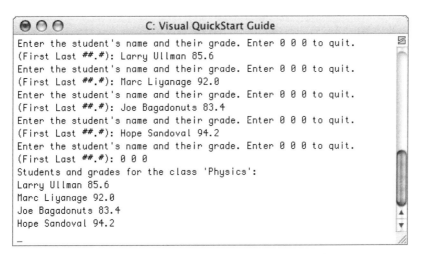

Figure 13.9 Several records are entered and then redisplayed by the application.

Introduction to Linked Lists

The problem with static arrays (like the array of structures in our previous example) is that they can have only a finite number of elements. This value is set during compilation, meaning that when you write the program, you must know and set the maximum number of elements to ever be stored. In Chapter 10, "Managing Memory," you learned how to make a dynamically sized array using realloc(), which increased the amount of available memory as needed. Linked lists allow you to combine these two concepts, creating a growing list of structures.

A linked list takes structures one step further by making them self-referential. This is accomplished by defining a structure as containing both data (the actual information being stored) and a pointer to the next item in the list (**Figure 13.10**).

The basic definition of a linked list is

```
struct my_list {
    char data[100];
    struct my_list *next;
};
```

You can have as many members in the structure as you like, and of any type, as long as you include one pointer member. That pointer must be of the struct my_list type (the same type as the structure itself).

To begin a linked list, the first item in the list should be declared as a pointer and initialized to NULL (**Figure 13.11**):

```
struct my_list *item = NULL;
```

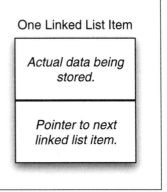

Figure 13.10 It helps to think of linked lists as blocks of memory that store both data and a pointer to the next memory block.

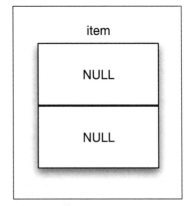

Figure 13.11 The first linked list item is created and set to NULL.

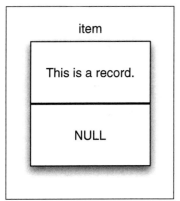

Figure 13.12 The first item in the linked list now stores a value but has a NULL pointer.

With only the one item in the list, this widget is both the start (sometimes called the *head*) and end (or *tail*) of the entire linked list. As the ending item, its value—or specifically its pointer's value—should be NULL (so you know no other items follow it).

The next step is to allocate the necessary memory to store all of the structure's data. The malloc() function will do this. That syntax is

```
item = (struct my_list *) malloc
→ (sizeof(struct my_list));
```

That line of code says that the required number of bytes for the structure (sizeof(struct my_list)) needs to be allocated. This should be *casted* as a pointer of type struct my_list. For detailed explanation of this process you can review Chapter 10, but all that is really happening here is that memory is being allocated for a structure instead of any array, number, or character.

Now that there is room in memory for item, the data can then be assigned to this first member of the structure, using the special *pointer->field* syntax, introduced in the sidebar "Structures and Pointers":

```
strncpy(item->data, "This is a record.",
→ 99);
item->next = NULL;
```

At this point, there is one structure in memory, containing some data and a NULL pointer (**Figure 13.12**).

To create another item, allocate the proper amount of memory:

```
struct my_list *new_item = NULL;
→ new_item = (struct my_list *) malloc
→ (sizeof(my_list));
```

This next item can then be assigned a value (**Figure 13.13**):

```
strncpy(new_item->data, "This is another
→ record.", 99);
new_item->next = NULL;
```

You could repeat this process, making as many new pointers as you want, for each added structure. But then you'll still be limited to the number of items set during compilation. To make this process limitless, you must be able to free up `new_item` so that it can be used again. To do that while still being able to find the `new_item` data, we need to store the address in memory where this information can be found. So, you assign `new_item`'s memory address to `item`'s pointer member.

This is done simply enough (**Figure 13.14**):

```
item->next = new_item;
```

Now you have a linked list. The `new_item` variable can be reused (to add another link) but you can still access every stored value as long as you retain the first item.

The concept behind linked lists can be confusing, so we'll paraphrase the idea. Simply put, a linked list stores blocks of information in memory. Each block holds both the data itself, and the address to where the next block is stored (this is the pointer). To access all of the stored data, all the C application needs to know is the address of the first block. There it can find the data and the address of the second block. At the second block it finds more data and the address to the third block. This continues until the address stored in a block is `NULL`, indicating there are no more records.

In this chapter's final example, we rewrite the *grades* application so that it can take any number of records. We include several illustrations here to help you visualize the process.

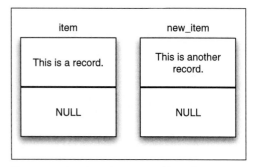

Figure 13.13 Two items now exist, although neither is linked to the other.

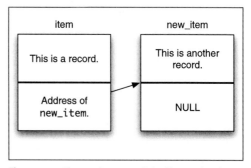

Figure 13.14 The two items are linked by storing the address of the one in the pointer member of the other.

Where to Add Items in a List

List items can be added at the beginning or end of the list (they can also be inserted into the middle but that requires a bit more work). The example in the introductory text added an item to the end of the list. To do so, the previous tail (last) item's pointer value is set to the newly added item. This method is conceptually easy to grasp but requires knowing the last item in the list, which means that the application must loop through each list item until it reaches the end. Alternatively, you could maintain two separate pointers: the head and the tail.

This next example (Script 13.4) adds items to the front of the list. It takes less effort in C (because you should always know which item is first) but is a little tricky to wrap your head around. If you have `first_item` (the head), `second_item` (the next item in the list), and `new_item` (the one being added), here is a descriptive version of the process:

1. The `new_item` pointer must be set to point to the address of `first_item`, so that `new_item` links to the rest of the chain. The `first_item` pointer stills points to the address of `second_item`.

2. The value of the `first_item` variable (which is a pointer to a structure) must be assigned the address of `new_item`, which is now the actual first item in the list.

3. Now you still have the `first_item` variable, which points to the first item in the list (which was just added), and the `new_item` variable can be reused.

If that wasn't clear, we hope the example—and its corresponding images—will help.

One other distinction between these two methods is that if you add items to the end of the list, the data will be in the same order as it was added. If you add items to the beginning of the lists, the data will be in the opposite order of how it was added.

To use linked lists:

1. Create a new file or project in your text editor or IDE.

2. Type the standard beginning lines of code (**Script 13.4**):

```
/* grades_list.c - Script 13.4 -
→ remake of grades.c (Script 13.3) */
#include <stdio.h>
```

3. Include the *string.h* and *stdlib.h* library files:

```
#include <string.h>
#include <stdlib.h>
```

In order to use the **strncpy()** function, we must include the *string.h* file. Since this application uses the **malloc()** function for dynamic memory allocation, the standard library is necessary as well.

4. Define one macro constant:

```
#define STR_LEN 20
```

The maximum string length is still necessary but the **NUM_STUDENTS** constant (used in the previous example) is unnecessary with this dynamically growing list.

5. Begin the **main** function:

```
int main (void) {
```

6. Define the structure:

```
struct student_grade {
    char first_name[STR_LEN];
    char last_name[STR_LEN];
    float grade;
    struct student_grade *next;
};
```

INTRODUCTION TO LINKED LISTS

```
 1    /* grades_list.c - Script 13.4 - remake
      → of grades.c (Script 13.3) */
 2
 3    #include <stdio.h>
 4    #include <string.h> /* For string
      → functions. */
 5    #include <stdlib.h> /* For memory
      → functions. */
 6
 7    #define STR_LEN 20
 8
 9    int main (void) {
10
11        /* Define the structure. */
12        struct student_grade {
13            char first_name[STR_LEN];
14            char last_name[STR_LEN];
15            float grade;
16            struct student_grade *next;
17        };
18
19        /* Rename the structure syntax. */
20        typedef struct student_grade sg;
21
22        /* Create two structure pointers. */
23        sg *first = NULL;
24        sg *new = NULL;
25        sg *temp = NULL;
26
27        int num; /* For counting the input.
      → */
28
29        /* Need a temporary float. */
30        float g; /* grade */
31
32        /* Need some strings to handle
      → the input. */
```

continues on next page

Script 13.4 By adding pointers to the definition of a structure, we can create a linked list of unlimited length (well, limited only by the amount of available memory).

```
33        char classname[12], fn[STR_LEN],
   → ln[STR_LEN];

34

35        /* Prompt the user. */

36        printf ("Enter the classname (without
   → spaces): ");

37        scanf ("%11s", classname);

38

39        /* Insert a check on the classname,
   → if you want. */

40

41        /* Prompt the user. */

42        printf ("Enter the student's name
   → and their grade. Enter 0 0 0 to
   → quit.\n(First Last ##.#): ");

43

44        /* Read in the input. */

45        num = scanf ("%11s %11s %f", fn, ln,
   → &g);

46

47        /* Check if the user is done. */

48        while (fn[0] != '0') {

49

50            /* Handle the input. */

51            if (num == 3) {

52

53                new = (sg *)
   → malloc(sizeof(sg));

54

55                /* Check that new is not
   → NULL. */

56

57                strncpy(new->first_name, fn,
   → STR_LEN-1);

58                new->first_name[STR_LEN-1] =
   → '\0';

59                strncpy(new->last_name, ln,
   → STR_LEN-1);

60                new->last_name[STR_LEN-1]
   → = '\0';
```

continues on next page

Script 13.4 *continued*

The structure is the same as it was before except for the addition of the pointer. The pointer is of type **struct student_grade**, since it will point to another structure (and pointers must match the data type they point to). The pointer itself is called **next**, appropriately enough.

7. Use **typedef** to rename the structure syntax:

   typedef struct student_grade sg;

   Again, the **typedef** simplifies the process of referring to a structure. This will be very useful in this example, where the text **struct student_grade** would be necessary in several places.

8. Define three structure pointers:

   sg *first = NULL;
   sg *new = NULL;
   sg *temp = NULL;

   The one pointer will always point to the first item in the list. The second will be used to add other items. The third will be used during the process of freeing up all the used memory.

9. Create the other variables:

   int num;
   float g;
   char classname[12], fn[STR_LEN],
   → **ln[STR_LEN];**

   All of these variables are the same as in the previous example. Two have been dropped. The **i** variable was used in a **for** loop before, but it's not necessary here as this application will use a **while** loop. The **count** variable is also no longer required as we don't need to count the number of items being stored.

continues on next page

10. Prompt the user and read in the class name:

```
printf ("Enter the classname
→ (without spaces): ");
scanf ("%11s", classname);
```

11. Prompt the user and read in the input:

```
printf ("Enter the student's name
→ and their grade. Enter 0 0 0 to
→ quit.\n(First Last ##.#): ");
num = scanf ("%11s %11s %f", fn, ln,
→ &g);
```

The while loop in this application (see Step 12) will keep running as long as the user keeps entering valid records. To enter that while, the user must be prompted to enter the first record. Hence, this prompt is outside the loop structure.

12. Define the while loop and create a conditional to check the validity of the input:

```
while (fn[0] != '0') {
    if (num == 3) {
```

The while loop checks if the first character of the first string is 0. As long as it isn't, the loop will be entered and the user can add another record.

The conditional checks the validity of the input.

13. Allocate memory for a new structure:

```
new = (sg *) malloc(sizeof(sg));
```

Following the example in the introductory text, this creates a memory block capable of storing one structure. The returned value is then type-cast to be of the same type as the structure itself.

Note also that this combination of malloc() and sizeof for the struct is a very common pattern that you will see and use again and again when working with dynamically allocated structures.

```
Script
61          new->grade = g;
62          new->next = first;
63          first = new;
64
65      } else {
66          printf ("The data was not
→ in the proper format.\n");
67      }
68
69      /* Prompt the user. */
70      printf ("Enter the student's name
→ and their grade. Enter 0 0 0 to
→ quit.\n(First Last ##.#): ");
71
72      /* Read in the input. */
73      num = scanf ("%11s %11s %f", fn,
→ ln, &g);
74
75  } /* End of while loop. */
76
77      /* Print the data and free the memory.
→ */
78      printf ("Students and grades for the
→ class '%s':\n", classname);
79
80  new = first; /* Start at the
→ beginning. */
81
82  while (new != NULL) { /* Stop when
→ the list is done. */
83
84      printf("%s %s %0.1f\n",
→ new->first_name, new->last_name,
→ new->grade);
85      temp = new->next;
86      free(new);
87      new = temp;
88
89  }
90
91  getchar(); /* Pause. */
```
continues on next page

Script 13.4 *continued*

```
92        getchar(); /* Pause. */
93        return 0;
94
95    }
```

Script 13.4 *continued*

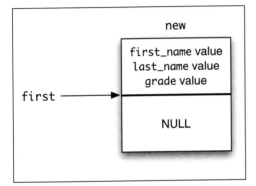

Figure 13.15 The structure of the linked list after running through the loop for the first time.

Finally, you could (and should) perform a check here to see that the memory was properly allocated, but that check has been skipped in the interest of simplicity. See Chapter 10 for details.

14. Assign the input to the structure:

```
strncpy(new->first_name, fn,
→ STR_LEN-1);
new->first_name[STR_LEN-1] = '\0';
strncpy(new->last_name, ln,
→ STR_LEN-1);
new->last_name[STR_LEN-1] = '\0';
new->grade = g;
```

The *structure_var->member* syntax is used to assign values to the structure. These lines store the inputted data in the allotted memory block.

15. Adjust the pointers accordingly:

```
new->next = first;
first = new;
```

The first time this loop is entered, `first` has no value but space has been allotted for a structure called `new` and data has been stored there (Step 14). The first line here assigns the `next` pointer member of `new` the value of `first`, which is `NULL`. This is desired since `new` is currently the tail of the list. The second line assigns the address of the new item (where the data is stored in memory) to `first`, since that's the first item in the list. **Figure 13.15** shows the result after the initial iteration of the loop.

continues on next page

INTRODUCTION TO LINKED LISTS

The second time this loop is entered, first has a value (it points to the first item in the list) and space has been allotted for a new structure (where data has been stored). The first line of code here will then assign the value of first to the new item's pointer member, so that the new item now points to the existing list. The second line then assigns the address of the new item to first, so that the first variable continues to point to the head of the list (**Figure 13.16**).

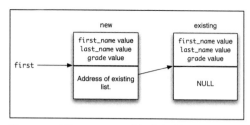

Figure 13.16 The structure of the linked list after adding another item (to the head of the list).

16. Complete the num conditional and the loop:

```
} else {
    printf ("The data was not in the
→ proper format.\n");
}
```

If the value returned by scanf()—num— is not equal to 3, the data wasn't entered properly and a message is printed. There's no need to break the loop because the user can be prompted again.

17. Re-prompt the user, read in the input, and complete the while loop:

```
    printf ("Enter the student's
→ name and their grade. Enter 0 0 0
→ to quit.\n(First Last ##.#): ");
    num = scanf ("%11s %11s %f", fn,
→ ln, &g);
} /* End of while loop. */
```

Now that the record has been stored in memory, the user should be prompted again. After these lines, the while loop will recheck the value of fn to see whether another record is being entered.

18. Begin printing all of the records:

```
printf ("Students and grades for the
→ class '%s':\n", classname);
```

This is the first line outside of the main while loop, which read in and stored all of the records.

19. Define a loop for accessing every list element:

```
new = first;
while (new != NULL) {
```

The first line takes the new pointer—which is no longer being used for anything—and assigns it the value of first. Now new can be used to access each list item.

The while loop checks that new is not equal to NULL. Within the loop, new will be assigned the pointer value to the next element; if there is no next element, it will be null. At that point, the end of the list has been reached.

20. Print the stored values:

```
printf("%s %s %0.1f\n", new-
→ new- >first_name, new->last_name,
→ new->grade);
```

Because new now represents a list item, its values can be printed easily.

21. Set temp to the next item:

```
temp = new->next;
```

To avoid problems on some systems, a temporary variable is assigned the value of the next list item (the memory address of that item).

22. Free up the memory being used:

```
free(new);
```

It's very, very, very (*very!*) important that you free up all memory an application reserved with malloc(). Since you don't have pointers for each individual block of memory that was set aside, each block must be released while going through the entire list. If you omit this process, it will lead to a memory leak.

continues on next page

INTRODUCTION TO LINKED LISTS

23. Set new to the next item:

```
new = temp;
```

To continue through the list, the new pointer is set to the address of the next list item. When the loop reaches the tail of the list, new will be assigned a value of NULL here (which is the value of the pointer member in the final list item).

24. Complete the while loop and the main function:

```
    }
    getchar();
    getchar();
    return 0;
}
```

25. Save the file as *grades_list.c*, compile, and debug as necessary.

26. Run the application, varying the number of entries (**Figure 13.17**).

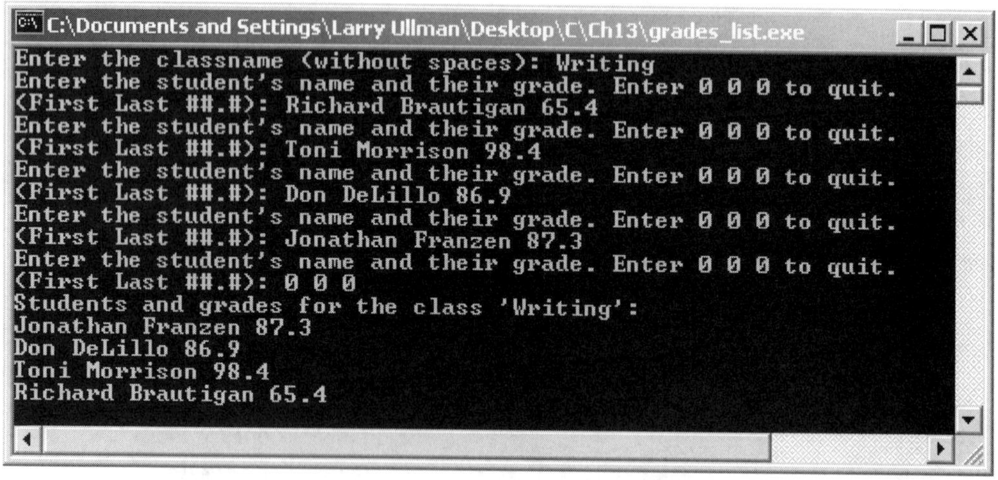

Figure 13.17 The application can now take as many records as there is memory space for. The entire list is then redisplayed, in inverse order.

✔ Tips

- Unlike the dynamically growing array example in Chapter 10, which used the `realloc()` function to consistently resize the memory block, this application adds new memory blocks. The difference is subtle, but it saves C from having to move around vast amounts of data (as with memory reallocation).

- If the data stored in a linked list is in some sort of order—alphabetical or numeric—this is an ordered list. When adding new items to such a list, the proper order (of the pointers) must be maintained, based on the value of the data.

- If you include two pointers in your structure definition, you can create a double-linked list, where each variable has a record of which item came before it and which comes after. With such a list you can move forward or backward through it.

- A structure with two pointers can also be used to create trees, where one pointer points to a left branch and the other pointer leads to the right. The branches are ordered in relation to the base value (so words that come before the base value would be in the left branch and those that come after would be in the right). Trees allow for faster searching through a list, since individual nodes (or limbs) of the list can be found more directly, without accessing every list element.

Linked Lists vs. Arrays

As you might suppose, linked lists and arrays are somewhat similar. Often, what can be accomplished with the one can also be accomplished with the other.

The arguments in favor of using arrays are

- Individual array elements can be accessed randomly (by referring to its index). Linked lists must be accessed in order.

- Arrays can be searched and sorted more easily.

The arguments for linked lists include

- Linked lists can grow dynamically, whereas arrays are limited to a fixed size (defined during compilation).

- It's faster and easier to insert records into the middle of a linked lists (or delete records from the middle of one).

Experience and practice will help you know which is the right tool for any particular job, but remembering the options you have is critical for using C optimally.

INSTALLING AND USING C TOOLS

Before you can begin programming with C, you'll need to make sure that you have the proper tools installed. At the very least, you need a text editor, a console or terminal window, and a compiler. The first two are already on your computer, and the third is freely available online. Still, we prefer and recommend that you use an integrated development environment (IDE) such as Dev-C++ for Windows and Xcode for Mac OS X. Both are free, and easy to use.

In this appendix, we'll go through quick demonstrations on how to use both applications. Then we'll quickly touch on what options our Unix and Linux friends have. After that, we'll introduce you to the popular GDB debugging tool. Finally, we'll mention a couple of other applications that might be of interest to you as you sink your teeth into C programming.

Dev-C++ for Windows

Dev-C++ is an open source application available from Bloodshed Software (www.bloodshed.net, **Figure A.1**). Not only is Dev-C++ free, but it runs nicely on any version of Windows since Windows 95, and requires just a mere 32 MB of RAM.

Dev-C++ is a syntax-highlighting text editor and it includes the required C compiler, letting you run the compiled applications directly from within Dev-C++. In short, if you're developing C applications on Windows, you can't go wrong with Dev-C++ (although it has *C++* in the name, it's also great for C). All of the examples in this book were written on and tested using Dev-C++ (on Windows 2000).

The following sequences constitute a mini "quickstart" guide to using Dev-C++. Also be sure to check out the debugging section, later in this appendix, since the full version of Dev-C++ comes with the popular Gnu Debugger (GDB) installed.

Customizing Dev-C++

Installing Dev-C++ is easy enough—just run the downloaded installer—but make sure that you download the full version, which includes the compiler. Once you have Dev-C++ on your computer, you'll want to set the preferences before using it too much. Specifically, we recommend the following instructions.

To customize Dev-C++:

1. Create a directory for your C files.

The best option is to create a simply titled directory in the root of the hard drive, like C:\c_code.

2. Open Dev-C++.

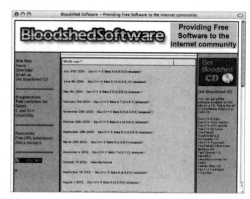

Figure A.1 The home page of Bloodshed Software.

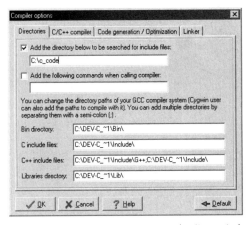

Figure A.2 Set your preferred directory (or directories) in the Compiler Options dialog.

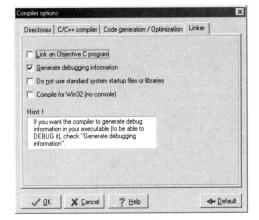

Figure A.3 In order to use the built-in debugger, you must have Dev-C++ generate debugging information.

3. Select Options > Compiler Options.

This will bring up the Compiler Options dialog.

4. Click the *Add the directory below to be searched for include files* check box.

In the long run, it will improve how easily you can develop applications if you use a set directory for storing all of your C code.

5. Type your C code directory in the box below that (**Figure A.2**).

You cannot use directory names here with spaces in them, but you can add multiple directories by separating each with a semicolon.

6. Click on the Linker tab and click the *Generate debugging information* check box (**Figure A.3**).

By doing this, you can use the debugging tools built into Dev-C++.

7. Click the OK button to exit.

✔ Tips

- Through the Dev-C++ Resource Site (http://bloodshed.net/dev/), you can download other packages, like GUI tool-kits for creating graphical interfaces for your applications.

- Once you've gotten through the first chapter, you may want to check out the Misc tab within the Environment Options panel (accessible by selecting Options > Environment options). There you can set the default code for creating a new source file.

- At the time of this writing, we were using version 4.x of Dev-C++. Version 5 should be available by the time you read this book (it was in beta at press time) and would be preferable, as it uses a newer compiler, among other benefits.

DEV-C++ FOR WINDOWS

355

Using Dev-C++

Although using Dev-C++ is pretty straight-forward, understanding how to use it with respect to the code and steps in this book merits discussion. The instructions for creating the examples are somewhat generic—so that users on any computer using any text editor or IDE can follow along—but here is how we envision Dev-C++ people going through the material.

To use Dev-C++:

1. Open Dev-C++.

2. Select File > New Project to create a whole new project.

   We like the idea of working with projects even though most of the applications in this book use only a single file at a time. Getting into the habit of creating projects will help you down the line when you're developing larger-scale C tools.

   Alternatively, you can select File > New Source file to begin creating a single C source document.

3. In the New Project window (**Figure A.4**), do the following:

   ▲ Click on the Console Application icon.

   ▲ Ensure that *C project* is selected.

   ▲ Ensure that *Make default language* is selected.

   Certainly Dev-C++ has more to offer— as you can tell from the New Project window—than a plain console application, but for the purposes of this book, that's where you'll want to start out.

4. Click OK.

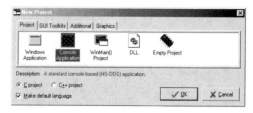

Figure A.4 The New Project window in Dev-C++.

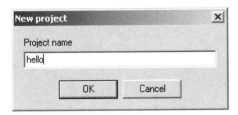

Figure A.5 Naming the new project.

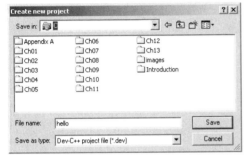

Figure A.6 Use the standard Windows interface to navigate to and select the desired location for your new project.

Figure A.7 The default C template.

5. Enter the project's name (**Figure A.5**) and click OK.

   For your project name, use the *basename* of whatever file is being created. So if the example is making a file called *hello.c*, name your project *hello*. Each example has its name near the very top of the step-by-step sequence, so you shouldn't have to go hunting around for that information.

6. Select the project's location (**Figure A.6**).

   You should use the same directory as you created in the Customizing Dev-C++ sequence. We also recommend using a separate directory for each project, to help maintain the organization of your work.

7. Click Save.

   After going through these steps, you'll be given a C source template (**Figure A.7**).

8. Enter your C code.

   You can now follow the particular instructions for an example, typing all of your code in the template so that it matches that in the book.

9. Select File > Save Unit.

   This will let you save the C source file itself. You can name it either *hello.c* (a name matching the project name) or *main.c*.

10. Select Execute > Compile or press Ctrl+F9.

   The compiler is linked to the Dev-C++ application, so you can compile your C code within it.

continues on next page

DEV-C++ FOR WINDOWS

11. If the application compiled successfully, select Execute > Run or press F9.

This will create a new console window (a DOS prompt) and begin running the compiled application.

12. If the application did not compile successfully, check the compiler tab (at the bottom of the screen) for error messages.

Any syntax errors in your code will be listed in the Compiler tab. The specific line number where the problem occurred is listed as well.

✔ Tips

- Steps 10 and 11 can be combined by selecting Execute > Compile and Run. Of course, you can always use the toolbar icons as well.

- On the Dev-C++ Resource Site (http://bloodshed.net/dev/), check out the Documentation page, which has links to various manuals, Web sites related to C and C++, and tutorials on using Dev-C++.

- You can create other templates that will appear in the New Project window by placing them in the Dev-C++\Templates directory.

Figure A.8 Xcode's New Project window.

Xcode on Mac OS X

Simply put, Apple's Xcode is the kind of development environment programmers are used to paying hundreds of dollars for. It's a top-notch IDE, with loads of features and support for many languages. All of the code in this book was written on and tested using Xcode, so we highly recommend Mac OS X users to use it as well.

Xcode is part of a series of Developer Tools Apple releases with the operating system. If you have a set of Mac OS X discs, you should check for the Developer Tools CD to save yourself a large download. If you don't already have a copy or if you want the latest version, Xcode is freely available from Apple's Developer Connection (ADC) Web site (http://developer.apple.com/tools/download/). You'll need to be an ADC member, but membership is free.

Once you've installed Xcode, take this quick tour to learn how to use it to create C applications.

To use Xcode:

1. Launch Xcode.

2. Select File > New Project.

3. In the resulting window (**Figure A.8**), select Standard Tool (the last item) and click Next.

   As you can see in the description (at the bottom), this option is intended for building command-line tools written in C, which is exactly what you're doing in this book.

continues on next page

4. Enter the project name, select the project directory, and click Finish (**Figure A.9**).

For your project name, use the *basename* of whatever file is being created. So if the example is making a file called *hello.c*, name your project *hello*. Each example has its name near the very top of the step-by-step sequence, so you shouldn't have to go hunting around for the name.

5. Click on *main.c* in the project window.

Xcode uses these project windows to manage your projects. After you choose a Standard Tool type of project, Xcode automatically creates some files for you. The most important in terms of this book is the *main.c* file, which is your main C source code.

6. Click the Show Editor button (to the right of the stop sign).

You can edit *main.c* by double-clicking on it—which will make it appear in its own window—or by using the built-in editor. If you click on Show Editor, the project window will be broken into three panes (**Figure A.10**).

7. After you've entered your code, select File > Save or press Command+S.

8. Select Build > Build and Run or press Command+R to compile and execute the application.

9. Press Command+R again to rerun your application.

Alternatively, you can double-click on the application's name in the top of the project window to run it in a terminal window.

Or, the executable application itself can be found in the *project_name/build* folder.

Figure A.9 Selecting the project's name and location.

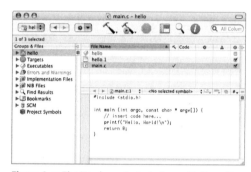

Figure A.10 The Xcode project window, with the editor in the lower-right panel.

✔ Tips

- Even if you don't want to use Xcode, you'll want to install the Developer Tools, which also installs the gcc compiler on your Mac.

- Cocoa is Apple's primary technology for creating Mac OS X applications. It uses Objective-C, a version of C that incorporates objects. Knowing C, after reading this book, you should be able to learn Cocoa with relative ease.

- The Developer Tools also include Interface Builder, for creating the graphical front end to an application. Search the Web for tutorials on creating applications using Xcode and Interface Builder.

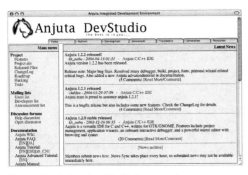

Figure A.11 Anjuta DevStudio is a popular open source IDE that runs on Unix.

Unix Tools

If your primary operating system is Unix (or a Unix derivative such as Linux), then learning C makes perfect sense. Large portions of Unix itself were written in C, and it's still a popular language for building Unix tools.

Unix people tend to be fanatical about their text editors (post a message to any newsgroup about emacs versus vi and watch the bullets fly), but there are worthy IDEs available too. Naturally, most of these are open source, such as Eclipse (www.eclipse.org), KDevelop (www.kdevelop.org), and Anjuta DevStudio (http://anjuta.sourceforge.net, **Figure A.11**).

✔ Tips

- If Eclipse, KDevelop, and Anjuta DevStudio aren't to your liking (or if they aren't available for your version of Unix), SourceForge (www.sf.net) has dozens upon dozens of IDEs for your consideration.

- This book doesn't discuss the make command, but it's a common tool for Unix. Although it's normally used with *Makefiles* to dictate how an application should be built, it can be used on its own. If you type make *myprogram* in the same directory as a *myprogram.c* file, make will compile the application for you, using the standard C compiler.

Debugging with GDB

Of the available tools for developing C applications, GDB (Gnu Debugger) is one of the more common. GDB is a command-line tool for C and C++, intended to help you find bugs in an application. It takes a while to learn how to make the most out of GDB, but if you do much C programming, doing so will pay off.

GDB will do the following:

◆ Show the source code of a file.

◆ Show the values of variables.

◆ Stop infinite loops.

◆ Demonstrate the logical progression through an application.

◆ Stop a program's execution at set points.

◆ Walk through a program, instruction by instruction.

◆ Allow you to inspect a program's state immediately after it crashes (to see what caused the crash).

GDB comes with Dev-C++ and is readily available on most variants of Unix, including Mac OS X. You can also download it and find out more information at www.gnu.org/software/gdb/gdb.html.

Showing you how to use GDB is beyond the scope of this book, but we can offer you a few starter tips:

◆ You cannot debug a file until you have tried to compile it. The compilation process generates the information GDB needs.

◆ On Dev-C++, be certain to click the *Generate debugging information* check box in your preferences panel (Figure A.3).

Programming for Easy Debugging

There are steps you can take to minimize the amount of debugging you have to do or to assist in the process when it does occur. The best practices include

◆ Use lots of comments to explain the purpose of variables and specific code.

◆ Avoid overly complex macros, functions, and statements.

◆ Make explicit use of parentheses or otherwise be careful with operator precedence.

◆ Make sure you're using = (the assignment operator) and == (the equals comparison operator) properly, particularly within conditionals and loops.

◆ Watch for array indexes and off-by-one errors.

◆ Provide a simple, consistent user interface.

◆ In `switch` conditionals, make sure you use `break` statements and a `default` case.

◆ Be careful about parentheses with function-like macros.

◆ Manage dynamic memory and pointers correctly.

◆ Pay attention to compiler warnings.

Obviously not making mistakes is the best way to simplify debugging, but we've found that it's tough to count on that policy.

Debug - hello (hello)
Build and Debug
Debug
Succeeded
Threads
Variable
Value
Summary
main.c:1
<No selected symbol>
#include <stdio.h>
int main (int argc, const char * argv[]) {
// insert code here...
printf("Hello, World!\n");
return 0;
}

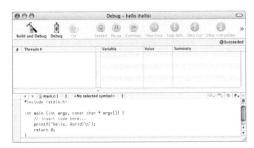

Figure A.12 Xcode's debugging interface.

- When using the command line gcc complier, always use the `-g` option to generate debugging data.
- In Dev-C++, select Execute > Debug or press F8 to bring up the debugger from the command line.
- In Xcode, you can select Debug > Show Debugger to bring up the graphical version of the debugger (**Figure A.12**).
- To use the debugger from the command line, type `gdb` *`application_name`*, where *`application_name`* is the name of the compiled executable.
- Get help by typing `help` in the console window (**Figure A.13**). Type `help` *`command-name`* to get help on a specific command.

Those are specific tips for working with GDB using the tools recommended by this book. Once you get to the point where you want to learn all about GDB, search the Web for "gdb tutorial" and peruse any of the thousands of results.

✔ Tips

- The Insight Debugger (http://sources.redhat.com/insight/) is a graphical interface to GDB for Unix.
- DDD (Data Display Debugger, www.gnu.org/software/ddd/) is another popular graphical interface to GDB.

C:\WINNT\system32\cmd.exe
(gdb) help
help
List of classes of commands:
aliases -- Aliases of other commands
breakpoints -- Making program stop at certain points
data -- Examining data
files -- Specifying and examining files
internals -- Maintenance commands
obscure -- Obscure features
running -- Running the program
stack -- Examining the stack
status -- Status inquiries
support -- Support facilities
tracepoints -- Tracing of program execution without stopping the program
user-defined -- User-defined commands
Type "help" followed by a class name for a list of commands in that class.
Type "help" followed by command name for full documentation.
Command name abbreviations are allowed if unambiguous.
(gdb)

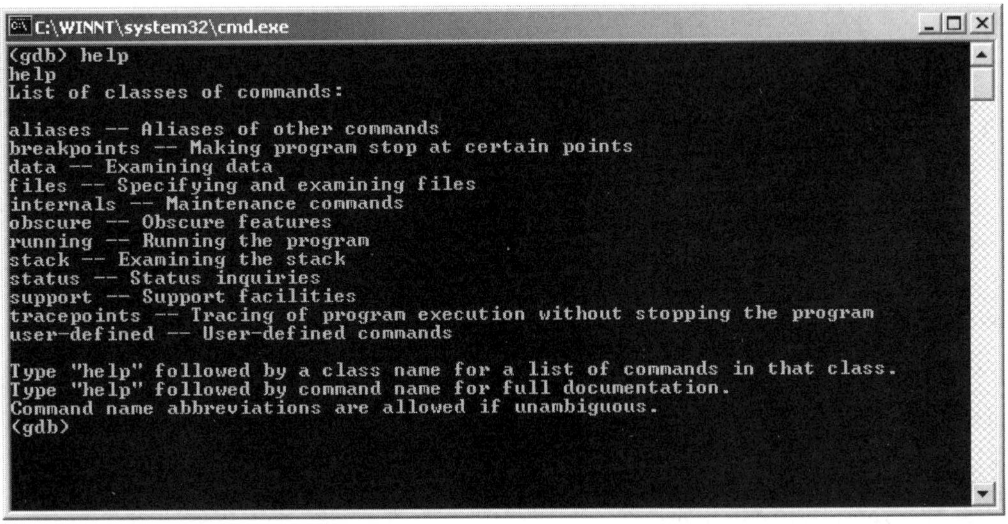

Figure A.13 The GDB help page.

Other Tools

The previously listed applications are just the tip of the iceberg when it comes to developing C applications. Due to the language's popularity, dozens of excellent and free other tools are available. Each takes a little effort to learn, but once you master them, they should improve the quality of your C programming and applications.

Eclipse

(www.eclipse.org)

Eclipse is an open source development environment written in Java, meaning it will run on practically every operating system. Although its initial purpose was for creating Java applications, by adding the C/C++ plug-in (see www.eclipse.org/tools/downloads.html), you can create C programs, too.

Splint

(www.splint.org)

Splint, short for *Secure Programming Lint*, helps to check your C applications for security concerns and other mistakes. It abides by the C99 standard and has a pretty good manual. Splint is freely available and can be run on most operating systems.

C Beautifier (cb)

cb is a special utility whose sole purpose is to reformat C code in a consistent style. You should probably back up a file before using one of these utilities for the first time, but the experience may give you a better appreciation for a professionally formatted document. One of the other features is to replace tabs—which are easier to type—with spaces—which are more portable. Of the available versions of cb, one is bcpp (http://freshmeat.net/projects/bcpp/).

RESOURCES

B

Because the C programming language has been around for so many years, there are ample resources for you to turn to for more information. In this appendix we'll highlight just a few of those options. As with most things, a simple Internet search (using Google or whatever you prefer) will always return a ton of results. But, to possibly save yourself that step, here's a list of useful Web sites and tables of helpful information.

Web Sites

Of the thousands and thousands of C-related Web sites, we've identified a few you might want to familiarize yourself with up front. But first, a couple of things you should know about C Web sites:

Because of the connectedness of the two languages, you'll often see sites that discuss both C and C++. From these you'll have to filter out the information that doesn't pertain to you (namely, the C++ stuff). Second, many of the available resources stem from university settings (which can be great, but specific in scope) or provide technical documentation, rather than detailed explanation (which can be less useful when you're just learning).

With that in mind, here are a few good C Web sites, with a brief description of each:

◆ Cprogramming.com
(www.cprogramming.com)
Has tutorials on many levels, information on different tools you can use, and resources for getting help (**Figure B.1**).

◆ How C Programming Works
(www.howstuffworks.com/c.htm)
Part of the How Stuff Works Web site (which talks about everything from automatic transmissions to nuclear bombs), these pages feature a good beginner's guide to C, one topic at a time.

◆ comp.lang.c Frequently Asked Questions
(www.eskimo.com/~scs/C-faq.top.html)
comp.lanc.c is *the* C newsgroup (see the sidebar). From years of use, the most frequently asked questions—and their answers—have been put together and posted here. Since you're a beginner, most of your questions will probably have been answered a hundred times already, so reading these pages can often get you the best, fastest solution to a problem.

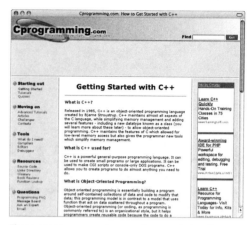

Figure B.1 Cprogramming.com is a good place for programmers of all levels to check out.

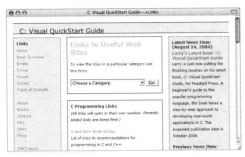

Figure B.2 This book's corresponding Web site contains a number of resources, such as links to ever more useful sites.

Newsgroups

If you're already a newsgroup fan, you're in luck. There's one really good available C newsgroup: comp.lang.c.

If you're not familiar with newsgroups, maybe it's time that you should be. Newsgroups are discussion groups on the Internet (Usenet primarily). They are a lot like mailing lists, except that every message is sent to, and stored on, a server (unlike mailing lists, which send the messages via email).

Using a newsreader application, you can view the messages that have been posted or post your own. Other readers can then respond to your questions, often in a relatively short period of time.

Newsgroups, like mailing lists, have a protocol to them. Abide by certain guidelines (see the "Asking Questions the Smart Way" sidebar in the Introduction) and you'll get a timely, useful response. Ask a question poorly or demonstrate a lack of effort on your part, and the responses won't be nearly as generous or useful. Still, newsgroups are a great resource and, when used properly, can be a real lifesaver.

◆ Dinkum C99 Library
(http://dinkumware.com/libc99.html)
The Dinkum C99 Library is simply a listing of the complete standard C library. In these pages you can find the contents and description of all of the C header files, like *stdio.h*, *string.h*, and *time.h*.

◆ World History.com
(www.worldhistory.com/wiki/C/
C-programming-language.htm)

A general introduction to the C language, including its history and how it relates to C++. The page includes lots of good references and links.

◆ C and C++ Style Guides
(www.chris-lott.org/resources/cstyle/)
Good programming style is more important than most people realize, greatly assisting the programmer in finding and preventing errors, understanding code, and more. On this page you'll find links to a couple of dozen guides to programming style.

✔ Tips

- For more Web sites, check out the links page at this book's support Web site: www.DMCInsights.com/cvqs (**Figure B.2**)

- When searching for C-related sites and information, it helps to begin your searches with either "C programming" or "C language".

- If you don't mind very technical descriptions, you can download a PDF of the official C standard at http://www. nirvani.net/docs/ansi_c.pdf.

Tables

This book contained a number of tables, and you may not want to go searching through the entire text to find them. We've included the most useful tables here, along with a couple of new ones.

Table B.1 This list of all C operators—including a couple that were not discussed in this book—ranks them from highest precedence to the lowest.

Operator Precedence	
OPERATORS	ASSOCIATIVITY
( ) □ - .	Left to right
! -- ++ - + * & {} (type-cast) sizeof (+, - and * are all unary, not arithmetic)	Right to left
* / %	Left to right
+ -	Left to right
<< >>	Left to right
< <= > >=	Left to right
== !=	Left to right
&	Left to right
^	Left to right
|	Left to right
&&	Left to right
||	Left to right
?:	Left to right
= += -= *= /= %= &= ^= |= <<= >>=	Right to left
,	Left to right

Table B.2 These escape sequences have special meaning when used within strings.

Escape Characters	
CHARACTER	MEANING
\b	backspace
\f	new page
\n	newline
\t	tab
\r	return
\'	single quotation mark
\"	double quotation mark

Table B.3 These signifiers act as placeholders for specific types of values. They are used in all the *f() functions: printf(), scanf(), fprintf(), sscanf(), sprintf(), and so forth.

printf(), scanf(), etc. Signifiers	
SIGNIFIER	MEANING
d	integer
f	floating point number
hd	short integer
ld	long integer
hu	unsigned short integer
u	unsigned integer
lu	unsigned long integer
lf	double
Lf	long double (not always available)
c	character
s	string
p	pointer

Table B.4 Choosing an appropriate number type affects the values a variable can store and how much memory it requires.

Number Types and Approximate Sizes		
TYPE	MEMORY USAGE	RANGE OF VALUES
short int	2 bytes	-32,768 to 32,767
unsigned short int	2 bytes	0 to 65,535
int	4 bytes	-2,147,483,648 to 2,147,483,647
unsigned int	4 bytes	0 to 4,294,967,295
long int	4 bytes	-2,147,483,648 to 2,147,483,647
unsigned long int	4 bytes	0 to 4,294,967,295
long long int	8 bytes	-9,223,372,036,854,775,808 to 9,223,372,036,854,775,807
unsigned long long int	8 bytes	0 to 18,446,744,073,709,551,615
float	4 bytes	-1e38 to +1e38
double	8 bytes	-1e308 to +1e308
long double	8 bytes	-1e308 to +1e308

Table B.5 In several places we stated that a character is actually an integer. Here are the corresponding decimal and character values. Those through number 32 are nonprinting characters.

ASCII Character Chart

DECIMAL	ASCII	DECIMAL	ASCII	DECIMAL	ASCII	DECIMAL	ASCII
0	NUL (null)	38	&	76	L	114	r
1	SOH (start of heading)	39	'	77	M	115	s
2	STX (start of text)	40	(	78	N	116	t
3	ETX (end of text)	41	)	79	O	117	u
4	EOT (end of transmission)	42	*	80	P	118	v
5	ENQ (enquiry)	43	+	81	Q	119	w
6	ACK (acknowledge)	44	,	82	R	120	x
7	BEL (bell)	45	-	83	S	121	y
8	BS (backspace)	46	.	84	T	122	z
9	HT (horizontal tab)	47	/	85	U	123	{
10	LF (line feed)	48	0	86	V	124		
11	VT (vertical tab)	49	1	87	W	125	}
12	FF (form feed)	50	2	88	X	126	~
13	CR (carriage return)	51	3	89	Y	127	DEL
14	SO (shift out)	52	4	90	Z		
15	SI (shift in)	53	5	91	[		
16	DLE (data link escape)	54	6	92	\		
17	DC1 (device control 1)	55	7	93	]		
18	DC2 (device control 2)	56	8	94	^		
19	DC3 (device control 3)	57	9	95	_		
20	DC4 (device control 4)	58	:	96	`		
21	NAK (negative acknowledge)	59	;	97	a		
22	SYN (synchronous idle)	60	<	98	b		
23	ETB (end of transmission block)	61	=	99	c		
24	CAN (cancel)	62	>	100	d		
25	EM (end of medium)	63	?	101	e		
26	SUB (substitute)	64	@	102	f		
27	ESC (escape)	65	A	103	g		
28	FS (file separator)	66	B	104	h		
29	GS (group separator)	67	C	105	i		
30	RS (record separator)	68	D	106	j		
31	US (unit separator)	69	E	107	k		
32	SP (space)	70	F	108	l		
33	!	71	G	109	m		
34		72	H	110	n		
35	#	73	I	111	o		
36	$	74	J	112	p		
37	%	75	K	113	q		

TABLES

INDEX

. (decimal point), 24, 37, 104
; (semicolon), 5–6, 165
& (address-of operator), 194–197
= (assignment operator), 24, 43, 61, 64, 362
* (asterisk), 204–207, 209
\ (backslash), 18, 172, 174, 289
* (dereference operator), 204–207, 229
|| (double pipe), 242
= (equal sign), 64
== (equal to operator), 61, 362
== (equality operator), 61
> (greater than operator), 61
>= (greater than or equal to operator), 61
(hash mark), 163, 165
++ (increment operators), 44–46, 214
< (less than operator), 61
<= (less than or equal to operator), 61
% (modulus operator), 40, 43
!= (not equal to operator), 61
|| (or operator), 61, 64
% (percent sign), 40, 43, 105
' (quote marks), 28–29
_ (underscore character), 21, 23
/ (forward slash), 289
" " (quotation marks)
  assigning values and, 24
  character arrays, 123
  enumerated types, 333
  including files, 184
  printing text, 5–6
  string pointers, 258

INDEX

INDEX

Peachpit
Essential books for the creative community

Visit Peachpit on the Web at www.peachpit.com

- Read the latest articles and download timesaving tipsheets from best-selling authors such as Scott Kelby, Robin Williams, Lynda Weinman, Ted Landau, and more!

- Join the Peachpit Club and save 25% off all your online purchases at peachpit.com every time you shop—plus enjoy free UPS ground shipping within the United States.

- Search through our entire collection of new and upcoming titles by author, ISBN, title, or topic. There's no easier way to find just the book you need.

- Sign up for newsletters offering special Peachpit savings and new book announcements so you're always the first to know about our newest books and killer deals.

- Did you know that Peachpit also publishes books by Apple, New Riders, Adobe Press, Macromedia Press, palmOne Press, and TechTV press? Swing by the Peachpit family section of the site and learn about all our partners and series.

- Got a great idea for a book? Check out our About section to find out how to submit a proposal. You could write our next best-seller!

You'll find all this and more at www.peachpit.com. Stop by and take a look today!